ATHENAEUS

VIII

LCL 519

ATHENAEUS

THE LEARNED BANQUETERS

BOOK 15 • INDEXES

EDITED AND TRANSLATED BY

S. DOUGLAS OLSON

HARVARD UNIVERSITY PRESS
CAMBRIDGE, MASSACHUSETTS
LONDON, ENGLAND
2012

First published 2012

LOEB CLASSICAL LIBRARY® is a registered trademark
of the President and Fellows of Harvard College

Library of Congress Control Number 2006041321
CIP data available from the Library of Congress

ISBN 978-0-674-99676-2

*Composed in ZephGreek and ZephText by
Technologies 'N Typography, Merrimac, Massachusetts.
Printed on acid-free paper and bound by
The Maple-Vail Book Manufacturing Group*

CONTENTS

PREFACE

For a general introduction to Athenaeus and *The Learned Banqueters* and to my citation conventions, see the beginning of Volume 1 (LCL 204). Much of the work on this volume and the one that preceded it was completed at the National Humanities Center, where I held a fellowship during the 2008–9 academic year. Thanks are again due my research assistant Timothy Beck and my undergraduate students Joseph MacDonald, William Blessing, Cameron Ferguson, and Debbie Sugarbaker for their many hours of reference checking, proofreading, formatting assistance, and the like. Andrew Seeley played a fundamental role in the creation of the overall index that appears at the end of this volume. My most heartfelt thanks, however, go to my wife, the beautiful Rachel of Woodbury; may we be granted many more happy years together. This volume is dedicated to my intelligent, articulate, free-spirited son, Nathaniel, who has grown into a person to whom I am proud to be related.

ABBREVIATIONS

Berve	H. Berve, *Das Alexanderreich auf prosopographischer Grundlage* ii *Prosopographie* (Munich, 1926)
Billows	R. A. Billows, *Antigonos the One-Eyed and the Creation of the Hellenistic State* (Berkeley, Los Angeles, and London, 1990)
Bradford	A. S. Bradford, *A Prosopography of Lacedaimonians from the Death of Alexander the Great, 323 B.C., to the Sack of Sparta by Alaric, A.D. 396* (Vestigia 27: Munich, 1977)
FGE	D. L. Page (ed.), *Further Greek Epigrams* (Cambridge, 1981)
FGrH	F. Jacoby (ed.), *Die Fragmente der Griechischen Historiker* (Leiden, 1923–69)
FHG	C. and T. Müller, *Fragmenta Historicorum Graecorum* (5 vols.: Paris, 1841–70)
HE	A. S. F. Gow and D. L. Page (eds.), *The Greek Anthology: Hellenistic Epigrams* (Cambridge, 1965)
O'Connor	J. B. O'Connor, *Chapters in the History of Actors and Acting in Ancient Greece together with a Prosopographia Histrionum Graecorum* (Chicago, 1908)

PAA	J. Traill (ed.), *Persons of Ancient Athens* (Toronto, 1994–)
PMG	D. L. Page (ed.), *Poetae Melici Graeci* (Oxford, 1962)
Poralla	P. Poralla, *A Prosopography of Lacedaimonians from the Earliest Times to the Death of Alexander the Great (X–323 B.C.)*[2] (revised by A. S. Bradford: Chicago, 1985)
SH	H. Lloyd-Jones and P. Parsons (eds.), *Supplementum Hellenisticum* (Texte und Kommentar, Band 11: Berlin and New York, 1983)
SSR	G. Giannantoni, *Socratis et Socraticorum Reliquiae* (4 vols.; n.p., 1990)
Stephanis	I. E. Stephanis, Διονυσιακοὶ Τεχνίται (Herakleion, 1988)
SVF	J. van Arnim (ed.), *Stoicorum Veterum Fragmenta* (3 vols.; Leipzig, 1921, 1903)
TrGF	B. Snell *et al.* (eds.), *Tragicorum Graecorum Fragmenta* (Göttingen, 1971–2004)

THE CHARACTERS

ATHENAEUS, the narrator; also a guest at the dinner party

TIMOCRATES, Athenaeus' interlocutor

AEMILIANUS MAURUS, grammarian (e.g. 3.126b)

ALCEIDES OF ALEXANDRIA, musician (1.1f; 4.174b)

AMOEBEUS, citharode (14.622d–e)

ARRIAN, grammarian (3.113a)

CYNULCUS, Cynic philosopher whose given name is Theodorus (e.g. 1.1d; 3.97c)

DAPHNUS OF EPHESUS, physician (e.g. 1.1e; 2.51a)

DEMOCRITUS OF NICOMEDIA, philosopher (1.1e; 3.83c)

DIONYSOCLES, physician (3.96d, 116d)

GALEN OF PERGAMUM, physician (e.g. 1.1e–f, 26c)

LARENSIUS, Roman official and also host of the party (e.g. 1.2b–3c; 2.50f)

LEONIDAS OF ELIS, grammarian (1.1d; 3.96d)

MAGNUS (e.g. 3.74c)

MASURIUS, jurist, poet, musician (e.g. 1.1c; 14.623e)

MYRTILUS OF THESSALY, grammarian (e.g. 3.83a)

PALAMEDES THE ELEATIC, lexicographer (9.379a)

PHILADELPHUS OF PTOLEMAIS, philosopher
   (1.1d)*
PLUTARCH OF ALEXANDRIA, grammarian (e.g.
   1.1c–d; 3.83b)
PONTIANUS OF NICOMEDIA, philosopher (1.1d;
   3.109b)
RUFINUS OF NICAEA, physician (1.1f)*
ULPIAN OF TYRE, grammarian and also symposiarch
   (e.g. 1.1d–e; 2.49a)
VARUS, grammarian (3.118d)
ZOILUS, grammarian (e.g. 1.1d; 7.277c)

* Neither Philadelphus nor Rufinus is said to speak any-
where in the preserved text of *The Learned Banqueters*,
and most likely some of the anonymous speeches in 1.2a–
3.73e (represented in the Epitome manuscripts only) belong to them.

THE LEARNED BANQUETERS

665 Εἴ μοι τὸ Νεστόρειον εὔγλωσσον μέλος
    Ἀντήνορός τε τοῦ Φρυγὸς δοίη θεός,

κατὰ τὸν πάνσοφον Εὐριπίδην, ἑταῖρε Τιμόκρατες,

    οὐκ ἂν δυναίμην

ἀπομνημονεύειν ἔτι σοι τῶν πολλάκις λεχθέντων ἐν
τοῖς περισπουδάστοις τούτοις συμποσίοις διά τε τὴν
ποικιλίαν καὶ τὴν ὁμοιότητα τῶν ἀεὶ καινῶς προσευ-
ρισκομένων. καὶ γὰρ καὶ περὶ τάξεως τῶν περιφορῶν |
b πολλάκις ἐλέχθη καὶ περὶ τῶν μετὰ τὸ δεῖπνον ἐπι-
τελουμένων, ἅπερ καὶ μόλις ἀναπεμπάζομαι, εἰπόντος
τινὸς τῶν ἑταίρων τὰ ἐκ τῶν Λακώνων Πλάτωνος
ἰαμβεῖα·

    (Α.) ἄνδρες δεδειπνήκασιν ἤδη; (Β.) σχεδὸν
        ἅπαντες. (Α.) εὖ γε·
    τί οὐ τρέχων ‹σὺ› τὰς τραπέζας ἐκφέρεις; ἐγὼ
        δὲ

BOOK XV

If a god were to grant me the eloquent
melodiousness of Nestor or Phrygian Antenor,

to quote the insightful Euripides (fr. 899),[1] my friend Timocrates,

I would be unable

even so to recall for you what was said on every occasion at
those brilliant parties, on account of both the diversity and
the similarity of the ever-new topics put forward. The fact
is that the conversation routinely involved the order of the
dishes served and the events that followed the meal, and I
can recount what was said only with difficulty, although
one member of our group quoted the iambic lines from
Plato's *Spartans* (fr. 71):

(A.) Have the men finished dinner yet? (B.) Almost
all of them. (A.) Good work!
Why don't you run and bring the tables out?
Meanwhile I'm

---

[1] The quotation continues in what follows. Nestor was the old-
est Achaean at Troy and much given to long speeches, while
Antenor was a Trojan elder (cf. *Il.* 3.148–53; Pl. *Smp.* 221c–d
[paired with Nestor]).

νίπτρον παραχέων ἔρχομαι. (Β.) κἀγὼ δὲ
  παρακορήσων.
(Α.) σπονδὰς δ' ἔπειτα παραχέας τὸν κότταβον
  παροίσω. |

c τῇ παιδὶ τοὺς αὐλοὺς ἐχρῆν ἤδη πρὸ χειρὸς
  εἶναι
καὶ προαναφυσᾶν. τὸ μύρον ἤδη παραχέω
  βαδίζων
Αἰγύπτιον κἆτ' ἴρινον· στέφανον δ' ἔπειθ' ἑκάστῳ
δώσω φέρων τῶν ξυμποτῶν. νεοκρᾶτά τις ποείτω.
(Β.) καὶ δὴ κέκραται. (Α.) τὸν λιβανωτὸν

d   ἐπιτιθεὶς | † εἶπε †

＊　　＊　　＊

σπονδὴ μὲν ἤδη γέγονε καὶ πίνοντές εἰσι πόρρω,
καὶ σκόλιον ᾖσται, κότταβος δ' ἐξοίχεται θύραζε.
αὐλοὺς δ' ἔχουσά τις κορίσκη Καρικὸν μέλος
  ⟨τι⟩
μελίζεται τοῖς συμπόταις, κἄλλην τρίγωνον εἶδον
ἔχουσαν, εἶτ' ᾖδεν πρὸς αὐτὸ μέλος Ἰωνικόν τι.

μετὰ ταῦτ', οἶμαι, καὶ περὶ κοττάβων ζήτησις ἦν καὶ
τῶν ἀποκοτταβιζόντων. οὓς οἰηθείς τις τῶν παρόντων
ἰατρῶν εἶναι τούτων οἳ ἀπὸ βαλανείου καθάρσεως
ἕνεκα τοῦ στομάχου πίνοντες ἄμυστιν ἀποβλύζουσιν,
ἔφη οὐκ εἶναι παλαιὰν ταύτην παράδοσιν οὐδ' εἰδέναι

---

[2] I offer the word in this form only where it clearly functions as
the name of the drinking game whose varieties are discussed below; where the sense is less clear-cut, I transliterate *kottabos*.

4

coming to pour the washing-water. (B.) And I'm
   coming to sweep up.
(A.) Then, after I pour the libations, I'll bring them
   the cottabus²-equipment.
The slave-girl should already have had her pipes
   ready at hand
and been practicing her playing. I'm going now to
   pour Egyptian perfume
for them, and then the kind that's scented with iris
   root. After that I'll bring
each guest a garland and give it to him. Someone
   should mix a fresh bowl of wine.
(B.) It's been mixed, in fact. (A.) After putting the
   frankincense on the (brazier) † he said †

                 *   *   *

The libation's already happened, and they're well into
   their drinking;
a skolion's been sung, and the cottabus-equipment's
   been removed from the room.
A little girl holding pipes is playing a Carian
song for the guests; I saw another one holding
a lyre, and then she started singing an Ionian song,
   with the lyre as accompaniment.

Afterward, I believe, there was a discussion of cottabus
and cottabus-players (*apokottabizontes*). One of the physicians present took this as a reference to people who have
a bath and then drink a large amount of wine and vomit
it up as a way of cleaning out their stomach; he said that
this was not an ancient tradition, and that he knew of no

τινὰ τῶν ἀρχαίων ταύτῃ τῇ καθάρσει χρησάμενον. διὸ
666 καὶ Ἐρασίστρατον τὸν Ἰουλιήτην ‖ ἐν τῇ Περὶ τῶν
Καθόλου πραγματείᾳ ἐπιτιμᾶν τοῖς τοῦτο ποιοῦσιν,
βλαπτικὸν ὀφθαλμῶν τὸ ἐπιχείρημα δεικνύων καὶ τῆς
κάτω κοιλίας ἐπισχετικόν. πρὸς ὃν Οὐλπιανὸς ἔφη·

ὄρσ᾽, Ἀσκληπιάδη, καλέει κρείων σε Χαρωνεύς.

οὐ γὰρ κακῶς τινι τῶν ἑταίρων ἡμῶν ἐλέχθη τὸ εἰ μὴ
ἰατροὶ ἦσαν, οὐδὲν ἂν ἦν τῶν γραμματικῶν μωρότε-
ρον. τίς γὰρ ἡμῶν οὐκ οἶδεν ὅτι οὐκ ἦν οὗτος ὁ
ἀποκοτταβισμὸς ἀρχαῖος; εἰ μή τι σὺ καὶ τοὺς Ἀμει-
ψίου ⟨Ἀποκοτταβίζοντας⟩[1] ἀποβλύζειν ὑπολαμβά-
b νεις. ἐπεὶ οὖν | ἄπειρος εἶ τῆς τοιαύτης θεωρίας, μάθε
παρ᾽ ἐμοῦ ὅτι πρῶτον μὲν ἡ τῶν κοττάβων εὕρεσις
Σικελική ἐστι παιδιά, ταύτην πρῶτων εὑρόντων Σικε-
λῶν, ὡς Κριτίας φησὶν ὁ Καλλαίσχρου ἐν τοῖς Ἐλεγείοις διὰ τούτων·

κότταβος ἐκ Σικελῆς ἐστι χθονός, ἐκπρεπὲς
    ἔργον,
ὃν σκοπὸν ἐς λατάγων τόξα καθιστάμεθα.

Δικαίαρχος ὁ Μεσσήνιος, Ἀριστοτέλους μαθητής, ἐν

[1] add. Meineke

---

[3] A parody of *Il.* 4.204 ("Get up, son of Asclepius; Lord Agamemnon is summoning (you)"); assigned to Timo Phliasius by
Wachsmuth, but not printed in *SH*. Asclepius was the god of heal-

one in the past who cleansed himself this way. This is why Erasistratus of Iulis in his treatise *On General Practice* (fr. 152 Garofalo) criticizes individuals who behave this way, pointing out that the practice damages the eyes and arrests the movement of the lower intestine. Ulpian responded to him:

> Get up, son of Asclepius; Lord Charoneus is calling you.[3]

For one of our fellow-guests wittily remarked that if it were not for the physicians, there would be nothing stupider than the grammarians. For who among us is unaware that this is not what the ancients meant by *apokottabismos*—unless you imagine that Amipsias' *Apokottabizontes* ("*Cottabus-Players*") spend their time vomiting? But since you are unacquainted with this line of research, allow me to begin by informing you that the game of cottabus was invented in Sicily, and that the Sicels came up with it, according to Critias the son of Callaeschrus in his *Elegies* (fr. B 2.1–2 West[2]), in the following passage:[4]

> The cottabus-stand is from the land of Sicily, a
>   preeminent manufacture;
>   we set it up as a target to shoot our wine-lees
>   (*latages*) at.

Aristotle's student Dicaearchus of Messene in his *On*

---

ing, hence the reference to him here, in an attack on a physician. Charoneus is presumably an otherwise unattested form of Charon, the ferryman of the Underworld.

[4] An excerpt from a much longer fragment preserved at 1.28b–c.

τῷ Περὶ Ἀλκαίου καὶ τὴν λατάγην φησὶν εἶναι Σικε-
c λικὸν ὄνομα. λατάγη δ' ἐστὶν τὸ ὑπολειπόμενον | ἀπὸ
τοῦ ἐκποθέντος ποτηρίου ὑγρόν, ὃ συνεστραμμένη τῇ
χειρὶ ἄνωθεν ἐρρίπτουν οἱ παίζοντες εἰς τὸ κοττάβιον.
Κλείταρχος δ' ἐν τῇ Περὶ Γλωττῶν πραγματείᾳ λάταγα Θεσσαλοὺς καὶ Ῥοδίους τὸν ἀπὸ τῶν ποτηρίων
κότταβον λέγειν. κότταβος δ' ἐκαλεῖτο καὶ τὸ τιθέμε-
νον ἆθλον τοῖς νικῶσιν ἐν τῷ πότῳ, ὡς Εὐριπίδης
παρίστησιν ἐν Οἰνεῖ λέγων οὕτως·

πυκνοῖς δ' ἔβαλλον Βακχίου τοξεύμασιν
κάρα γέροντος· τὸν βαλόντα δὲ στέφειν
ἐγὼ 'τετάγμην, ἆθλα κότταβον² διδούς. |

d ἐκαλεῖτο δὲ κότταβος καὶ τὸ ἄγγος εἰς ὃ ἔβαλλον τὰς
λάταγας, ὡς Κρατῖνος ἐν Νεμέσει δείκνυσιν.³ Πλάτων
δὲ ἐν Διὶ Κακουμένῳ παιδιᾶς εἶδος παροίνιον τὸν
κότταβον εἶναι ἀποδίδωσιν, ἐν ᾗ ἐξίσταντο καὶ τῶν
σκευαρίων οἱ δυσκυβοῦντες. λέγει δ' οὕτως·

(Α.) πρὸς κότταβον παίζειν, ἕως ἂν σφῷν ἐγὼ

---

² But κοσσάβων (Nauck, followed by Kannicht) ought probably to be read, meaning that Athenaeus' interpretation of the
word merely reflects a manuscript error.

³ Kaibel misguidedly added ὅτι δὲ καὶ χαλκοῦν ἦν, Εὔπολις
ἐν Βάπταις λέγει χαλκῷ περὶ κοττάβῳ (drawn from the Σ Ar.).

---

⁵ Closely related fragments of Dicaearchus' discussion are
preserved at 11.479d; 15.667b; cf. Alc. fr. 322 (quoted at 11.481a).

Alcaeus (fr. 95 Wehrli = fr. 106 Mirhady)[5] says that *latagê*[6] is a Sicilian word. *Latagê* is the liquid left in a cup after its contents have been drunk; people playing the game would twist their hand and toss it upward in the direction of the *kottabion*.[7] But Cleitarchus in his essay *On Vocabulary* (claims that) Thessalians and Rhodians refer to the clatter (*kottabos*) produced by the cups as a *latax*.[8] *Kottabos* was also the term for the prize awarded the winners of any contest at a drinking party, as Euripides establishes in *Oeneus* (fr. 562), where he says the following:

> They tried to hit the old man's head with a barrage
> of Bacchic missiles; I myself was assigned
> to garland whoever hit him, offering a *kottabos* as the
>   prize.

The vessel into which they tried to throw the *latages* was also referred to as a *kottabos*,[9] as Cratinus shows in *Nemesis* (fr. 124).[10] Plato in *Zeus Abused* (fr. 46) proves that cottabus was a type of game played by drunks, in the course of which those who made bad throws lost their clothing. He puts it as follows:

> (A.) to play cottabus, until I get dinner

6 A first-declension form of the word, which appears in the third-declension form *latax* in the quotation from Critias above.

7 Apparently "the cottabus-stand," i.e. "the target"; see Eub. fr. 15.2 (quoted at 15.666f).

8 Cf. Hsch. λ 388 "*latagê*: the *kottabos* that is thrown from the cups and produces a sound."   9 Referring to arrangements for the variant of the game discussed at 15.667e–f and described in the fragment of Plato Comicus below.

10 Quoted at 15.667f.

τὸ δεῖπνον ἔνδον σκευάσω. (Ηρ.) πάνυ βούλομαι.
† ἀλλα νεμος ἐστ †. (Α.) ἀλλ' εἰς θυείαν
    παιστέον.
(Ηρ.) φέρε τὴν θυείαν, αἶρ' ὕδωρ, ποτήρια |
e παράθετε. παίζωμεν δὲ περὶ φιλημάτων.
(Α.) <   . . .   > ἀγεννῶς οὐκ ἐῶ
παίζειν. τίθημι κοττάβεια σφῶν ἐγὼ
τασδί τε τὰς κρηπῖδας, ἃς αὕτη φορεῖ,
καὶ τὸν κότυλον τὸν σόν. (Ηρ.) βαβαιάξ· οὑτοσὶ
μείζων ἀγὼν τῆς Ἰσθμιάδος ἐπέρχεται.

ἐκάλουν δὲ καὶ κατακτούς τινας κοττάβους· ἐστὶν δὲ
λυχνία ἀναγόμενα πάλιν τε συμπίπτοντα. Εὔβουλος
Βελλεροφόντῃ·

τίς ἂν λάβοιτο τοῦ σκέλους κάτωθέ μου; |
f ἄνω γὰρ ὥσπερ κοττάβειον αἴρομαι.

Ἀντιφάνης δ' ἐν Ἀφροδίτης Γοναῖς·

(Α.) τονδὶ λέγω, σὺ δ' οὐ συνιεῖς; κότταβος
τὸ λυχνεῖόν ἐστι. πρόσεχε τὸν νοῦν· ᾠὰ μὲν
<   . . .   > πέντε νικητήριον.
(Β.) περὶ τοῦ; γελοῖον. κοτταβιεῖτε τίνα τρόπον;

---

11 Here apparently "cottabus-prizes," as at 15.667e.
12 I.e. the Isthmian Games, celebrated at Corinth in honor of
Poseidon every other year.
13 Cf. 15.667d–e.
14 Probably spoken by Bellerophon himself, as he takes flight
on Pegasus' back for the first time.

ready for the two of you inside. (Heracles) I'm quite
    willing;
[corrupt]. (A.) But you have to play in a mortar.
(Heracles) Fetch the mortar! Bring water! Put
cups beside us! Let's play for kisses.
(A.) . . . I'm not letting you play
in such an unrefined way. I'm setting these platform
    shoes here that
she's wearing as *kottabeia*[11] for the two of you,
and also your drinking cup. (Heracles) Damn! This
    contest
that's coming up here is bigger than the one at the
    Isthmus![12]

They also referred to something known as *kottabos kataktos*; these are lampstands that are set up and then collapse
again.[13] Eubulus in *Bellerophon* (fr. 15):

    Will somebody please grab my leg from down below?
    Because I'm being lifted up like a *kottabeion*![14]

Antiphanes in *The Birth of Aphrodite* (fr. 57, encompassing both quotations):[15]

    (A.) I'm talking about *this*, don't you understand?
        The "lampstand"
    is the cottabus-equipment. Pay attention! Eggs, on
        the one hand
    . . . five as a prize.
    (B.) For what? This is ridiculous. How are you going
        to play cottabus?

15 Verses 5–13 are quoted also at 11.487d–e.

11

(Α.) ἐγὼ διδάξω· καθ᾽ ὅσον τὸν κότταβον
ἀφεὶς ἐπὶ τὴν πλάστιγγα < . . . >
<(Β.) . . . >⁴ ποίαν; (Α.) τοῦτο τοὐπικείμενον
ἄνω τὸ μικρόν (Β.) τὸ πινακίσκιον λέγεις; ‖

667   (Α.) τοῦτ᾽ ἔστι πλάστιγξ – οὗτος ὁ κρατῶν
           γίγνεται.

(Β.) πῶς δ᾽ εἴσεταί τις τοῦτ᾽; (Α.) ἐὰν θίγῃ μόνον
αὐτῆς, ἐπὶ τὸν μάνην πεσεῖται καὶ ψόφος
ἔσται πάνυ πολύς. (Β.) πρὸς θεῶν, τῷ κοττάβῳ
πρόσεστι καὶ Μάνης τις ὥσπερ οἰκέτης;

καὶ μετ᾽ ὀλίγα·

(Β.) ᾧ δεῖ λαβὼν τὸ ποτήριον δεῖξον νόμῳ.
(Α.) αὐλητικῶς δεῖ καρκινοῦν τοὺς δακτύλους
οἶνόν τε μικρὸν ἐγχέαι καὶ μὴ πολύν· |

b   ἔπειτ᾽ ἀφήσεις. (Β.) τίνα τρόπον; (Α.) δεῦρο
           βλέπε·

τοιοῦτον. (Β.) <ὦ> Πόσειδον, ὡς ὑψοῦ σφόδρα.
(Α.) οὕτω ποήσεις. (Β.) ἀλλ᾽ ἐγὼ μὲν σφενδόνῃ
οὐκ ἂν ἐφικοίμην αὐτόσ᾽. (Α.) ἀλλὰ μάνθανε.

ἀγκυλοῦντα γὰρ δεῖ σφόδρα τὴν χεῖρα εὐρύθμως
πέμπειν τὸν κότταβον, ὡς Δικαίαρχός φησιν καὶ Πλά-

---

⁴ The Scholiast to Lucian has the words ποιήσῃ πεσεῖν. (Β.)
πλάστιγγα, which are missing from both of Athenaeus' quotations of this passage and must therefore have been lost already in
his source.

(A.) I'll teach you. To the extent that someone throws
his *kottabos*[16] onto the disk . . .
(B.) . . . What disk? (A.) This tiny object
set on top— (B.) Are you talking about the little
    platter?
(A.) That's the disk;—he's the winner.
(B.) How's anyone going to know this? (A.) If he just
    touches
it, it'll fall onto the *manês*,[17] and there'll be
an enormous clatter. (B.) By the gods—does the
    kottabos
also have a Manês to be its slave?

And shortly thereafter:

(B.) Take the cup and show me how.
(A.) You have to curl your fingers like a crab's claws,
    like
playing the pipes; pour in a little wine, not too much;
and then let it go! (B.) How? (A.) Look here!
Like this. (B.) Poseidon! How remarkably high it
    went!
(A.) You can do it just like that. (B.) I wouldn't reach
    there
if I was using a sling. (A.) Alright—practice-time!

For you need to bend your wrist very gracefully and toss
the *kottabos*, according to Dicaearchus (fr. 96 Wehrli = fr.

16 Here "wine-lees," as repeatedly below.
17 Also a common Athenian slave name, hence the joke that
follows; cf. the feminine form Mania in Amips. fr. 2.1 (quoted at
15.667f).

τῶν δ' ἐν τῷ Διὶ τῷ Κακουμένῳ· παρακελεύεται δέ τις
τῷ Ἡρακλεῖ μὴ σκληρὰν ἔχειν τὴν χεῖρα μέλλοντα
c κοτταβίζειν. ἐκάλουν | δ' ἀπ' ἀγκύλης τὴν τοῦ κοττά-
βου πρόεσιν διὰ τὸ ἐπαγκυλοῦν τὴν δεξιὰν χεῖρα ἐν
τοῖς ἀποκοτταβισμοῖς· οἱ δὲ ποτηρίου εἶδος τὴν ἀγκύ-
λην φασί. Βακχυλίδης ἐν Ἐρωτικοῖς·

εὖτε

τὴν ἀπ' ἀγκύλης ἵησι τοῖσδε τοῖς νεανίαις
λευκὸν ἀντείνασα πῆχυν.

καὶ Αἰσχύλος δ' ἐν Ὀστολόγοις ἀγκυλητοὺς λέγει
κοττάβους διὰ τούτων·

Εὐρύμαχος † οὐκ ἄλλος † οὐδὲν ἧσσον ⟨ . . . ⟩
ὕβριζ' ὑβρισμοὺς οὐκ ἐναισίους ἐμοί· |
d ἦν μὲν γὰρ αὐτῷ † κότταβος ἀεὶ † τοὐμὸν κάρα,
τοῦ δ' ἀγκυλητοῦ κοσσάβιός ἐστι σκοπὸς
⟨ . . . ⟩ ἐκτεμὼν ἡβῶσα χεὶρ ἐφίετο.

ὅτι δὲ ἆθλον προὔκειτο τῷ εὖ προεμένῳ τὸν κότταβον
προείρηκε μὲν καὶ ὁ Ἀντιφάνης· ᾠὰ γάρ ἐστι καὶ
πεμμάτια καὶ τραγήματα. ὁμοίως δὲ διεξέρχονται
Κηφισόδωρος ἐν Τροφωνίῳ καὶ Καλλίας ἢ Διοκλῆς ἐν
Κύκλωψι καὶ Εὔπολις Ἕρμιππός τε ἐν τοῖς Ἰάμβοις.

---

18 Cf. 11.782d–e.

19 Quoted also at 11.782e.

20 One of Penelope's suitors (cf. 1.17a–b, with a seemingly related fragment of Aeschylus quoted at 1.17c), suggesting that the
speaker is the disguised Odysseus himself.

107 Mirhady) and Plato in his *Zeus Abused* (fr. 47); someone there tells Heracles not to keep his wrist stiff, if he intends to play cottabus. They referred to the *kottabos* as
hurled from a bent wrist (*ankulê*), because they twisted
(*epankuloun*) their right hand when they played the game;
but other authorities claim that an *ankulê* is a type of cup.[18]
Bacchylides in the *Erotica* (fr. 17 Snell–Maehler):[19]

> when
> she extends her white forearm and makes the from-
> the-*ankulê* toss
> for these young men.

So too Aeschylus in *Bone-Gatherers* (fr. 179) refers to *an-
kulêtoi kottaboi*, in the following passage:

> Eurymachus[20] † no other † insulted me
> no less . . . inappropriately.
> Because my head served him † a *kottabos*
>   constantly †,
> and his bent wrist's (*ankulêtos*) cottabus-target is . . .
> Cutting away . . . , his youthful hand let fly.

That a prize was offered to anyone who threw his *kottabos*
well was noted earlier by Antiphanes (fr. 57.2–3, quoted at
15.666f); for (the prizes) were eggs, pastries, and snacks.
Cephisodorus in *Trophonius* (fr. 5), Callias (fr. 12) or Diocles in *Cyclopes*,[21] Eupolis (fr. 399), and Hermippus in

---

[21] Athenaeus (or his source) also expresses doubts about the
authorship of the play at 4.140e; 7.306a; 12.524f, but assigns it unambiguously to Callias at 7.285e, 286a; 11.487a, as do other authorities.

τὸ δὲ καλούμενον κατακτὸν κοττάβιον τοιοῦτόν ἐστιν·
e λυχνίον ἐστὶν ὑψηλόν, | ἔχον τὸν μάνην καλούμενον,
ἐφ᾽ ὃν τὴν καταβαλλομένην ἔδει πεσεῖν πλάστιγγα,
ἐντεῦθεν δὲ πίπτειν εἰς λεκάνην ὑποκειμένην πληγεῖ-
σαν τῷ κοττάβῳ· καί τις ἦν ἀκριβὴς εὐχέρεια τῆς
βολῆς. μνημονεύει δὲ τοῦ μάνου Νικοχάρης ἐν Λάκω-
σιν. ἕτερον δ᾽ ἐστὶν εἶδος παιδιᾶς τῆς ἐν λεκάνῃ. αὕτη
δ᾽ ὕδατος πληροῦται ἐπινεῖ τε ἐπ᾽ αὐτῆς ὀξύβαφα
κενά, ἐφ᾽ ἃ βάλλοντες τὰς λατάγας ἐκ καρχησίων
ἐπειρῶντο καταδύειν· ἀνῃρεῖτο δὲ τὰ κοττάβια ὁ πλείω
καταδύσας. Ἀμειψίας Ἀκοκοτταβίζουσιν· |

f   ἡ Μανία, φέρ᾽ ὀξύβαφα καὶ κανθάρους
     καὶ τὸν ποδανιπτῆρ᾽, ἐγχέασα θὕδατος.

Κρατῖνος ἐν Νεμέσει· † τὸ δὲ κοττάβῳ προθέντας ἐν
πατρικοῖσι νόμοις τὸ κεινεου ὀξυβάφοις βάλλειν μὲν
τῷ πόντῳ δὲ βάλλοντι νέμω πλεῖστα τύχης τὸ δ᾽
ἆθλον. † Ἀριστοφάνης Δαιταλεῦσιν· † ἔγνωκ᾽, ἐγὼ δὲ
χαλκίον, τοῦτ᾽ ἐστὶν κοττάβειον, ἱστάναι καὶ μυρ-
668 ρίνας. † ‖ Ἕρμιππος Μοίραις·

     χλανίδες δ᾽ οὖλαι καταβέβληνται,
     θώρακα δ᾽ ἅπας ἐμπερονᾶται,

---

22 Cf. 15.666e, 667a with n.
23 Either this is a hybrid version of the two forms of the game
or Athenaeus' source is garbled or confused.
24 Identified by Kaibel as a (partially corrupt) fragment of an
adespota trochaic verse.

his *Iambs* (fr. 7 West²) offer similar details. The so-called *kottabos kataktos* is something of the following sort: There is a high lampstand, which supports the so-called *manês*.²² When the disk was knocked down, it had to strike the *manês*; then it had to fall into the basin set underneath, after it was struck by the *kottabos*.²³ The throw involved a certain degree of dexterity.²⁴ Nicochares in *Spartans* (fr. 13) mentions the *manês*. A separate variety of the game is played in a basin. The basin is filled with water, and empty vinegar cruets are floated inside it; they threw the wine-lees from their cups (*karchêsiai*) at the cruets and tried to sink them; and whoever sank the most got the prizes (*kottabia*). Amipsias in *Cottabus-Players* (fr. 2):

> Mania! Bring vinegar cruets and some large cups (*kantharoi*),
> along with the foot-washing basin, after you pour the water into it!

Cratinus in *Nemesis* (fr. 124, corrupt and unmetrical): † after setting out the *kottabos* following our ancestral rules the [corrupt] to strike with cruets, but to the sea (?) that strikes I apportion the most luck, but the prize. † Aristophanes in *Banqueters* (fr. 231, corrupt and unmetrical): † he realized, but I (said) to set up a piece of bronze—that is a *kottabeion*—and myrtle branches. † Hermippus in *Fates* (fr. 48):²⁵

> The wool cloaks have been thrown off,
> and everyone's fastening on his breastplate;

²⁵ Verses 5–10 are quoted also at 11.487e–f.

κνημὶς δὲ περὶ σφυρὸν ἀρθροῦται,
βλαύτης δ' οὐδεὶς ἔτ' ἔρως λευκῆς,
ῥάβδον δ' ὄψει τὴν κοτταβικὴν
ἐν τοῖς ἀχύροισι κυλινδομένην,
μάνης δ' οὐδὲν λατάγων ἀίει,
τὴν δὲ τάλαιναν πλάστιγγ' ⟨ἂν⟩ ἴδοις
παρὰ τὸν στροφέα τῆς κηπαίας
    ἐν τοῖσι κορήμασιν οὖσαν.

Ἀχαιὸς δ' ἐν Λίνῳ περὶ τῶν σατύρων λέγων φησίν·

    ῥιπτοῦντες ἐκβάλλοντες ἀγνύντες, τί μ' οὐ |
b   λέγοντες· ὦ κάλλιστον Ἡρακλεί⟨διον⟩
    λάταξ.

τοῦτο δὲ "λέγοντες" παρ' ὅσον τῶν ἐρωμένων ἐμέμνηντο, ἀφιέντες ἐπ' αὐτοῖς τοὺς λεγομένους κοσσάβους.
διὸ καὶ Σοφοκλῆς ἐν Ἰνάχῳ Ἀφροδισίαν εἴρηκε τὴν
λάταγα·

    ξανθὰ δ' Ἀφροδισία λάταξ
    πᾶσιν ἐπεκτύπει δόμοις.

καὶ Εὐριπίδης ἐν Πλεισθένει·

    πολὺς δὲ κοσσάβων ἀραγ-
        μὸς Κύπριδος προσῳδὸν ἀ-
        χεῖ μέλος ἐν δόμοισιν.

greaves are being fitted around ankles,
and there's no longer any interest in a white slipper.
You'll see the cottabus-stand
rolling around in the dust,[26]
and the *manês* no longer pays attention to the wine-
　　lees.
You'd also notice the poor disk
lying in the trash beside
　　the hinge of the back door.

Achaeus in *Linus* (*TrGF* 20 F 26), discussing the satyrs,
says:

Tossing me, hurling me out, shattering me, calling
　　me every
name imaginable! O lovely little Heracles,
wine-lees!

He uses the term "calling" because they mentioned those
they loved, throwing what are referred to as *kossaboi*[27] in
their honor. This is why Sophocles in *Inachus* (fr. 277) refers to the wine-lees as belonging to Aphrodite:

Aphrodite's blond wine-lees
echoed throughout the house.

Also Euripides in *Pleisthenes* (fr. 631):

The loud clatter of Cypris'[28]
　　kossaboi produces its harmonious
　　tune in the house.

26 Literally "the chaff, the husks."
27 A variant form of *kottaboi*.
28 Aphrodite's.

καὶ Καλλίμαχος δέ φησι·

πολλοὶ καὶ φιλέοντες Ἀκόντιον ἧκαν ἔραζε |
οἰνοπόται Σικελὰς ἐκ κυλίκων λάταγας.

c

ἦν δέ τι καὶ ἄλλο κοτταβίων εἶδος προτιθέμενον ἐν
ταῖς παννυχίσιν, οὗ μνημονεύει Καλλίμαχος[5] ἐν Παννυχίδι διὰ τούτων·

ὁ δ' ἀγρυπνήσας < . . . >
τὸν πυραμοῦντα λήψεται <καὶ> τὰ κοττάβεια
καὶ τῶν παρουσῶν ἣν θέλει < . . . > φιλήσει.

ἐγίνετο δὲ καὶ πεμμάτιά τινα ἐν ταῖς παννυχίσιν, ἐν
αἷς πλεῖστον ὅσον χρόνον διηγρύπνουν χορεύοντες·
καὶ διωνομάζετο τὰ πεμμάτια τότε χαρίσιοι ἀπὸ τῆς
d   τῶν ἀναιρουμένων χαρᾶς. μνημονεύει | Εὔβουλος ἐν
Ἀγκυλίωνι λέγων οὑτωσί·

καὶ γὰρ πάλαι πέττει τὰ νικητήρια.

εἶθ' ἑξῆς φησιν·

ἐξεπήδησ' ἀρτίως
πέττουσα τὸν χαρίσιον.

ὅτι δὲ καὶ φίλημα ἦν ἆθλον ἑξῆς λέγει ὁ Εὔβουλος·

5 Καλλίμαχος Wilamowitz: Κάλλιππος A

---

29 A papyrus preserves a more complete version of the verses.
30 For the *charisios*, cf. 14.646b.

Callimachus (fr. 69 Pfeiffer) as well says:

> And many wine-drinkers, out of love for Acontius,
>   threw
> Sicilian lees from their cups onto the ground.

There was also another type of *kottabia* that were offered as the prize at all-night festivals. Callimachus mentions them in *The All-Night Festival* (fr. 227.5–7 Pfeiffer), in the following passage:[29]

> Whoever stays awake . . .
> will get the *puramous* and the *kottabeia*,
> and will kiss any woman he wishes of those who are
>   there.

There were also pastries available at their all-night festivals, during which they stayed awake dancing for as long as they could; the pastries were referred to as *charisioi* in those days, because of the joy (*chara*) the individuals awarded them experienced.[30] Eubulus in *Ankulion* (fr. 1, encompassing both quotations) mentions them, saying the following:

> In fact, she's been baking the victory-cakes for a long
>   time now.

Then immediately after this he says:

> > She leapt out just now
> as she was baking the *charisios*.

Immediately after this, Eubulus (fr. 2) notes that kisses served as a prize:

εἶέν γυναῖκες· νῦν ὅπως τὴν νύχθ' ὅλην
ἐν τῇ δεκάτῃ τοῦ παιδίου χορεύσετε.
θήσω δὲ νικητήριον τρεῖς ταινίας
καὶ μῆλα πέντε καὶ φιλήματ' ἐννέα.

e ὅτι δὲ ἐσπούδαστο παρὰ τοῖς Σικελιώταις ὁ | κότ-
ταβος δῆλον ἐκ τοῦ καὶ οἰκήματα ἐπιτήδεια τῇ παιδιᾷ
κατασκευάζεσθαι, ὡς ἱστορεῖ Δικαίαρχος ἐν τῷ Περὶ
Ἀλκαίου. οὐκ ἀπεικότως οὖν οὐδ' ὁ Καλλίμαχος Σικε-
λὴν τὴν λάταγα προσηγόρευσεν. μνημονεύει τῶν
λατάγων καὶ τῶν κοττάβων καὶ ὁ Χαλκοῦς καλούμενος Διονύσιος ἐν τοῖς Ἐλεγείοις διὰ τούτων·

κότταβον ἐνθάδε σοι τρίτον ἑστάναι οἱ
δυσέρωτες |
f   ἡμεῖς προστίθεμεν γυμνασίῳ Βρομίου
κώρυκον. οἱ δὲ παρόντες ἐνείρετε χεῖρας ἅπαντες
ἐς σφαίρας κυλίκων· καὶ πρὶν ἐκεῖνον ἰδεῖν,
ὄμματι βηματίσασθε τὸν αἰθέρα τὸν κατὰ
κλίνην,
εἰς ὅσον αἱ λάταγες χωρίον ἐκτατέαι.

ἐπὶ τούτοις ὁ Οὐλπιανὸς ᾔτει πιεῖν μεγάλῃ κύλικι,
ἐπιλέγων ἐκ τῶν αὐτῶν Ἐλεγείων καὶ τόδε· ||

669   ὕμνους οἰνοχοεῖν ἐπιδέξια σοί τε καὶ ἡμῖν·
τόν τε σὸν ἀρχαῖον τηλεδαπόν τε φίλον

---

[31] When friends and family were invited for a celebration, and
the child was given a name.   [32] Quoted at 15.668c.
[33] Discussed by Borthwick, *JHS* 84 (1964) 49–53.

Alright, ladies—be sure to dance all
night long at the baby's tenth-day celebration![31]
I'll offer three ribbons, five apples,
and nine kisses as a victory prize.

That the inhabitants of Sicily were enthusiastic about cottabus is apparent from the fact that they built rooms specifically intended for the game, according to Dicaearchus in his *On Alcaeus* (fr. 94 Wehrli = fr. 108 Mirhady). It was therefore not unreasonable for Callimachus (fr. 69.2 Pfeiffer)[32] to refer to the wine-lees as "Sicilian." The Dionysius known as Chalcous mentions wine-lees and *kottaboi* in his *Elegies* (fr. 3 West[2]), in the following passage:[33]

We who are unhappy in love are adding for you a
        third
    kottabos to stand here in Bromius' school as a
punching bag. All of you who belong to our group
        must wrap your hands
    in the boxing-thongs the cups represent; even
        before you see it,
pace off with your eye the space from there to your
        couch,
    over which the wine-lees must extend.

After Ulpian completed these remarks, he asked to drink from a large cup, appending the following passage from the same *Elegies* (Dionys. Eleg. fr. 4 West[2]):

to pour hymns like wine from left to right for you and
        us;
    and we will send your old friend from another
        country

εἰρεσίη γλώσσης ἀποπέμψομεν εἰς μέγαν αἶνον
τοῦδ' ἐπὶ συμποσίου· δεξιότης δὲ λόγου
Φαίακος Μουσῶν ἐρέτας ἐπὶ σέλματα πέμπει.

κατὰ γὰρ τὸν νεώτερον Κρατῖνον, ὃς ἐν Ὀμφάλῃ
φησίν·

πίνειν μένοντα τὸν καλῶς εὐδαίμονα |
b   κρεῖττον· μάχαι δ' ἄλλοισι καὶ πόνος μέλοι.

πρὸς ὃν ὁ Κύνουλκος ἀεὶ τῷ Σύρῳ ἀντικορυσσόμενος
καὶ οὐδέποτε τῆς φιλονεικίας παυόμενος ἧς εἶχε πρὸς
αὐτόν, ἐπεὶ θόρυβος κατεῖχε τὸ συμπόσιον, ἔφη· τίς
οὗτος ὁ τῶν συρβηνέων χορός; καὶ αὐτὸς δὲ τούτων
τῶν ἐπῶν μεμνημένος τινῶν ἐρῶ, ἵνα μὴ ὁ Οὐλπιανὸς
βρενθύηται ὡς ἐκ τῶν ἀποθέτων τοῖς Ὁμηρίδαις
μόνος ἀνασπάσας ⟨λήψεται⟩[6] τὰ κοττάβεια·

ἀγγελίας ἀγαθῆς δεῦρ' ἴτε πευσόμενοι, |
c   καὶ κυλίκων ἔριδας διαλύσατε, καὶ κατάθεσθε
τὴν ξύνεσιν παρ' ἐμοί, καὶ τάδε μανθάνετε,

εἰς τὴν παροῦσαν ζήτησιν ἐπιτήδεια ὄντα· ὁρῶ γὰρ
καὶ τοὺς παῖδας ἤδη φέροντας ἡμῖν στεφάνους καὶ
μύρα. διὰ τί δὲ λέγονται, τῶν ἐστεφανωμένων ἐὰν

6 add. Wilamowitz

34 Ulpian. The same odd expression (literally "going helmet to
helmet") is used at 15.701b, again of Cynulcus' attitude toward
Ulpian.

off to great praise with the rowing of tongues
> that takes place at this party. The cleverness of
> > Phaeacian
speech sends the Muses' oarsmen to their benches.

For to quote Cratinus Junior, who says in *Omphale* (fr. 4):

> It's better for someone who's genuinely happy to stay
> > at home
> and drink; let other people worry about battles and
> > hard work!

The party descended into shouting, and Cynulcus, who was constantly butting heads with the Syrian[34] and never abandoned the quarrel he had with him, responded: What is this chorus of pipers (*surbênes*)?[35] I myself too remember some of these verses and will recite them, to prevent Ulpian from acting haughty on the ground that he alone can draw on the treasures that belong to the Homeridae[36] and will therefore receive the prize (*kottabeia*) (Dionys. Eleg. fr. 2 West[2]):

> Come here to hear good news;
> put a stop to the quarrels that go with drinking; pay
> > attention to me; and learn the following,

which is relevant to the topic we are currently discussing. I see that the slaves are now bringing us garlands and perfumes. Why is it, that when the garlands people are wear-

---

[35] Perhaps part of a comic iambic trimeter line; the word is used again at 15.671c, 697e.

[36] An echo of Pl. *Phdr.* 252b.

λύωνται οἱ στέφανοι, ὅτι ἐρῶσιν; τοῦτο γὰρ ἐν παισὶ
τὰ Καλλιμάχου ἀναγινώσκων Ἐπιγράμματα, ὧν ἐστι
d καὶ τοῦτο, ἐπεζήτουν μαθεῖν, | εἰπόντος τοῦ Κυρη-
ναίου·

τὰ δὲ ῥόδα φυλλοβολεῦντα
τῶνδρὸς ἀπὸ στεφάνων πάντ' ἐγένοντο χαμαί.

σὸν οὖν ἐστιν, ὦ μουσικώτατε, τὴν χιλιέτη μου ταύτην
ζήτησιν ἀπολύσασθαι, Δημόκριτε, καὶ διὰ τί οἱ ἐρῶντες στεφανοῦσι τὰς τῶν ἐρωμένων θύρας. καὶ ὁ Δημόκριτος, ἀλλ' ἵνα κἀγώ, φησίν, μνημονεύσω τῶν τοῦ
Χαλκοῦ ποιητοῦ καὶ ῥήτορος Διονυσίου – Χαλκοῦς δὲ
προσηγορεύθη διὰ τὸ συμβουλεῦσαι Ἀθηναίοις
χαλκῷ νομίσματι χρήσασθαι, καὶ τὸν λόγον τοῦτον
e ἀνέγραψε | Καλλίμαχος ἐν τῇ τῶν Ῥητορικῶν Ἀνα-
γραφῇ – λέξω τι καὶ αὐτὸς ἐκ τῶν Ἐλεγείων. σὺ δέ, ὦ
Θεόδωρε (τοῦτο γάρ σου τὸ κύριον ὄνομα),

δέχου τήνδε προπινομένην
τὴν ἀπ' ἐμοῦ ποίησιν· ἐγὼ δ' ἐπιδέξια πέμπω
σοὶ πρώτῳ, Χαρίτων ἐγκεράσας χάριτας.
καὶ σὺ λαβὼν τόδε δῶρον ἀοιδὰς ἀντιπρόπιθι,
συμπόσιον κοσμῶν καὶ τὸ σὸν εὖ θέμενος. |

---

37 *PAA* 336985; the speech in question was probably made
around 443 BCE, when Dionysius was one of the leaders of the
Athenian colony sent to Thurii.

ing fall apart, they are said to be in love? Because when I read Callimachus' *Epigrams*, from which the following passage is drawn, in school, I attempted to understand this point, since the Cyrenean said (Call. *AP* 12.134.3–4 = *HE* 1105–6):

> The roses all shed their petals
> from the man's wreaths and lay on the ground.

Your task, therefore, my most learned Democritus, is to resolve this millennium-old question of mine, along with the problem of why people place garlands at the doors of those they are in love with. And Democritus said: Well, in order that I too may quote from the works of the poet and orator Dionysius Chalcous[37]—he was called Chalcous because he advised the Athenians to use bronze (*chalkos*) coins, and Callimachus recorded this speech in his *List of Rhetorical Pieces* (fr. 430 Pfeiffer)—I myself will recite a passage from the *Elegies* (Dionys. Eleg. fr. 1 West²). As for you, Theodorus—for this is your given name:[38]

> Accept this poetry I am offering you
> as a toast; I am sending it to you first, moving from
> left to right, and I have mixed the grace of the
> Graces into it.
> As for you, take this gift and offer me a toast of song
> in return,
> adding brilliance to our party and improving your
> own situation.

---

[38] Cf. 15.692b. Elsewhere the character is consistently referred to as Cynulcus; see 1.1d with n.

f φῂς οὖν, διὰ τί, τῶν ἐστεφανωμένων ἐὰν λύηται ὁ
στέφανος, ἐρᾶν λέγονται. πότερον ὅτι ὁ ἔρως τοῦ τῶν
ἐρώντων ἤθους περιαιρεῖται τὸν κόσμον, διὰ τοῦτο τὴν
τοῦ ἐπιφανοῦς κόσμου περιαίρεσιν φρυκτόν τινα,
φησὶ Κλέαρχος ἐν πρώτῳ Ἐρωτικῶν, καὶ σημεῖον
νομίζουσιν τοῦ καὶ τὸν τοῦ ἤθους κόσμον περιῃρῆ-
σθαι τοὺς τοιούτους; ἢ καθάπερ ἐπὶ τῆς μαντικῆς
670 ἄλλα πολλά, καὶ τοῦτο σημειοῦνταί τινες; ‖ ὁ γὰρ ἐκ
τοῦ στεφάνου κόσμος οὐδὲν ἔχων μόνιμον σημεῖόν
ἐστι πάθους ἀβεβαίου μέν, κεκαλλωπισμένου δέ. τοιοῦτος δ᾽ ἐστὶν ὁ ἔρως· οὐδένες γὰρ μᾶλλον τῶν ἐν τῷ
ἐρᾶν ὄντων καλλωπίζονται. εἰ μὴ ἄρα ἡ φύσις οἱονεί
τι δαιμόνιον δικαίως βραβεύουσα τῶν πραγμάτων
ἕκαστον οἴεται δεῖν τοὺς ἐρῶντας μὴ στεφανοῦσθαι
πρὶν κρατήσωσιν τοῦ ἔρωτος· τοῦτο δ᾽ ἐστὶν ὅταν
κατεργασάμενοι τὸν ἐρώμενον ἀπαλλαγῶσιν τῆς ἐπι-
θυμίας. τὴν ἀφαίρεσιν οὖν τοῦ στεφάνου σημεῖον τοῦ
b ἔτι ἐν τῷ διαγωνίζεσθαι εἶναι ποιούμεθα. | ἢ ὁ Ἔρως
αὐτὸς οὐκ ἐῶν καθ᾽ αὑτοῦ στεφανοῦσθαι καὶ ἀνακη-
ρύττεσθαι τῶν μὲν τὸν στέφανον περιαιρεῖ, τοῖς δὲ
λοιποῖς ἐνδίδωσιν αἴσθησιν μηνύων ὅτι ἡττῶνται ὑπὸ
αὐτοῦ; διὸ ἐρᾶν οἱ λοιποὶ τοὺς τοιούτους φασίν. ἢ ὅτι
λύεται μὲν πᾶν τὸ δεδεμένον, ὁ δὲ ἔρως στεφανου-
μένων τινῶν δεσμός ἐστιν (οὐθένες γὰρ ἄλλοι τῶν
δεδεμένων περὶ τὸ στεφανοῦσθαι σπουδάζουσιν πλὴν
οἱ ἐρῶντες), τὴν τοῦ στεφάνου δὴ λύσιν σημεῖον τοῦ

Your question, then, is why, when the garlands people are wearing fall apart, such individuals are said to be in love. Is it because love strips lovers of the decent behavior that normally characterizes them, and on that account people regard the stripping of the decency that is conspicuously theirs as a signal of a sort, and as evidence that such individuals have been stripped of their normal decent behavior, as Clearchus puts it in Book I of the *Erotica* (fr. 24 Wehrli, extending to the quotation from Lycophronides)? Or, as in the case of prophecy, are there many different signs, and are only some people distinguished by this one? For the decency represented by the garland has no enduring character, and it thus signifies a feeling that is fleeting, even if attractive. This is what love is like; no one is more concerned about being physically attractive than people in love. Unless nature, in fact, acting as a divine power and offering a correct assessment of all matters, regards it as necessary that lovers wear no garlands until they are victorious over love, which is to say, when they overcome the person they are in love with and escape their desire. We accordingly consider the decay of the garland evidence that someone is still involved in the struggle. Or is it the case that, because Eros himself does not allow anyone to be garlanded and proclaimed victorious over him, he strips such individuals of their garlands, while allowing everyone else to understand the situation, by informing them that he has defeated the lovers? This is why everyone else says that such people are in love (*eran*). Or is it because everything that is bound together can also be torn apart, and that when people are garlanded, it is love that binds them—for no one else who is bound this way is as enthusiastic about wearing garlands as lovers are—and that people regard the

περὶ τὸν ἔρωτα δεσμοῦ νομίζοντες ἐρᾶν φασιν τοὺς
c τοιούτους; | ἢ διὰ τὸ πολλάκις τοὺς ἐρῶντας διὰ τὴν
πτοίησιν, ὡς ἔοικεν, στεφανουμένους περιαιρεῖν αὐτῶν τὸν στέφανον ἀντιστρέφομεν τῇ ὑπονοίᾳ τὸ πά-
θος, ὡς οὐκ ἄν ποτε τοῦ στεφάνου περιρέοντος, εἰ μὴ
ἤρων; ἢ ὅτι ἀναλύσεις περὶ μόνους μάλιστα τοὺς
ἐρῶντας καὶ καταδεδεμένους γίνονται, τὴν δὲ τοῦ
στεφάνου ἀνάλυσιν καταδεδεμένων τινῶν εἶναι νομίζοντες ἐρᾶν φασι τοὺς τοιούτους; καταδέδενται γὰρ οἱ
ἐρῶντες. εἰ μὴ ἄρα διὰ τὸ κατεστέφθαι τῷ Ἔρωτι τοὺς
ἐρῶντας οὐκ ἐπίμονος αὐτῶν ὁ στέφανος γίνεται· |
d χαλεπὸν γὰρ ἐπὶ μεγάλῳ καὶ θείῳ στεφάνῳ μικρὸν
καὶ τὸν τυχόντα μεῖναι. στεφανοῦσιν δὲ τὰς τῶν
ἐρωμένων θύρας ἤτοι τιμῆς χάριν καθαπερεί τινος
θεοῦ τὰ πρόθυρα,[7] ἢ οὐ τοῖς ἐρωμένοις ἀλλὰ τῷ
Ἔρωτι ποιούμενοι τὴν τῶν στεφάνων ἀνάθεσιν τοῦ
μὲν Ἔρωτος τὸν ἐρώμενον ἄγαλμα, τούτου δὲ ναὸν
ὄντα τὴν οἴκησιν στεφανοῦσι·[8] διὰ ταῦτα δὲ καὶ θύου-
σιν ἔνιοι ἐπὶ ταῖς τῶν ἐρωμένων θύραις. ἢ μᾶλλον ὑφ᾽
e ὧν οἴονταί | τε καὶ πρὸς ἀλήθειαν τὸν τῆς ψυχῆς
κόσμον ἐσκύλευνται, καὶ τούτοις[9] καὶ τὸν τοῦ σώμα-
τος κόσμον ὑπὸ τοῦ πάθους ἐξαγόμενοι καὶ σκυλεύ-
οντες ἑαυτοὺς ἀνατιθέασιν. πᾶς δ᾽ ὁ ἐρῶν τοῦτο δρᾷ
μὲν ⟨παρόντος⟩,[10] μὴ παρόντος δὲ τοῦ ἐρωμένου τοῦ

---

[7] τὰ πρόθυρα στεφανοῦσιν αὐτῶν A: del. Wilamowitz: στεφανοῦσιν αὐτῶν tantum del. Kaibel
[8] στεφανοῦσι τὰ τῶν ἐρωμένων πρόθυρα A: τὰ . . . πρόθυρα del. Wilamowitz

30

decay of the garland as evidence pertaining to the binding associated with love, and say that such individuals are in love? Or, as a consequence of the fact that lovers, on account of their excitement, apparently, frequently pluck the petals from the garlands they are wearing, do we reverse our interpretation of the situation, reasoning that the garland would never have fallen apart, unless they were in love? Or is it that only lovers and individuals under a spell can be released, and that people who regard the decay of the wreath as connected with those who have been bound somehow say that such individuals are in love? For lovers are under a spell. Unless, perhaps, the fact that lovers have been garlanded by Eros means that their garland does not last long; since it is difficult for something small and ordinary to last when it is connected with a large garland associated with a god. They garland their lovers' doors either to honor them, as if this was the front door of some god, or else they dedicate the garlands not to their lovers but to Eros, and garland their beloved as if he were a statue of Eros, and his house as if it were the god's temple. This is why some people offer sacrifices at their lovers' doors. Or else they believe instead that they have been robbed of their soul's decency—and they actually have been!—and having been separated from physical decency by what they have suffered, they plunder themselves and make a dedication to the ones who robbed them. Every lover does this when his lover is present, whereas if his lover is absent, he makes his dedication to anyone he encounters. This

---

9 τούτοις Musurus: τοῦτον A
10 add. Schweighäuser

ἐμποδὼν ποιεῖται τὴν ἀνάθεσιν. ὅθεν Λυκοφρονίδης
τὸν ἐρῶντα ἐκεῖνον αἰπόλον ἐποίησε λέγοντα·

> τόδ' ἀνατίθημί σοι ῥόδον,
> καλὸν ἄνθημα, καὶ πέδιλα καὶ κυνέαν
> καὶ τὰν θηροφόνον λογχίδ', ἐπεί μοι νόος ἄλλᾳ
> κέχυται
f   ἐπὶ τὰν Χάρισιν | φίλαν παῖδα καὶ καλάν.

ἀλλὰ μὴν καὶ ὁ ἱερώτατος Πλάτων ἐν ἑβδόμῳ Νόμων
πρόβλημά τι προβάλλει στεφανωτικόν, ὅπερ ἄξιόν
ἐστιν ἐπιλύσασθαι, οὕτως λέγοντος τοῦ φιλοσόφου·
μήλων τέ τινων διανομαὶ καὶ στεφάνων πλείοσιν ἅμα
καὶ ἐλάττοσιν ἁρμοττόντων τῶν ἀριθμῶν τῶν αὐτῶν. ὁ
μὲν Πλάτων οὕτως εἶπεν, ἔστιν δ' ὃ λέγει τοιοῦτον·
ἕνα βούλεσθαι ἀριθμὸν εὑρεῖν, ᾧ ἕως τοῦ τελευταίου
εἰσελθόντος ἐξ ἴσου πάντες ἕξουσιν ἤτοι μῆλα ἢ
671   στεφάνους. ‖ φημὶ οὖν τὸν τῶν ἑξήκοντα ἀριθμὸν εἰς
ἓξ συμπότας δύνασθαι τὴν ἰσότητα πληροῦν. οἶδα
γὰρ ὅτι κατ' ἀρχὰς ἐλέγομεν μὴ συνδειπνεῖν τῶν
πέντε γε πλείους· ὅτι δ' ἡμεῖς ψαμμακόσιοι ἐσμὲν
δῆλον. ὁ οὖν ⟨τῶν⟩¹¹ ἑξήκοντα ἀριθμὸς εἰς ἓξ συμ-
πληρωθέντος τοῦ συμποσίου ἀρκέσει οὕτως. εἰσῆλθεν
εἰς τὸ συμπόσιον ὁ πρῶτος καὶ ἔλαβεν στεφάνους
ἑξήκοντα· ἐπεισελθόντι τῷ δευτέρῳ δίδωσιν τοὺς ἡμί-
σεις καὶ ἑκατέρῳ γίνονται τριάκοντα· καὶ τρίτῳ ἐπ-
b   εισελθόντι | συνδιαιρούμενοι τοὺς πάντας ἐξ εἴκοσιν
ἔχουσι, τετάρτῳ πάλιν ὁμοίως κοινωνήσαντες ἐκ

is why Lycophronides (*PMG* 844) represented his well-known love-sick goatherd as saying:

> I dedicate this rose, a beautiful
> flower, to you, along with my sandals and my cap
> and the javelin with which I kill wild beasts, since my
>   thoughts have been turned in another direction,
> toward the beautiful girl the Graces love.

The most holy Plato in Book VII of the *Laws* (819b), moreover, poses a puzzle that involves garlands, which deserves to be explicated. The philosopher puts it as follows: distributions of certain apples and garlands, with the same quantities working for both larger and smaller numbers of people. This is what Plato said, but what he means is something along the following lines: Try to identify a single number that will allow everyone, including the last person to enter the room, to have an equal number of apples or garlands. I claim, then, that the number 60 can provide up to six guests with an equal share. For I am aware that initially (1.4e, quoting Archestr. fr. 4 Olson–Sens = *SH* 191) we said that a dinner party should consist of no more than five people; but that we are more numerous than the grains of sand is obvious. The number 60, at any rate, will be large enough for a party that includes up to six guests, in the following way. The first man came to the party and took 60 garlands; when the second man came in, he gave him half, and they each had 30; when the third man came in, they divided them all up again and had 20 apiece; so too they shared them with the fourth man and had 15 apiece, and

---

11 add. Kaibel

δεκαπέντε,[12] πέμπτῳ δὲ ἐκ δώδεκα καὶ τῷ ἕκτῳ ἐκ δέκα. καὶ οὕτως ἰσότης ἀναπληροῦται τῶν στεφάνων.

Ταῦτ᾽ εἰπόντος τοῦ Δημοκρίτου ὁ Οὐλπιανὸς ἀπο-βλέψας πρὸς τὸν Κύνουλκον,

οἵῳ μ᾽ ὁ δαίμων (ἔφη) φιλοσόφῳ συνῴκισεν,

κατὰ τὸ Θεογνήτου τοῦ κωμῳδιοποιοῦ Φάσμα.

ἐπαρίστερ᾽ ἔμαθες, ὦ πόνηρε, γράμματα· |
c   ἀνέστροφέν σου τὸν βίον τὰ βιβλία.
πεφιλοσόφηκας γῇ τε κοὐρανῷ λαλῶν,
οἷς οὐθέν ἐστιν ἐπιμελὲς τῶν σῶν λόγων.

πόθεν γάρ σοι καὶ ὁ τῶν συρβηνέων ἐπῆλθεν χορός; τίς τῶν ἀξίων λόγου μέμνηται τοῦ μουσικοῦ τούτου χοροῦ; καὶ ὅς, οὐ πρότερον, ἔφη, ὦ οὗτος, διδάξω σε, πρὶν ἂν τὸν ἄξιον παρὰ σοῦ λάβω μισθόν· οὐ γὰρ ἐγὼ τὰς ἐκ τῶν βιβλίων ἀκάνθας ὥσπερ σὺ ἀναγινώσκων ἐκλέγω, ἀλλὰ τὰ χρησιμώτατα καὶ ἀκοῆς ἄξια. ἐπὶ d   τούτοις ὁ Οὐλπιανὸς | δυσχεράνας ἀνεβόησεν τὰ ἐξ Ὕπνου Ἀλέξιδος·

οὐδ᾽ ἐν Τριβαλλοῖς ταῦτά γ᾽ ἐστὶν ἔννομα·
οὗ φασι τὸν θύοντα τοῖς κεκλημένοις

[12] ἐκ δεκαπέντε γίνονται ACE: γίνονται del. Kaibel

---

[39] Quoted at greater length at 3.104b–c.
[40] Literally "from right to left."   [41] See 15.669b with n.
[42] For the image, cf. 3.97c–d with n.; 8.347d with n.; 15.678f.

34

with the fifth man and had 12 apiece, and with the sixth man and had 10 apiece. In this way an equal division of the wreaths can be maintained.

After Democritus completed these remarks, Ulpian glanced at Cynulcus and said:

> What a philosopher the gods forced me to share a
> house with!,

to quote the *Phantom* of the comic poet Theognetus (fr. 1.6–10):[39]

> You learned your letters backwards,[40] fool!
> Your books turned your life upside-down!
> You've offered your philosophical babbling to earth
> and heaven,
> and they're completely uninterested in what you have
> to say.

Where did you get this "chorus of pipers (*surbênes*)"?[41] What authority that deserves mention refers to a musical group of this sort? Cynulcus replied: I will offer you no answer, sir, until you pay me the appropriate amount. For I do not pick out the thorny passages from my books when I read, as you do;[42] I look instead for those that are most useful and worth hearing. This upset Ulpian, and he shouted out the passage from Alexis' *Sleep* (fr. 243):

> Not even Triballians[43] are allowed to act like this!
> In their country, they say, someone who's making a
> sacrifice shows

[43] A notoriously barbaric Illyrian or Thracian tribe (e.g. Ar. *Av.* 1520–9).

35

δείξαντ᾽ ἰδεῖν τὸ δεῖπνον εἰς τὴν αὔριον
πωλεῖν ἀδείπνοις ἃ παρέθηκ᾽ αὐτοῖς ἰδεῖν.

τὰ αὐτὰ ἰαμβεῖα φέρεται καὶ παρὰ Ἀντιφάνει ἐν
e Ὕπνῳ. καὶ ὁ Κύνουλκος· ἐπεὶ περὶ στεφάνων | ζητή-
σεις ἤδη γεγόνασιν, εἰπὲ ἡμῖν τίς ἐστιν ὁ παρὰ τῷ
χαρίεντι Ἀνακρέοντι Ναυκρατίτης στέφανος, ὦ Οὐλπιανέ. φησὶν γὰρ οὕτως ὁ μελιχρὸς ποιητής·

στεφάνους δ᾽ ἀνὴρ τρεῖς ἕκαστος εἶχεν,
τοὺς μὲν ῥοδίνους, τὸν δὲ Ναυκρατίτην.

καὶ διὰ τί παρὰ τῷ αὐτῷ ποιητῇ λύγῳ τινὲς στεφα-
νοῦνται; φησὶν γὰρ ἐν τῷ δευτέρῳ τῶν Μελῶν·

f <ὁ> Μεγιστῆς δ᾽ ὁ φιλόφρων δέκα δὴ | μῆνες
ἐπεί τε
στεφανοῦταί τε λύγῳ καὶ τρύγα πίνει μελιηδέα.

ὁ γὰρ τῆς λύγου στέφανος ἄτοπος· πρὸς δεσμοὺς γὰρ
καὶ πλέγματα ἡ λύγος ἐπιτήδειος. εἰπὲ οὖν ἡμῖν τι
περὶ τούτων ζητήσεως ἀξίων ὄντων καὶ μὴ ὀνόματα
θήρα, φιλότης. σιωπῶντος δ᾽ αὐτοῦ καὶ ἀναζητεῖν
προσποιουμένου ὁ Δημόκριτος ἔφη· Ἀρίσταρχος ὁ

---

[44] Ancient authorities were unsure whether the various fragments of a play or plays entitled *Sleep* were to be attributed to
Alexis or Antiphanes (cf. 13.572b), and K–A do not assign this
fragment an Antiphanes-number.

[45] Ulpian responds to Cynulcus' second question (below) first
and only takes up the problem of the Naucratean garland at
15.675f.

the dinner to his guests, so they can see it; and the
    next day,
after they've had no dinner, he sells them the meal he
    served them to look at.

The same iambic lines are found in Antiphanes' *Sleep*.[44]
And Cynulcus said: Since we have begun discussing garlands, tell us what the Naucratean garland referred to by
the witty Anacreon is, Ulpian.[45] For the delightful poet
puts it as follows (*PMG* 434):

Each man had three garlands,
two made of roses, the other a Naucratean.

And why do some individuals mentioned by the same poet
wear garlands made of willow branches? For he says in
Book II of his *Lyric Poems* (*PMG* 352):[46]

For ten months now the good-hearted Megistes has
    been
wearing a willow-garland and drinking honey-sweet
    grape-must.

Since a garland made of willow-branches is unusual; for
willow-branches are suited to tying objects up and to wick-
erwork. So offer us information on these topics, which deserve consideration, and do not merely hunt for vocabulary,[47] my dear friend. When Ulpian remained silent and
appeared to be racking his brain, Democritus said: The
gifted grammarian Aristarchus, my friend, in his exege-

---

[46] Quoted again at 15.673d.
[47] Cf. 3.97f (of Pompeianus of Philadelphia); 14.649b (of
Ulpian).

672   γραμματικώτατος, ἑταῖρε, ἐξηγούμενος ‖ τὸ χωρίον
ἔφη ὅτι καὶ λύγοις ἐστεφανοῦντο οἱ ἀρχαῖοι. † Τενα-
ρος¹³ † δὲ ἀγροίκων εἶναι λέγει στεφάνωμα τὴν λύγον,
καὶ οἱ ἄλλοι δὲ ἐξηγηταὶ ἀπροσδιόνυσά τινα εἰρήκα-
σιν περὶ τοῦ προκειμένου. ἐγὼ δ᾽ ἐντυχὼν τῷ Μηνοδότου τοῦ Σαμίου συγγράμματι, ὅπερ ἐπιγράφεται
Τῶν Κατὰ τὴν Σάμον Ἐνδόξων Ἀναγραφή, εὗρον τὸ
ζητούμενον. Ἀδμήτην γάρ φησιν τὴν Εὐρυσθέως ἐξ
Ἄργους φυγοῦσαν ἐλθεῖν εἰς Σάμον, θεασαμένην δὲ
τὴν τῆς Ἥρας ἐπιφάνειαν καὶ τῆς οἴκοθεν σωτηρίας
b   χαριστήριον βουλομένην ἀποδοῦναι | ἐπιμεληθῆναι
τοῦ ἱεροῦ τοῦ καὶ νῦν ὑπάρχοντος, πρότερον δὲ ὑπὸ
Λελέγων καὶ νυμφῶν καθιδρυμένου· τοὺς δ᾽ Ἀργείους
πυθομένους καὶ χαλεπαίνοντας πεῖσαι χρημάτων
ὑποσχέσει Τυρρηνοὺς ληστρικῷ¹⁴ βίῳ χρωμένους ἁρ-
πάσαι τὸ βρέτας, πεπεισμένους τοὺς Ἀργείους ὡς, εἰ
τοῦτο γένοιτο, πάντως τι κακὸν πρὸς τῶν τὴν Σάμον
κατοικούντων ἡ Ἀδμήτη πείσεται. τοὺς δὲ Τυρρηνοὺς
ἐλθόντας εἰς τὸν Ἡραῖτην ὅρμον καὶ ἀποβάντας
εὐθέως ἔχεσθαι τῆς πράξεως. ἀθύρου δὲ ὄντος τότε
c   τοῦ νεὼ | ταχέως ἀνελέσθαι τὸ βρέτας καὶ διακο-
μίσαντας ἐπὶ θάλασσαν εἰς τὸ σκάφος ἐμβαλέσθαι·
λυσαμένους δ᾽ αὐτοὺς τὰ πρυμνήσια καὶ τὰς ἀγκύρας
ἀνελομένους εἰρεσίᾳ τε πάσῃ χρωμένους ἀπαίρειν οὐ

¹³ Ταίναρος Meineke
¹⁴ ληστρικῷ τε A: τε del. Schweighäuser

sis of this passage, claimed that the ancients wore garlands made of willow-branches; and † Tenarus[48] † asserts that country-people use willow-branches to make garlands, while other interpreters offer various irrelevant[49] remarks on the topic. But I stumbled upon the treatise by Menodotus of Samos entitled *A List of the Notable Objects*[50] *on Samos* (*FGrH* 541 F 1) and discovered the answer. He claims that when Eurystheus' daughter Admete,[51] who had been exiled from Argos, arrived on Samos, she had a vision of Hera and wanted to make a thank-offering in return for her successful escape from her homeland, and she therefore took charge of the temple that still exists today and that was originally founded by the Leleges and the nymphs. The Argives heard about this and were upset, and they accordingly promised money to the Etruscans, who lived off piracy, and convinced them to steal the statue, since the Argives were convinced that if this happened, the inhabitants of Samos would certainly punish Admete. The Etruscans entered Hera's port, disembarked, and immediately got to work. Because the temple had no doors in those days, they quickly picked up the statue, carried it down to the sea, and loaded it into their boat; and after they loosed their mooring-cables and pulled up their anchors, they began to row as hard as they could—but were unable to leave. They therefore decided

---

48 No historian or grammarian by this name (probably corrupt in any case) is known.   49 Literally "nothing-to-do-with-Dionysus."   50 Or "*Notable Individuals*"; see also 15.673b n.

51 Otherwise known only for having wanted Heracles to capture the belt of the Amazon queen Hippolyte ([Apollod.] *Bib.* 2.5.9).

δύνασθαι. ἡγησαμένους οὖν θεῖόν τι τοῦτ' εἶναι πάλιν
ἐξενεγκαμένους τῆς νεὼς τὸ βρέτας ἀποθέσθαι παρὰ
τὸν αἰγιαλόν· καὶ ψαιστὰ αὐτῷ ποιήσαντας περιδεεῖς
ἀπαλλάττεσθαι. τῆς δὲ Ἀδμήτης ἕωθεν δηλωσάσης
ὅτι τὸ βρέτας ἠφανίσθη καὶ ζητήσεως γενομένης
d εὑρεῖν μὲν αὐτὸ τοὺς ζητοῦντας ἐπὶ | τῆς ἠόνος, ὡς δὲ
δὴ βαρβάρους Κᾶρας ὑπονοήσαντας αὐτόματον ἀπο-
δεδρακέναι πρός τι λύγου θωράκιον ἀπερείσασθαι καὶ
τοὺς εὐμηκεστάτους τῶν κλάδων ἑκατέρωθεν ἐπισπα-
σαμένους περιειλῆσαι πάντοθεν. τὴν δὲ Ἀδμήτην
λύσασαν αὐτὸ ἁγνίσαι καὶ στῆσαι πάλιν ἐπὶ τοῦ
βάθρου, καθάπερ πρότερον ἵδρυτο. διόπερ ἐξ ἐκείνου
καθ' ἕκαστον ἔτος ἀποκομίζεσθαι τὸ βρέτας εἰς τὴν
ἠόνα καὶ ἀφαγνίζεσθαι ψαιστά τε αὐτῷ παρατίθε-
e σθαι· καὶ καλεῖσθαι Τόναια τὴν ἑορτήν, ὅτι | συν-
τόνως συνέβη περιειληθῆναι τὸ βρέτας ὑπὸ τῶν τὴν
πρώτην αὐτοῦ ζήτησιν ποιησαμένων. ἱστορεῖται δ'
ὑπ' αὐτὸν ἐκεῖνον τὸν χρόνον τῶν Καρῶν δεισιδαι-
μονίᾳ περισχεθέντων ἐπὶ τὸ μαντεῖον τοῦ θεοῦ παρα-
γενομένων εἰς Ὕβλαν καὶ πυνθανομένων περὶ τῶν
ἀπηντημένων, θεσπίσαι τὸν Ἀπόλλωνα ποινὴν αὐτοὺς
ἀποδοῦναι τῇ θεῷ δι' ἑαυτῶν ἑκούσιον καὶ χωρὶς
δυσχεροῦς συμφορᾶς, ἣν ἐν τοῖς ἔμπροσθεν χρόνοις
f ἀφώρισεν ὁ Ζεὺς τῷ Προμηθεῖ χάριν τῆς κλοπῆς | τοῦ
πυρός, λύσας αὐτὸν ἐκ τῶν χαλεπωτάτων δεσμῶν· καὶ
τίσιν ἑκούσιον ἐν ἀλυπίᾳ κειμένην δοῦναι θελήσαν-
τος, ταύτην ἐκείνῳ ἐπιτάξαι τὸν καθηγούμενον τῶν
θεῶν. ὅθεν αὐτίκα τὸν δεδηλωμένον στέφανον τῷ Προ-

that a god was involved somehow, and they took the statue
out of the boat again and set it on the shore; after making
cakes of ground barley (*psaista*) for it, they left, terrified.
At dawn Admete spread the news that the statue had dis-
appeared, and after a search was mounted, the people who
went out looking for it discovered it on the seashore. Being
barbarians, however, the Carians imagined that it had run
off under its own power, so they set it on a mat made of willow-branches, pulled the longest branches around it from
either side, and wrapped it up completely. After Admete
untied it, she purified it and set it once again on the base
where it had rested previously. This is why every year since
then the statue is taken out of the temple down to the seashore, where it is purified and served barley-cakes. The
festival is called the Tonaia, because the statue was tightly
(*suntonôs*) wrapped by the people who searched for it originally. There is also a story that around that same time the
Carians, who were deeply superstitious, visited the god's
oracle in Hybla[52] and asked about these events. Apollo
prophesied that they should pay the goddess a penalty they
selected themselves that involved no particular suffering.
This is the same penalty that in earlier times Zeus imposed
on Prometheus on account of his theft of fire, after he released him from his extraordinarily painful bonds; because
Prometheus was willing to offer a satisfaction he chose
himself that involved no suffering, this is the one the chief
god assigned him. As a consequence, the garland Prome-

----

52 Otherwise unknown.

μηθεὶ περιγενέσθαι καὶ μετ᾽ οὐ πολὺ τοῖς εὐεργετη-
θεῖσιν ἀνθρώποις ὑπ᾽ αὐτοῦ κατὰ τὴν τοῦ πυρὸς δωρεάν. διόπερ καὶ τοῖς Καρσὶ κατὰ τὸ παραπλήσιον ὁ
θεὸς παρεκελεύσατο στεφανώματι χρωμένοις τῇ λύγῳ
καταδεῖν τὴν ἑαυτῶν κεφαλὴν τοῖς κλάδοις οἷς αὐτοὶ
673 κατέλαβον τὴν θεόν. ‖ καταλῦσαι δὲ καὶ τἄλλα γένη
τῶν στεφάνων ἐπέταξε χωρὶς τῆς δάφνης· τὴν δ᾽
αὐτὸς ἔφη τοῖς τὴν θεὸν θεραπεύουσι μόνοις ἀπονέ-
μειν δῶρον. τοῖς τε χρησθεῖσιν ἐκ τῆς μαντείας κατα-
κολουθήσαντας αὐτοὺς ἀβλαβεῖς ἔσεσθαι δίκην[15] ἐν
εὐωχίαις ἀποδιδόντας τῇ θεῷ τὴν προσήκουσαν. ὅθεν
τοὺς Κᾶρας ὑπακοῦσαι βουλομένους τοῖς ἐκ τοῦ χρη-
στηρίου καταλῦσαι τὰς ἔμπροσθεν εἰθισμένας στεφα-
νώσεις αὐτούς τε κατὰ πλῆθος χρῆσθαι μὲν τῇ λύγῳ,
b τοῖς δὲ θεραπεύουσιν τὴν θεὸν ἐπιτρέψαι | φορεῖν τὸν
καὶ νῦν ἔτι διαμένοντα τῆς δάφνης στέφανον. μνημο-
νεύειν δ᾽ ἔοικεν ἐπὶ ποσόν τι τῆς κατὰ τὴν λύγον
στεφανώσεως καὶ Νικαίνετος ὁ ἐποποιὸς ἐν τοῖς Ἐπι-
γράμμασιν, ποιητὴς ὑπάρχων ἐπιχώριος καὶ τὴν
ἐπιχώριον ἱστορίαν ἠγαπηκὼς ἐν πλείοσιν. λέγει δ᾽
οὕτως·

οὐκ ἐθέλω, Φιλόθηρε, κατὰ πτόλιν ἀλλὰ παρ᾽
    Ἥρῃ
    δαίνυσθαι Ζεφύρου πνεύμασι τερπόμενος. |

[15] καὶ δίκην A: καὶ del. Wilamowitz

42

theus specified prevailed at once, as well as shortly thereafter among the human beings who had benefited from his
gift of fire.[53] This is why Apollo similarly urged the Carians
to wear willow-garlands and to bind their heads with the
branches they had used to restrain the goddess. He also ordered them to give up all other types of garlands except for
those made of laurel, and said that he personally was as-
signing the latter as a gift exclusively to the goddess' servants. And if they followed the prophecies his oracle issued, they would suffer no injury, provided they offered
the goddess the appropriate penalty at their feasts. As a
consequence the Carians, who wanted to obey the orders
the oracle issued, abandoned the styles of garlanding they
had practiced previously and by and large used willow-
branches, although they allowed the goddess' servants to
wear garlands made of laurel, as they continue to do even
today. Reference of some sort to the use of willow-
branches for garlands appears to be made by the epic poet
Nicaenetus, who was a local poet[54] and frequently expresses his fondness for local history, in his *Epigrams* (fr. 6,
p. 3 Powell = *HE* 2703–10). He puts it as follows:

> I do not wish to dine in the city, Philotherus,
>> but with Hera instead, enjoying the West Wind's
>> breezes.

[53] Cf. 15.674d.

[54] Cf. 13.590b "Nicaenetus of Samos or Abdera." Gow–Page,
HE ii.417, speculate that the information preserved here comes
from the work by Menodotus of Samos cited at 15.672a, where
see n.

c   ἀρκεῖ μοι λιτὴ μὲν ὑπὸ πλευροῖσι χάμευνα,
    ἐγγύθι γὰρ προμάλου δέμνιον ἐνδαπίης
    καὶ λύγος, ἀρχαῖον Καρῶν στέφος. ἀλλὰ
        φερέσθω
    οἶνος καὶ Μουσέων ἡ χαρίεσσα λύρη,
    θυμῆρες πίνοντες ὅπως Διὸς εὐκλέα νύμφην
    μέλπωμεν, νήσου δεσπότιν ἡμετέρης.

ἐν τούτοις γὰρ ἀμφιβόλως εἰρηκὼς ὁ Νικαίνετος πότε-
d ρον στρωμνῆς ἕνεκεν ἢ στεφανώσεως ἀρκεῖται | τῇ
λύγῳ, τῷ λέγειν[16] αὐτὴν τῶν Καρῶν ἀρχαῖον στέφος
πρόδηλον καθίστησι τὸ ζητούμενον. συνέβη δὲ τὴν
τῆς λύγου στεφάνωσιν καὶ μέχρι τῶν κατὰ Πολυ-
κράτην χρόνων, ὡς ἄν τις εἰκάσειε, τῇ νήσῳ συνηθε-
στέραν ὑπάρχειν. ὁ γοῦν Ἀνακρέων φησίν·

    ⟨ὁ⟩ Μεγιστῆς ὁ φιλόφρων δέκα δὴ μῆνες
      ἐπειδὴ[17]
    στεφανοῦταί τε λύγῳ καὶ τρύγα πίνει μελιηδέα.

ταῦτα ἴσασιν οἱ θεοὶ ὡς πρῶτος αὐτὸς ἐν τῇ καλῇ
Ἀλεξανδρείᾳ εὗρον κτησάμενος τὸ τοῦ Μηνοδότου
συγγραμμάτιον καὶ ἐπιδείξας πολλοῖς ἐξ αὐτοῦ τὸ |

[16] τῷ δὲ λέγειν A: δὲ del. Musurus
[17] ἐπεί τε 15.671e–f

---

[55] Probably a willow variety of some sort.
[56] Hera, the guardian deity of Samos.

I am satisfied with a simple pallet-bed beneath my
 ribs,
  since a bed made of *promalos*[55] that grows on the
   spot is close at hand,
as are willow-branches, the Carians' ancient garland.
  Let someone fetch
   wine and the Muses' lovely lyre,
so that we may drink as much as our hearts desire
  and sing in honor of Zeus'
   famous bride, the lady to whom our island
    belongs![56]

For although Nicaenetus does not specify in this passage
whether he intends to use the willow-branches for bedding
or to produce a garland, he makes the answer to the question obvious by referring to them as "the ancient garland of
the Carians." The use of willow-branches for garlanding
turned out to have been quite common on the island, so it
seems, until Polycrates' time.[57] Anacreon, at any rate, says
(*PMG* 352):[58]

 For ten months now the good-hearted Megistes
 has been wearing a willow-garland and drinking
  honey-sweet grape-must.

The gods are my witness, that I myself was the first person
in beautiful Alexandria to discover this, after I acquired
Menodotus' little treatise and cited it to many people for

---

[57] The tyrant Polycrates controlled Samos *c*.535–*c*.522 BCE;
Anacreon spent time in his court.

[58] Quoted also (with several minor variants in verse 1) at
15.671e–f.

e παρὰ τῷ Ἀνακρέοντι ζητούμενον. λαβὼν δὲ παρ᾽ ἐμοῦ
ὁ πᾶσιν κλοπὴν ὀνειδίζων Ἡφαιστίων ἐξιδιοποιήσατο
τὴν λύσιν καὶ σύγγραμμα ἐξέδωκεν ἐπιγράψας Περὶ
τοῦ Παρ᾽ Ἀνακρέοντι Λυγίνου Στεφάνου· ὅπερ νῦν ἐν
τῇ Ῥώμῃ εὕρομεν παρὰ † τῇ ἀντικοττυραι Δημητρίῳ
†. τοιοῦτος δέ τις καὶ[18] περὶ τὸν καλὸν ἡμῶν Ἄδρα-
στον ἐγένετο· ἐκδόντος γὰρ τούτου πέντε μὲν βιβλία
Περὶ τῶν Παρὰ Θεοφράστῳ Ἐν τοῖς Περὶ Ἠθῶν Καθ᾽
Ἱστορίαν καὶ Λέξιν Ζητουμένων, ἕκτον δὲ Περὶ τῶν
f Ἐν τοῖς | Ἠθικοῖς Νικομαχείοις Ἀριστοτέλους, ἐννοί-
ας ἀμφιλαφεῖς παραθεμένου περὶ τοῦ παρὰ Ἀντι-
φῶντι τῷ τραγῳδιοποιῷ Πληξίππου καὶ πλεῖστα ὅσα
καὶ περὶ αὐτοῦ τοῦ Ἀντιφῶντος εἰπόντος, σφετερι-
σάμενος καὶ ταῦτα ἐπέγραψέν τι βιβλίον Περὶ τοῦ
Παρὰ Ξενοφῶντι Ἐν τοῖς Ἀπομνημονεύμασιν Ἀντιφῶντος, οὐδὲν ἴδιον προσεξευρών, ὥσπερ κἂν τῷ Περὶ
τοῦ Λυγίνου Στεφάνου. μόνον γὰρ τοῦτ᾽ ἴδιον εἴρηκεν,
ὅτι Φύλαρχος ἐν τῇ ἑβδόμῃ τῶν Ἱστοριῶν οἶδεν τὴν
κατὰ <τὴν>[19] λύγον ἱστορίαν καὶ ὅτι οὔτε τὰ Νικαι-
674 νέτου ‖ οἶδεν οὔτε τὰ Ἀνακρέοντος ὁ συγγραφεύς.
ἀπέδειξε δὲ καὶ διαφωνοῦντα αὐτὸν κατ᾽ ἔνια τῶν

[18] τοιοῦτος δέ τις καὶ ὁ Ἥφαιστίων συγγραφεὺς καὶ A: ὁ
Ἥφαιστίων συγγραφεὺς καὶ del. Casaubon
[19] add. Wilamowitz

[59] Adrastus of Aphrodisias was a Peripatetic philosopher of
the first half of the 2nd century CE. Casaubon speculated that he
might have been the historical Athenaeus' teacher.

46

the question involving Anacreon. But Hephaestion, who accuses everyone else of plagiarism, took the solution from me and appropriated it for himself, by publishing a treatise he entitled *On the Willow-Branch Garland in Anacreon*; I recently discovered the work in Rome at † the [corrupt] Demetrius †. He behaved in a similar fashion toward our noble Adrastus;[59] for after Adrastus published *On Historical and Lexical Questions in Theophrastus' On Manners* in five Books (= Thphr. fr. 437 Fortenbaugh), with a sixth Book *On Questions in Aristotle's Nicomachean Ethics*, in which he offered a wealth of ideas about the Plexippus[60] who appears in the tragic poet Antiphon (*TrGF* 55 F 1b), and also made numerous comments regarding Antiphon himself, Hephaestion appropriated this material for himself and produced a book with the title *On the Antiphon Who Appears in Xenophon's Memorabilia*,[61] after doing no additional research of his own, precisely as he did in the case of *On the Willow-Branch Garland*. The only observation of his own that he offered was that Phylarchus in Book VII of his *History* (*FGrH* 81 F 14) is familiar with the story involving the willow-branches, but that this author knows neither the passage from Nicaenetus nor the one from Anacreon; he also showed that Phylarchus disagreed with

60 Plexippus was the maternal uncle of Meleager, the eponymous hero of one of the tragic poet Antiphon's plays. This is a different Antiphon (*PAA* 138165) from Antiphon the Sophist mentioned below.

61 Cf. X. *Mem.* 1.6; the Antiphon in question is Antiphon the Sophist (*PAA* 138190), and this reference is 87 A 4 D–K = T4 Pendrick.

ἱστορηθέντων παρὰ τῷ Μηνοδότῳ. δύναται δέ τις
λέγειν περὶ τῆς λύγου ἁπλούστερον, ὅτι ὁ Μεγίστης
τῇ λύγῳ ἐστεφανοῦτο, ὡς παρακειμένης ἐκ τοῦ δαψι-
λοῦς ἐν ᾧ εὐωχεῖτο τόπῳ, συνδέσεως ἕνεκα τῶν κροτάφων. καὶ γὰρ καὶ Λακεδαιμόνιοι καλάμῳ στεφα-
νοῦνται ἐν τῇ τῶν Προμαχείων ἑορτῇ, ὥς φησι
Σωσίβιος ἐν τοῖς Περὶ τῶν ἐν Λακεδαίμονι Θυσιῶν
b γράφων οὕτως· ἐν ταύτῃ συμβαίνει τοὺς | μὲν ἀπὸ τῆς
χώρας καλάμοις στεφανοῦσθαι ἢ στλεγγίδι, τοὺς δ'
ἐκ τῆς ἀγωγῆς παῖδας ἀστεφανώτους ἀκολουθεῖν.
Ἀριστοτέλης δ' ἐν δευτέρῳ Ἐρωτικῶν καὶ Ἀρίστων ὁ
περιπατητικός, Κεῖος δὲ τὸ γένος, ἐν δευτέρῳ Ἐρωτικῶν Ὁμοίων φασὶν ὅτι οἱ ἀρχαῖοι διὰ τοὺς περὶ τὸν
οἶνον πόνους τῶν κεφαλαλγιῶν δεσμοὺς εὕρισκον
τοὺς τυχόντας, τῆς τῶν κροτάφων συνδέσεως ὠφελεῖν
δοκούσης· οἱ δ' ὕστερον ἅμα τῷ κροτάφῳ προσέβαλόν
τινα καὶ κόσμον οἰκεῖον τῇ παρὰ τὸν οἶνον διαγωγῇ,
c μηχανησάμενοι | τὸν στέφανον. βέλτιον δὲ διὰ τὸ
πάσας τὰς αἰσθήσεις ἐν τῇ κεφαλῇ εἶναι ταύτην
στεφανοῦσθαι ἢ διὰ τὸ συμφέρειν ἐσκεπάσθαι καὶ
συνδεδέσθαι τοὺς κροτάφους πρὸς τὸν οἶνον. ἐστεφανοῦντο δὲ καὶ τὸ μέτωπον, ὡς ὁ καλὸς Ἀνακρέων ἔφη·

> ἐπὶ δ' ὀφρύσιν σελίνων στεφανίσκους
> θέμενοι θάλειαν ἑορτὴν ἀγάγωμεν
> Διονύσῳ.

---

[62] stlegis; cf. 4.128e.
[63] The Spartan system of public education.

some parts of the account offered in Menodotus. A less complicated comment on the willow-branches might also be offered, to the effect that Megistes used them to garland himself because there were plenty available in the place where he was feasting, and that he used them to bind his temples. The Spartans in fact wear garlands made of reeds at the Promacheia festival, according to Sosibius in his *On the Sacrificial Festivals in Sparta* (*FGrH* 595 F 4), where he writes as follows: What goes on at this festival is that the boys from the countryside wear a reed-garland or a tiara,[62] while those being brought up in the *agôgê*[63] follow without garlands. Aristotle in Book II of the *Erotica* (fr. 41) and Ariston the Peripatetic, whose family was from Ceos, in Book II of the *Erotic Comparisons* (fr. 22 Wehrli = fr. 10 Fortenbaugh–White) claim that the ancients came up with the idea of wrapping themselves with whatever they could find to deal with the headaches caused by wine, since wrapping their temples appeared to help; those who came after them added a bit of decoration to their temples appropriate to how they spent their time when they were drinking, creating the garland. Given that all our senses reside in our heads, it is better to garland them than to have our temples covered and wrapped tight to guard against the wine because of the trouble it causes. They also wore garlands around their foreheads, as the noble Anacreon (*PMG* 410) said:

> And placing little garlands of celery upon
> our brows, let us celebrate a rich festival
> in honor of Dionysus.

ἐστεφανοῦντο δὲ καὶ τὰ στήθη καὶ ἐμύρουν ταῦτα,
ἐπεὶ αὐτόθι ἡ καρδία. ἐκάλουν δὲ καὶ οἷς περιεδέοντο
d τὸν τράχηλον στεφάνους ὑποθυμίδας, ὡς Ἀλκαῖος | ἐν
τούτοις·

> ἀλλ᾽ ἀνήτω μὲν περὶ ταῖς δέραισι
> περθέτω πλέκταις ὑπαθύμιδάς τις.

καὶ Σαπφώ·

> καὶ πόλλαις ὑπαθύμιδας
> πλέκταις ἀμφ᾽ ἀπάλᾳ δέρᾳ.

καὶ Ἀνακρέων·

> πλεκτὰς
> δ᾽ ὑποθυμίδας περὶ στήθεσι λωτίνας ἔθεντο.

Αἰσχύλος δ᾽ ἐν τῷ Λυομένῳ Προμηθεῖ σαφῶς φησιν
ὅτι ἐπὶ τιμῇ[20] τοῦ Προμηθέως τὸν στέφανον περι-
τίθεμεν τῇ κεφαλῇ, ἀντίποινα τοῦ ἐκείνου δεσμοῦ, καίτοι ἐν τῇ ἐπιγραφομένῃ Σφιγγὶ εἰπών·

> τῷ δὲ ξένῳ γε στέφανον, ἀρχαῖον στέφος, |
e > δεσμῶν ἄριστον ἐκ Προμηθέως λόγου.

Σαπφὼ δ᾽ ἁπλούστερον τὴν αἰτίαν ἀποδίδωσιν τοῦ
στεφανοῦσθαι ἡμᾶς, λέγουσα τάδε·

> σὺ δὲ στεφάνοις, ὦ Δίκα, πέρθεσθ᾽ ἐράτοις
> φόβαισιν

[20] ἐπὶ τιμῇ CE: ἐπί τε τιμῇ A

50

They put garlands around their chests as well, and covered them with perfume, since that is where the heart is located. They referred to the garlands they wrapped around their necks as *hupothumides*, as for example Alcaeus (fr. 362.1–2)[64] in the following passage:

But let someone place *upathumides* woven of anise about our necks.

Also Sappho (fr. 94.15–16):

and many woven
upathumides around my soft neck.

And Anacreon (*PMG* 397):

They placed
hupothumides made of *lôtos* about their chests.

Aeschylus in his *Prometheus Released* (fr. 202) says explicitly that we place garlands about our heads to honor Prometheus, as recompense for his bondage,[65] although in his play entitled *The Sphinx* (fr. 235) he said:

But for the stranger a garland, an ancient wreath, the best bond there is, as Prometheus put it.

Sappho (fr. 81.4–7) offers a simpler explanation of why we wear garlands, saying the following:

Wrap anise shoots together into garlands, Dica,

64 Two additional verses of what appear to be the same fragment are preserved at 15.687d–e, where see n.
65 Cf. 15.672e–f.

ὄρπακας ἀνήτω συναέρραισ᾽ ἀπάλαισι χέρσιν·
εὐάνθεα † γὰρ πέλεται † καὶ Χάριτες μάκαιραι
μᾶλλον † προτερην †, ἀστεφανώτοισι δ᾽
ἀπυστρέφονται.

ὡς εὐανθέστερον γὰρ καὶ κεχαρισμένον μᾶλλον τοῖς
θεοῖς παραγγέλλει στεφανοῦσθαι τοὺς θύοντας. Ἀρι-
f στοτέλης δ᾽ ἐν τῷ Συμποσίῳ φησὶν ὅτι | οὐδὲν κολο-
βὸν προσφέρομεν πρὸς τοὺς θεούς, ἀλλὰ τέλεια καὶ
ὅλα. τὸ δὲ πλῆρες τέλειόν ἐστιν, τὸ δὲ στέφειν πλή-
ρωσίν τινα σημαίνει. Ὅμηρος·

κοῦροι δὲ²¹ κρητῆρας ἐπεστέψαντο ποτοῖο.

καί·

ἀλλὰ θεὸς μορφὴν ἔπεσι στέφει.

τοὺς γὰρ αὖ τὴν ὄψιν ἀμόρφους, φησίν, ἀναπληροῖ ἡ
675 τοῦ λέγειν πιθανότης· ‖ ἔοικεν οὖν ὁ στέφανος τοῦτο
ποιεῖν βούλεσθαι. διὸ καὶ περὶ τὰ πένθη τοὐναντίον
παρασκευάζομεν· ὁμοπαθείᾳ γὰρ τοῦ κεκμηκότος κο-
λοβοῦμεν ἡμᾶς αὐτοὺς τῇ τε κουρᾷ τῶν τριχῶν καὶ τῇ
τῶν στεφάνων ἀφαιρέσει. Φιλωνίδης δ᾽ ὁ ἰατρὸς ἐν τῷ
Περὶ Μύρων καὶ Στεφάνων, ἐκ τῆς Ἐρυθρᾶς, φησίν,
θαλάσσης ὑπὸ Διονύσου μετενεχθείσης εἰς τὴν Ἑλ-

---

²¹ The traditional text of Homer has μέν.

---

⁶⁶ Cited also, less precisely, at 1.13e.

with your soft hands, and place them around your
    lovely hair;
with fine flowers † for it is † and the blessed Graces
more [corrupt], but turn away from those who wear
    no garlands.

For she recommends that people making a sacrifice wear
garlands, because whatever has more flowers is more ap-
pealing to the gods. Aristotle in his *Symposium* (fr. 48)
notes that we offer the gods nothing imperfect, but only
what is perfect and whole; and what is full is perfect, and
the act of garlanding implies a type of filling. Homer (*Il.*
1.470):[66]

And the young men crowned the mixing-bowls with
    drink.

And (*Od.* 8.170):

But a god garlands his words with beauty.

Because individuals who are not good-looking, he[67] says,
are filled out by the persuasiveness with which they speak,
which is apparently what a garland is intended to accomplish. This is also why we make the opposite arrangements
in the case of mourning; for as a way of sharing the dead
person's suffering, we disfigure ourselves by cutting our
hair and removing our garlands. The physician Philonides
says in his *On Perfumes and Garlands*: After Dionysus introduced the grapevine to Greece from the area around

[67] Aristotle (continuing the paraphrase of the *Symposium* after the reference to Homer); the discussion as a whole is probably
drawn once again from Clearchus.

b λάδα | τῆς ἀμπέλου καὶ πρὸς ἄμετρον ἀπόλαυσιν τῶν
πολλῶν ἐκτρεπομένων ἄκρατόν τε προσφερομένων
αὐτῶν, οἱ μὲν μανιωδῶς ἐκτρεπόμενοι παρέπαιον, οἱ δὲ
νεκροῖς ἐῴκεσαν ἀπὸ τῆς καρώσεως. ἐπ᾽ ἀκτῆς δέ
τινων πινόντων ἐπιπεσὼν ὄμβρος τὸ μὲν συμπόσιον
διέλυσεν, τὸν δὲ κρατῆρα, ὃς εἶχεν ὀλίγον οἶνον ὑπο-
λελειμμένον, ἐπλήρωσεν ὕδατος. γενομένης δ᾽ αἰθρίας
c εἰς τὸν αὐτὸν ὑποστρέψαντες | τόπον, γευσάμενοι τοῦ
μίγματος προσηνῆ καὶ ἄλυπον ἔσχον ἀπόλαυσιν. καὶ
διὰ τοῦθ᾽ οἱ Ἕλληνες τῷ μὲν παρὰ δεῖπνον ἀκράτῳ
προσδιδομένῳ τὸν Ἀγαθὸν ἐπιφωνοῦσι Δαίμονα,
τιμῶντες τὸν εὑρόντα δαίμονα[22]· ἦν δ᾽ οὗτος ὁ Διό-
νυσος. τῷ δὲ μετὰ δεῖπνον κεκραμένῳ πρώτῳ διδο-
μένῳ ποτηρίῳ Δία Σωτῆρα ἐπιλέγουσι, τῆς ἐκ τοῦ
μίγματος ἀλύπου κράσεως τὸν καὶ τῶν ὄμβρων ἀρχη-
γὸν αἴτιον ὑπολαβόντες. ἔδει μὲν οὖν βοηθημάτων
τοῖς ἐν τῷ πότῳ κεφαλὴν ἐπιθλιβεῖσιν, ἦν δὲ δεσμὸς
ἐξ αὐτῶν προχειρότατος καὶ τῆς φύσεως ἐπὶ τοῦτο
ὁδηγούσης· ἀλγήσας γάρ τις κεφαλήν, ὥς φησιν
d Ἀνδρέας, εἶτα πιέσας καὶ κουφισθεὶς εὗρεν | κεφα-
λαλγίας δεσμὸν φάρμακον. τούτῳ οὖν βοηθήματι
πρὸς πότους χρώμενοι τοῖς παραπίπτουσι τὴν κεφαλὴν ἐδέσμευον· καὶ ἐπὶ τὸν κίσσινον στέφανον ἦλθον
αὐτόματόν τε καὶ πολὺν ὄντα καὶ κατὰ πάντα τόπον
γεννώμενον, ἔχοντα καὶ πρόσοψιν οὐκ ἀτερπῆ, χλω-

---

[22] εὑρόντα δαίμονα A: εὑρόντα Διόνυσον CE: δαίμονα/
Διόνυσον del. Meineke

the Red Sea, and many people misguidedly enjoyed unlim-
ited quantities of wine and consumed it unmixed, some of
them became delirious and began to act like madmen,
while others grew drowsy and resembled corpses. When a
group of them were drinking on the seashore, a sudden
rainstorm broke up the party and filled their mixing-bowl,
which contained a small quantity of left-over wine, with
water. After the sky cleared, they returned to the same
place, and when they tasted the mixture, they derived a
soothing, painless pleasure from it. As a consequence of
this, the Greeks invoke the Good Divinity when unmixed
wine is distributed at their dinner parties, as a way of
honoring the deity—that is, Dionysus—who discovered it.
And when they are offered the first cup of mixed wine after
dinner, they call upon Zeus the Savior, since they regard
him, in his capacity as marshaller of the storms, as respon-
sible for the painless mixing that results from mingling
(wine and water). They accordingly needed help for those
whose heads were oppressed as a result of drinking, and
the handiest help of those available, and one that nature
itself directed them to, was to wrap them. For when someone's head hurt, according to Andreas,[68] he applied pres-
sure to it and got relief, and he thus discovered that wrapping cures a headache. At their drinking parties, therefore,
they used this form of assistance and began to bind the par-
ticipants' heads. They settled on ivy garlands because the
plant grows without having to be cultivated and in large
quantities; is found everywhere; has an attractive appear-

[68] Cf. 15.680d n.

ροῖς πετάλοις καὶ κορύμβοις σκιάζοντα τὸ μέτωπον
καὶ τοὺς ἐν τῷ σφίγγειν τόνους ὑπομένοντα, προσέτι
δὲ ψύχοντα χωρὶς ὀδμῆς καρούσης. καὶ ταύτῃ μοι
δοκεῖ Διονύσῳ ὁ βίος ἀνεῖναι τὸ στέφος, τὸν εὑρετὴν
τοῦ πώματος καὶ τῶν δι᾽ αὐτὸ ἐλασσωμάτων ἀλεξη-
τῆρα βουλόμενος εἶναι. ἐντεῦθεν δὲ εἰς ἡδονὴν τρα-
e πέντες | τὸ μὲν εἰς συμφέρον καὶ τοῖς ἐκ μέθης
παραβοηθοῦν ἐλαττώμασιν[23] τοῦ πρὸς ὄψιν ἢ πρὸς
ὀσμὴν ἐπιτερποῦς ἐφρόντισαν. διὸ μυρσίνης μὲν
στέφανον στύφοντα καὶ τὴν οἴνων ἀναθυμίασιν ἀπο-
κρουόμενον, ἔτι δὲ ῥόδινον ἔχοντά τι καὶ κεφαλαλγίας
παρηγορικὸν σὺν τῷ καὶ κατὰ ποσὸν ψύχειν, πρὸς δὲ
τοῖς δάφνινον οὐκ ἀλλότριον πότου ἡγητέον. λευ-
κόϊνον δὲ κινητικὸν ὄντα κεφαλῆς καὶ ἀμαράκινον καὶ
ἅπαντας τοὺς καροῦν δυναμένους ἢ βαρύνειν ἄλλως
κεφαλὴν περιστατέον. τὰ αὐτὰ εἴρηκεν καὶ Ἀπολλόδωρος ἐν τῷ Περὶ Μύρων καὶ Στεφάνων ⟨ταῖς⟩[24]
f αὐταῖς λέξεσι. καὶ | περὶ μὲν τούτων, ὦ ἑταῖροι, ταῦτα.
περὶ δὲ τοῦ Ναυκρατίτου στεφάνου τίς ἐστι τὴν ἄνθην
πολλὰ ἀναζητήσας καὶ πολλῶν πυθόμενος, ὡς οὐδὲν
ἐμάνθανον, ἐνέτυχον ὀψέ ποτε Πολυχάρμου Ναυκρατίτου ἐπιγραφομένῳ βιβλίῳ Περὶ Ἀφροδίτης, ἐν ᾧ
ταυτὶ γέγραπται· κατὰ δὲ τὴν τρίτην πρὸς ταῖς εἴκο-

---

[23] ἐλαττώμασιν ὁ στέφανος CE: ἐλαττώματος ὁ στέφανος
A: ὁ στέφανος del. Olson, ducente Kaibelo
[24] add. Kaibel

ance; shades one's brow with pale leaves and berry-clusters; stands up to the tension when wrapped tight; and on top of all that, cools without producing a stupefying scent. This is why, in my opinion, our society dedicates the garland to Dionysus, in the conviction that he invented wine and protects us from the disadvantages associated with it. From that point on, they devoted themselves to pleasure, and as for what was useful and helped them with the disadvantages associated with getting drunk . . . and paid attention to what looked or smelled pleasant. As a result of which a myrtle garland, which is astringent and tends to drive away the vapors wine produces, as well as a garland made of roses, which has the power to soothe headaches, in addition to some capacity to cool, and laurel garlands in addition to these, should not be regarded as inappropriate for drinking parties. Whereas garlands made of gillyflower (which makes the head spin), marjoram, or any other flowers capable of stupefying a person or making one's head heavy in some other way, should be avoided. Apollodorus in his *On Perfumes and Garlands* offers the same observations, using identical words. But enough on this topic, my friends. As for the type of flower used in a Naucratean garland,[69] although I did considerable research on the matter and questioned many people, I learned nothing. But then eventually I came upon a book by Polycharmus of Naucratis entitled *On Aphodite* (*FGrH* 640 F 1), which contains the following passage: During the 23rd Olympiad,[70]

---

[69] Finally responding to Cynulcus' first question at 15.671d–e.
[70] 688–685 BCE. In fact, Naucratis was only founded as a trading station well after this, during the reign of Psammetichus I (664–610 BCE).

σιν Ὀλυμπιάδα ὁ Ἡρόστρατος, πολίτης ἡμέτερος
676 ἐμπορίᾳ χρώμενος καὶ χώραν πολλὴν ‖ περιπλέων,
προσσχὼν ποτε καὶ Πάφῳ τῆς Κύπρου ἀγαλμάτιον
Ἀφροδίτης σπιθαμιαῖον, ἀρχαῖον τῇ τέχνῃ, ὠνη-
σάμενος ᾖει φέρων εἰς τὴν Ναύκρατιν. καὶ αὐτῷ πλη-
σίον φερομένῳ τῆς Αἰγύπτου ἐπεὶ χειμὼν αἰφνίδιον
ἐπέπεσεν καὶ συνιδεῖν²⁵ οὐκ ἦν ὅπου γῆς ἦσαν,
κατέφυγον ἅπαντες ἐπὶ τὸ τῆς Ἀφροδίτης ἄγαλμα
σῴζειν αὐτοὺς αὐτὴν δεόμενοι. ἡ δὲ θεὸς (προσφιλὴς
γὰρ τοῖς Ναυκρατίταις ἦν) αἰφνίδιον ἐποίησε πάντα
τὰ παρακείμενα αὐτῇ μυρρίνης χλωρᾶς πλήρη ὀδμῆς
b τε ἡδίστης | ἐπλήρωσεν τὴν ναῦν ἤδη ἀπειρηκόσι τοῖς
ἐμπλέουσιν τὴν σωτηρίαν διὰ τὴν πολλὴν ναυτίαν
γενομένου τε ἐμέτου πολλοῦ, καὶ ἡλίου ἐκλάμψαντος
κατιδόντες τοὺς ὅρμους ἧκον εἰς τὴν Ναύκρατιν. καὶ ὁ
Ἡρόστρατος ἐξορμήσας τῆς νεὼς μετὰ τοῦ ἀγάλ-
ματος, ἔχων καὶ τὰς αἰφνίδιον αὐτῷ ἀναφανείσας
χλωρὰς μυρρίνας, ἀνέθηκεν ἐν τῷ τῆς Ἀφροδίτης
ἱερῷ, θύσας δὲ τῇ θεῷ καὶ ἀναθεὶς τῇ Ἀφροδίτῃ
τἄγαλμα, καλέσας δὲ καὶ ἐφ᾽ ἑστίασιν ἐν αὐτῷ τῷ
c ἱερῷ τοὺς προσήκοντας καὶ τοὺς οἰκειοτάτους | ἔδωκεν
ἑκάστῳ καὶ στέφανον ἐκ τῆς μυρρίνης, ὃν καὶ τότε
ἐκάλεσε Ναυκρατίτην. ὁ μὲν οὖν Πολύχαρμος ταῦτα·
οἷς κἀγὼ πείθομαι, ἡγούμενος οὐκ ἄλλον τινὰ εἶναι
Ναυκρατίτην στέφανον ἢ τὸν ἐκ τῆς μυρρίνης, τῷ καὶ
μετὰ τῶν ῥόδων ὑπὸ τοῦ Ἀνακρέοντος φορεῖσθαι. καὶ

²⁵ οὐ συνιδεῖν A: οὐ del. edd.

58

our fellow-citizen Herostratus, who was involved in trade and sailed to various places, put in at one point to Paphos on Cyprus, where he purchased a small statue of Aphrodite that was less than a foot[71] tall and of archaic workmanship, and headed off to Naucratis with it. As he was approaching Egypt, a sudden storm hit; since it was impossible to tell where they were, they all fled to the statue of Aphrodite and begged her to protect them. The goddess—who was well-disposed to the inhabitants of Naucratis—immediately filled all the vessels that had been set before her with fresh myrtle, and the entire ship with a delicious scent, even though everyone on board had given up any hope of surviving, because they were so seasick, and there was a great deal of vomiting. The sun came out, and they spotted the harbor basin and arrived in Naucratis. Herostratus emerged from the ship holding the statue, as well as the fresh myrtle-branches that had abruptly appeared to him, and dedicated them in Aphrodite's temple. After he made a sacrifice to the goddess and dedicated the statue to her, he invited his relatives and closest friends to a feast in the temple itself and gave them all myrtle garlands, to which he at that point gave the name Naucratean. Thus Polycharmus; and I accept his account, since I believe that there is only one type of Naucratean garland, which is the one made of myrtle, given that Anacreon wears it along with the roses (*PMG* 434, quoted at 15.671e). Philonides[72]

71 Literally "a span," i.e. the distance between the tip of the thumb and the tip of the little finger when the hand is outstretched.

72 Quoted at 15.675e.

ὁ Φιλωνίδης δὲ εἴρηκεν ὡς ὁ τῆς μυρρίνης στέφανος
τὴν ἐκ τῶν οἴνων ἀναθυμίασιν ἀποκρούεται καὶ ὁ τῶν
ῥόδων ἔχει τι κεφαλαλγίας παρηγορικὸν πρὸς τῷ καὶ
ἐμψύχειν. γελοῖοι οὖν εἰσιν καὶ οἱ λέγοντες Ναυ-
d κρατίτην εἶναι στέφανον | τὸν ἐκ τῆς βύβλου τῆς
στεφανωτρίδος καλουμένης παρ' Αἰγυπτίοις,[26] παρα-
τιθέμενοι Θεοπόμπου ἐκ τῆς τρι‹σ›καιδεκάτης τῶν
Φιλιππικῶν καὶ τῆς ἑνδεκάτης[27] τῶν Ἑλληνικῶν, ὅς
φησιν Ἀγησιλάῳ τῷ Λάκωνι παραγενομένῳ εἰς Αἴγυπτον δῶρα πέμψαι τοὺς Αἰγυπτίους ἄλλα τέ τινα
καὶ δὴ καὶ τὴν στεφανωτρίδα βύβλον. ἐγὼ δὲ οὐκ
οἶδα τίνα ὠφέλειαν ἢ ἡδονὴν ἔχει τὸ βύβλῳ στεφανοῦσθαι μετὰ ῥόδων, πλὴν εἰ μή τι οἱ τούτοις
χαίροντες στέψονται ὁμοῦ ῥόδοις καὶ σκόροδα. παμ-
πόλλους δὲ οἶδα λέγοντας τὸν ἐκ τῆς σαμψύχου |
e στέφανον εἶναι τὸν Ναυκρατίτην· πολὺ δὲ τὸ ἄνθος
τοῦτο κατὰ τὴν Αἴγυπτον. διάφορος δὲ γίνεται κατὰ
τὴν ὀδμὴν ἡ ἐν Αἰγύπτῳ μυρρίνη παρὰ τὰς ἐν ἄλλαις
χώραις, ὡς καὶ Θεόφραστος ἱστορεῖ.

Ἔτι τούτων λεγομένων ἐπεισῆλθον παῖδες στεφάνους φέροντες τῶν ἀκμαζόντων κατὰ τοὺς καιρούς.
καὶ ὁ Μυρτίλος, λέγε, καλέ, εἶπεν, Οὐλπιανέ, στεφάνων ὀνόματα· οἱ γὰρ παῖδες, κατὰ τὸν Χαιρήμονος
Κένταυρον,

---

[26] παρ' Αἰγυπτίοις στεφόμενον A: παρ' Αἰγυπτίοις tantum
CE: στεφόμενον del. Kaibel
[27] suppl. Grenfell–Hunt ex 9.384a

too maintains that myrtle-garlands dispel the vapors wine produces, and that rose-garlands have a soothing effect on headaches, in addition to being cooling. Sarcastic laughter is accordingly an appropriate response to those authorities who claim that a Naucratean garland is the type made of what the Egyptians refer to as "garland-papyrus," and who cite a passage from Book XIII of Theopompus' *History of Philip* and Book XI of his *History of Greece* (*FGrH* 115 F 106b),[73] where he reports that when Agesilaus of Sparta visited Egypt, the Egyptians sent him various gifts, including garland-papyrus. I myself have no idea what benefit or pleasure could be derived from wearing a garland that combines papyrus and roses—unless, perhaps, people who like garlands of this sort also intend to wear a combination of garlic and roses! I am aware that numerous authorities claim that a Naucratean garland is the type made of *sampsuchos*,[74] which is a common flower in Egypt. Egyptian myrtle has a stronger scent than the varieties found elsewhere, according to Theophrastus (*HP* 6.8.5).

In the midst of these remarks, slaves entered the room carrying garlands made of the flowers that were in season at the moment, and Myrtilus said: Offer us a list, my good Ulpian, of names of garlands! For the slaves, to quote Chaeremon's *Centaur* (*TrGF* 71 F 11),

[73] The same passage of Theopompus appears to be referred to at 9.384a; 14.657b (where see n.). The Agesilaus in question is Agesilaus II (Poralla #9; reigned 400–360/59 BCE).

[74] Seemingly a non-Greek word for marjoram (normally *amarakon*); cf. 15.681b, 684b, 689c; Andrews, *CP* 56 (1961) 78.

στεφάνους ἑτοιμάζουσιν, οὓς εὐφημίας
κήρυκας εὐχαῖς προὐβάλοντο δαιμόνων.

καὶ ἐν τῷ Διονύσῳ δὲ ὁ αὐτὸς ἔφη ποιητής·

στεφάνους τεμόντες ἀγγέλους εὐφημίας. |

f σὺ δὲ μὴ τὰ ἐκ τῶν ἐπιγραφομένων Αἰλίου Ἀσκλη-
πιάδου Στεφάνων φέρε ἡμῖν ὡς ἀνηκόοις αὐτῶν, ἀλλ'
ἄλλο τι παρ' ἐκεῖνα λέγε. δεῖξαι γὰρ οὐκ ἔχεις ὅτι †
διαλελυμένως † τις εἴρηκε ῥόδων στέφανον καὶ ἴων
στέφανον· τὸ γὰρ παρὰ Κρατίνῳ κατὰ παιδιὰν εἴρη-
ται· † ναρκισσίνους ὀλίσκους. † καὶ ὃς γελάσας,
πρῶτον ἐν τοῖς Ἕλλησι στέφανος ὠνομάσθη, ὥς
φησι Σῆμος ὁ Δήλιος ἐν τετάρτῳ Δηλιάδος, τὸ παρὰ ‖
677 μὲν ἡμῖν στέφος, παρὰ δέ τισι στέμμα προσαγορευό-
μενον, διὸ καὶ τούτῳ πρώτῳ στεφανωσάμενοι δεύτερον
περιτιθέμεθα τὸν δάφνινον. κέκληται δὲ στέφανος ἀπὸ
τοῦ στέφειν. σὺ δὲ οἴει με, ἔφη,

Θετταλὲ ποικιλόμυθε,

τῶν κοινῶν τούτων καὶ κατημαξευμένων ἐρεῖν τι; διὰ
δὲ τὴν σὴν γλῶσσαν τῆς ὑπογλωττίδος μνησθήσομαι, ἧς Πλάτων ἐμνήσθη ἐν Διὶ Κακουμένῳ·

---

[75] Literally "the call for *euphêmia*" ("the use of good words
only," and thus practically "the use of no words at all"), which was
issued just before a sacrifice was made.

[76] Cf. 15.679b with n.   [77] The words are in fact cognate.

[78] A fragment of a dactylic hexameter line, probably borrowed

are preparing garlands, which they set out as heralds of the call for silence,[75] to guard the prayers we offer the gods.

So too in his *Dionysus* (*TrGF* 71 F 6) the same poet said:

cutting garlands to serve as messengers of the call for silence.

Do not offer us material drawn from Aelius Asclepiades' work entitled *Garlands*,[76] as if we had never heard of it, but cite something different. For you cannot demonstrate that anyone ever referred to a garland made of roses or violets † using an uncontracted form †; for Cratinus' (fr. 394, unmetrical) † narcissus-[corrupt] † is a joke. Ulpian laughed (and said): According to Semus of Delos in Book IV of the *History of Delos* (*FGrH* 396 F 8), the Greeks originally used the term *stephanos* ("garland") to refer to what we know as a *stephos*, although some people call it a *stemma*; this is why we garland ourselves with this first, and then put a laurel-garland on our head. The noun *stephanos* ("garland") is derived from *stephein* ("to put around").[77] But do you expect me, he said,

my eloquent Thessalian,[78]

to discuss pedestrian commonplaces of this sort? On account of this tongue (*glôssa*) of yours, however, I will mention the *hupoglôttis*, to which Plato referred in *Zeus Abused* (fr. 51):[79]

or adapted from an oracle, as at 13.568d, where Myrtilus (who is from Thessaly) is again being addressed.   [79] The second verse is referred to again (but not quoted) at 15.678d.

63

καίτοι φορεῖτε γλῶτταν ἐν ὑποδήμασιν,
στεφανοῦσθ᾽ ὑπογλωττίσιν, ὅταν πίνητέ που· |
b   κἂν καλλιερῆτε, γλῶτταν ἀγαθὴν πέμπετε.

Θεόδωρος δ᾽ ἐν ταῖς Ἀττικαῖς Φωναῖς, ὥς φησιν
Πάμφιλος ἐν τοῖς Περὶ Ὀνομάτων, πλοκῆς στεφάνων
γένος τι τὴν ὑπογλωττίδα ἀποδίδωσιν. λαβὲ οὖν καὶ
παρ᾽ ἐμοῦ κατὰ τὸν Εὐριπίδην·

ἐκ παντὸς (γὰρ) ἄν τις πράγματος δισσῶν
   λόγων
ἀγῶνα θεῖτ᾽ ἄν, εἰ λέγειν εἴη σοφός.

Ἰσθμιακόν. οὕτως τοῦτον καλούμενον στέφανον
Ἀριστοφάνης μνήμης ἠξίωσεν ἐν Ταγηνισταῖς λέγων
οὕτως· |

c   τί οὖν ποῶμεν; χλανίδ᾽ ἐχρῆν λευκὴν λαβεῖν·
εἶτ᾽ Ἰσθμιακὰ λαβόντες ὥσπερ οἱ χοροὶ
ᾄδωμεν ἐς τὸν δεσπότην ἐγκώμιον.

Σιληνὸς δ᾽ ἐν ταῖς Γλώσσαις φησίν· Ἴσθμιον· στέφανον. Φιλητᾶς δέ φησι· στέφανος ἤγουν ὁμωνυμία
ἀμφοτέρωθι οἷον τῆς κεφαλῆς καὶ τοῦ † πρώτου †
κόσμου. λέγω δὲ τὸ ἐπὶ τοῦ φρέατος καὶ τοῦ ἐγχει-

---

80 Cited again at 15.678d (under the title *Attic Glossary*, as
also at 14.646c), along with a reference to the passage of Plato
Comicus quoted above.

81 Identified by Stobaeus as coming from *Antiope*.

82 Silenus, like Philitas and the other scholars cited below, ap-

In fact you have a tongue (*glôtta*) on your shoes;
you wear garlands made of *hupoglôttides* whenever
  you drink somewhere;
and if your sacrifices produce favorable omens, you
  give tongue to your joy.

According to Pamphilus in his *On Words* (fr. XXXVII
Schmidt), Theodorus in his *Attic Terms* (*FGrH* 346 F 3a)[80]
defines a *hupoglôttis* as a style of weaving garlands. So accept from me the following passage from Euripides (fr.
189);[81] for

If someone was a clever speaker, he could develop
two sides to the argument in any situation.

Isthmiakon. Aristophanes regarded the garland referred to this way as deserving mention in *Frying-Pan Men*
(fr. 505), where he says the following:

What should we do, then? We should've got a white
  cloak.
So let's get *Isthmiaka*, like the choruses do,
and sing a song of praise in our master's honor.

Silenus says in his *Vocabulary*: *Isthmion*:[82] a garland. Philetas[83] (fr. 13 Dettori = fr. 41 Spanoudakis) says: A garland,
i.e., a word with a double sense, used ambiguously to refer
to the head and to the † first † ornament.[84] I also note the
use of *isthmion* to refer to part of a well or a dagger.

pears to be commenting on *Od*. 18.299–300, where the suitor
Pisander is said to bring Penelope an *isthmion*.
  [83] Thus Athenaeus throughout; the correct spelling of the
name appears to be "Philitas."
  [84] Sc. that is placed around it.

ριδίου ἴσθμιον. Τιμαχίδας δὲ καὶ Σιμμίας οἱ Ῥόδιοι
ἀποδιδόασιν ἐν ἀνθ᾽ ἑνός· Ἴσθμιον· στέφανον. οὗ
μνημονεύει καὶ Καλλίξεινος ὁ Ῥόδιος καὶ αὐτὸς |
d γένος ἐν τοῖς Περὶ Ἀλεξανδρείας γράφων οὕτως· < . . . >
ἐπεὶ δὲ Ἀλεξανδρείας ἐμνημόνευσα, οἶδά τινα ἐν τῇ
καλῇ ταύτῃ πόλει καλούμενον στέφανον Ἀντινόειον
γινόμενον ἐκ τοῦ αὐτόθι καλουμένου λωτοῦ. φύεται δ᾽
οὗτος ἐν λίμναις θέρους ὥρᾳ, καὶ εἰσὶν αὐτοῦ χροιαὶ
δύο. ἡ μὲν τῷ ῥόδῳ ἐοικυῖα· ἐκ τούτου δὲ ὁ πλεκόμενος
στέφανος κυρίως Ἀντινόειος καλεῖται· ὁ δὲ ἕτερος
λώτινος ὀνομάζεται, κυανέαν ἔχων τὴν χροιάν. καὶ
Παγκράτης τις τῶν ἐπιχωρίων ποιητής, ὃν καὶ ἡμεῖς
e ἔγνωμεν, Ἀδριανῷ τῷ αὐτοκράτορι | ἐπιδημήσαντι τῇ
Ἀλεξανδρείᾳ μετὰ πολλῆς τερατείας ἐπέδειξεν τὸν
ῥοδίζοντα λωτόν, φάσκων αὐτὸν δεῖν καλεῖν Ἀντινόειον, ἀναπεμφθέντα ὑπὸ τῆς γῆς ὅτε τὸ αἷμα
ἐδέξατο τοῦ Μαυρουσίου λέοντος, ὃν κατὰ τὴν πλη-
σίον τῇ Ἀλεξανδρείᾳ Λιβύην ἐν κυνηγίῳ καταβεβλή-
κει ὁ Ἀδριανός, μέγα χρῆμα ὄντα καὶ πολλῷ χρόνῳ
κατανεμηθέντα πᾶσαν τὴν Λιβύην, ἧς καὶ πολλὰ
ἀοίκητα ἐπεποιήκει οὗτος ὁ λέων. ἡσθεὶς οὖν ἐπὶ τῇ
τῆς ἐννοίας εὑρέσει καὶ καινότητι τὴν ἐν Μουσῶν
f αὐτῷ σίτησιν ἔχειν | ἐχαρίσατο. καὶ Κρατῖνος δ᾽ ὁ

---

85 The quotation has fallen out of the text. 86 Named
after the emperor Hadrian's boyfriend Antinous, who accompanied him to Egypt and drowned in the Nile in 130 CE.
87 *RE* (5); to be distinguished from the Hellenistic poet
Pancrates of Arcadia (*RE* (3); quoted at e.g. 7.283a).

Timachidas (fr. 28 Blinkenberg) and Simmias (fr. 27, p. 120
Powell), both of Rhodes, gloss it with a single word: *Isthmion*: a garland. Callixeinus, whose family was again from
Rhodes, mentions it in his *On Alexandria* (*FGrH* 627 F 4),
writing as follows:[85] . . . But since I mentioned Alexandria:
I am familiar with a type of garland referred to in that
lovely city as an Antinoeian,[86] which is produced from what
is known there as *lôtos*. This plant grows in the marshes in
the spring, and comes in two colors. One variety resembles
a rose, and the garlands woven from it are properly referred to as Antinoeians, whereas the other is known as
a *lôtinos* and is a dark blue color. A certain Pancrates[87]
(*FGrH* 625 T 1), who was a local poet with whom I was personally acquainted, showed the rose-colored *lôtos* to the
emperor Hadrian when he was visiting Alexandria, and
presented it as a great marvel, claiming that it ought to be
referred to as an *Antinoeios*, since the earth had produced
it when it was drenched with the blood of the Mauretanian
lion Hadrian had killed while hunting in the part of Libya
near Alexandria; this lion was a huge creature, which had
ravaged all of Libya for a long time and rendered much
of it uninhabitable.[88] Hadrian was delighted by this novel
and original idea, and rewarded Pancrates with mainte-
nance in the Museum. So too the comic poet Cratinus in

[88] A substantial papyrus fragment of the poem (from which
the claim that the lion had made much of Libya uninhabitable before the emperor intervened—probably an echo of Hdt. 1.36.1—
is presumably drawn) is preserved (Pancrates fr. 2, pp. 52–4
Heitsch) and makes it clear that Antinous too was supposed to
have participated in the hunt.

κωμῳδιοποιὸς ἐν Ὀδυσσεῦσι κέκληκεν τὸν λωτὸν στεφάνωμα διὰ τὸ πάντα τὰ φυλλώδη ὑπὸ τῶν Ἀθηναίων
στεφανώματα λέγεσθαι. ὁ δὲ Παγκράτης ἐν τῷ ποιή-
ματι οὐκ ἀγλαφύρως εἴρηκεν·

οὔλην ἔρπυλλον, λευκὸν κρίνον ἠδ᾽ ὑάκινθον
πορφυρέην γλαυκοῦ τε χελιδονίοιο πέτηλα
καὶ ῥόδον εἰαρινοῖσιν ἀνοιγόμενον Ζεφύροισιν·
οὔπω γὰρ φύεν ἄνθος ἐπώνυμον Ἀντινόοιο. ||

678   Πυλεών. οὕτως καλεῖται ὁ στέφανος ὃν τῇ Ἥρᾳ
περιτιθέασιν Λάκωνες, ὥς φησιν Πάμφιλος. ἀλλὰ μὴν
καὶ Ἴακχα τινὰ καλούμενον οἶδα στέφανον ὑπὸ Σικυ-
ωνίων, ὥς φησι Τιμαχίδας ἐν ταῖς Γλώσσαις. Φιλητᾶς δ᾽ οὕτως γράφει· Ἴακχα· ἐν τῇ Σικυωνίᾳ στεφάνωμα εὐῶδες.

ἕστηκ᾽ ἀμφὶ κόμας εὐώδεας ἀγχόθι πατρὸς
καλὸν Ἰακχαῖον θηκαμένη στέφανον.

Σέλευκος δ᾽ ἐν ταῖς Γλώσσαις Ἑλλωτίδα καλεῖ-
σθαί φησι τὸν ἐκ μυρρίνης πλεκόμενον στέφανον, |
b   ὄντα τὴν περίμετρον πηχῶν εἴκοσι, πομπεύειν τε ἐν τῇ
τῶν Ἑλλωτίων ἑορτῇ. φασὶ δ᾽ ἐν αὐτῷ τὰ τῆς Εὐρώ-
πης ὀστᾶ κομίζεσθαι, ἣν ἐκάλουν Ἑλλωτίδα· ἄγεσθαι
δὲ καὶ ἐν Κορίνθῳ τὰ Ἑλλώτια.

---

[89] An intrusive remark, which interrupts the anecdote about
Hadrian and Pancrates and presumably belongs with the lexico-
graphical material cited above.   [90] Cf. 15.680f–1a with n.

Odysseuses (fr. 157) refers to the *lôtos* as a *stephanôma*, since the Athenians call anything that has leaves a *stephanôma*.[89] Pancrates remarks quite elegantly in his poem (fr. 3, p. 54 Heitsch):

> woolly thyme, white lily, and purple
> hyacinth, and the petals of the gray-blue *chelidonios*,
> and the rose, which opens when the West Winds
>   blow in spring;
> for the flower named for Antinous had not yet
>   appeared.

Puleôn. This is the term for the garland with which the Spartans crown Hera, according to Pamphilus (fr. XXXII Schmidt).[90] But I am also familiar with a garland the inhabitants of Sicyon refer to as an *Iakcha*,[91] according to Timachidas in his *Vocabulary* (fr. 19 Blinkenberg). Philetas (Philit. fr. 12 Dettori = fr. 40 Spanoudakis) writes as follows: *Iakcha*: a fragrant garland in Sicyonian territory.

> She stood close to her father, after placing a lovely
>   *Iakchaios* garland about her fragrant hair.[92]

Seleucus in his *Glossary* (fr. 52 Müller) says that *Hellôtis* is the term for the garland woven out of myrtle that is about 30 feet[93] in circumference and is carried in the procession at the Hellôtia festival. They say that the bones of Europa, whom they referred to as Hellôtis, are transported in it; the Hellôtia are celebrated in Corinth.

---

91 Presumably connected to the divine name Iacchus (closely associated with Dionysus).   92 Author unknown (= [Philit.] fr. 27, p. 95 Powell; printed by neither Spanoudakis nor Sbardella).   93 Literally "20 cubits."

Θυρεατικοί. οὕτω καλοῦνταί τινες στέφανοι παρὰ
Λακεδαιμονίοις, ὥς φησι Σωσίβιος ἐν τοῖς Περὶ Θυσιῶν, ψιλίνους αὐτοὺς φάσκων νῦν ὀνομάζεσθαι, ὄν-
τας ἐκ φοινίκων· φέρειν δ' αὐτοὺς ὑπόμνημα τῆς ἐν
Θυρέᾳ γενομένης νίκης τοὺς προστάτας τῶν ἀγομέ-
νων χορῶν ἐν τῇ ἑορτῇ ταύτῃ, ὅτε καὶ τὰς γυμνοπαι-
c δίας | ἐπιτελοῦσιν. χοροὶ δ' εἰσὶν τὸ μὲν πρόσω
παίδων, ⟨τὸ δ' ἐκ δεξίου . . . ⟩,[28] τὸ δ' ἐξ ἀρίστου
ἀνδρῶν, γυμνῶν ὀρχουμένων καὶ ἀδόντων Θαλητᾶ καὶ
Ἀλκμᾶνος ᾄσματα καὶ τοὺς Διονυσοδότου τοῦ Λάκω-
νος παιᾶνας.

Μελιλωτίνων δὲ στεφάνων μνημονεύει Ἄλεξις ἐν
Κρατείᾳ ἢ Φαρμακοπώλῃ οὕτως·

στεφάνους τε πολλοὺς κρεμαμένους
μελιλωτίνους.

Ἐπιθυμίς. Σέλευκός φησι· τὰ πάντα στεφανώματα.
Τιμαχίδας δέ φησιν τὰ παντοδαπὰ στεφανώματα ἃ |
d τὰς γυναῖκας φορεῖν οὕτως καλεῖσθαι. ὑποθυμὶς δὲ
καὶ ὑποθυμίδες στέφανοι παρ' Αἰολεῦσιν καὶ Ἴωσιν,
οὓς περὶ τοὺς τραχήλους περιετίθεντο, ὡς σαφῶς
ἔστιν μαθεῖν ἐκ τῆς Ἀλκαίου καὶ Ἀνακρέοντος ποιή-
σεως. Φιλητᾶς δ' ἐν τοῖς Ἀτάκτοις ὑποθυμίδα Λεσβί-
ους φησὶν καλεῖν μυρσίνης κλῶνα, περὶ ὃν πλέκειν ἴα

---

[28] add. Wyttenbach

[94] Literally "Naked-boy (Festival)"; cf. 14.630d–e, 631c.

Thureatikoi. This is a Spartan term for a type of garland, according to Sosibius in his *On Sacrifices* (*FGrH* 595 F 5), where he claims that they are referred to today as *psilinoi* and are made of palm-fronds; the leaders of the choruses that perform at this festival, during which they also celebrate the Gumnopaidiai,[94] hold them to commemorate the victory that took place at Thyrea.[95] A chorus of boys is in front, a chorus of . . . on the right, and a chorus of men on the left; they dance naked and sing songs by Thaletas[96] and Alcman, as well as the paeans of Dionysodotus of Sparta.[97]

Alexis in *Crateia or the Pharmacist* (fr. 119) mentions garlands made of *melilôt*,[98] as follows:

and many garlands made of *melilot* hanging there.

Epithumis. Seleucus (fr. 54 Müller) says: Garlands of all sorts. But Timachidas (fr. 25 Blinkenberg) claims that garlands of all sorts that women wear are referred to this way. *Hupothumis* and *hupothumides* are Aeolian and Ionian terms for the garlands they put around their necks, as is apparent from the poetry of Alcman and Anacreon.[99] Philetas in his *Miscellany* (Philit. fr. 14 Dettori = fr. 42 Spanoudakis) claims that the Lesbians refer to a twig of

---

[95] *c.*545 BCE, when the Spartans defeated the Argives and took control of the area; cf. Hdt. 1.82.

[96] Thaletas of Gortyn (7th century BCE) is supposed to have founded the Gumnopaidiai Festival in Sparta (Plu. *Mor.* 1134b–c).   [97] Poralla #240; otherwise unknown.

[98] A type of clover.

[99] Quoted (along with a relevant fragment of Sappho) at 15.674c–d.

καὶ ἄλλα ἄνθη. καὶ ὑπογλωττὶς δὲ στεφάνου ἐστὶν
εἶδος. Θεόδωρος δ' ἐν Ἀττικαῖς Γλώσσαις στεφάνων
πλοκῆς γένος παρὰ Πλάτωνι ἐν Διὶ Κακουμένῳ.

e   Εὑρίσκω δὲ καὶ παρὰ τοῖς κωμικοῖς | κυλιστόν τινα
καλούμενον στέφανον καὶ μνημονεύοντα αὐτοῦ Ἄρ-
χιππον ἐν Ῥίνωνι διὰ τούτων·

ἀθῷος ἀποδοὺς θοἰμάτιον ἀπέρχεται,
στέφανον ἔχων τῶν ἐκκυλίστων, οἴκαδε.

Ἄλεξις δ' ἐν μὲν Ἀγωνίδι ἢ Ἱππίσκῳ·

               (Α.) ὁ τρίτος οὗτος δ' ἔχει
σύκων κυλιστὸν στέφανον. (Β.) ἀλλ' ἔχαιρε καὶ
ζῶν τοῖς τοιούτοις.

ἐν δὲ τῷ Σκίρωνί φησι·

ὥσπερ κυλιστὸς στέφανος αἰωρούμενος.

μνημονεύει δ' αὐτοῦ καὶ Ἀντιφάνης ἐν Ἑαυτοῦ Ἐρῶν-
f τι, | Εὔβουλος δ' ἐν Οἰνομάῳ ἢ Πέλοπι·

             περιφοραῖς κυκλούμενος
ὥσπερ κυλιστὸς στέφανος.

τίς οὖν οὗτος ὁ κυλιστός; οἶδα γὰρ τὸν Θυατειρηνὸν
Νίκανδρον ἐν τοῖς Ἀττικοῖς Ὀνόμασι λέγοντα τάδε·
ἐκκύλιστοι στέφανοι· καὶ μάλιστα οἱ ἐκ ῥόδων. καὶ τὸ
εἶδος ὁποῖον ζητῶ, ὦ Κύνουλκε. καὶ μή μοι εἴπῃς ὅτι

myrtle that has violets and other flowers wrapped around it as a *hupothumis*. A *hupoglôttis* is also a type of garland; Theodorus in the *Attic Glossary* (*FGrH* 346 F 3b) (says that) Plato in *Zeus Abused* (fr. 51.2) uses the word to refer to a style of weaving garlands.[100]

I also find a type of garland known as a *kulistos* mentioned in the comic poets; Archippus refers to it in *Rhinon* (fr. 42), in the following passage:

> He surrenders his robe and goes off home
> scot-free, wearing an *ekkulistos* garland.

Alexis in *Agonis or The Brooch* (fr. 4):

> (A.) The third guy here has
> a *kulistos* garland of figs. (B.) Well, he liked
> food like this when he was alive too!

And in his *Sciron* (fr. 210) he says:

> hung up high like a *kulistos* garland.

Antiphanes in *The Man Who Was in Love with Himself* (fr. 53) also mentions it, as does Eubulus in *Oenomaus or Pelops* (fr. 73):

> rolling around in circles,
> like a *kulistos* garland.

So what is this *kulistos* garland? For I know that Nicander of Thyateira in his *Attic Words* (*FGrH* 343 F 7) says the following: *Ekkulistoi* garlands: in particular those made of roses. What I am wondering, Cynulcus, is what they look

---

100 Cf. 15.677a–b (citing Pamphilus for this information, and giving the quotation from Plato) with n.

δεῖ τοὺς ἁδροὺς ἀκούειν· σὺ γὰρ εἶ ὁ τὰ ἐν τοῖς
βιβλίοις ἀπόρρητα οὐ μόνον ἐκλέγων ἀλλὰ καὶ ἀνορύττων,[29] καθάπερ οἱ παρὰ Βάτωνι τῷ κωμῳδιοποιῷ ἐν
Συνεξαπατῶντι φιλόσοφοι, περὶ ὧν καὶ Σοφοκλῆς
Συνδείπνοις[30] φησίν, οὖσί σοι παραπλησίοις· ||

679   οὗτοι γένειον ὧδε χρὴ διηλιφὲς
       φοροῦντα κἀντίπαιδα καὶ γένει μέγαν
       γαστρὸς καλεῖσθαι παῖδα, τοῦ πατρὸς παρόν.

ἐπειδὴ οὖν ἤδη καὶ σὺ πεπλήρωσαι οὐ μόνον τῶν τοῦ
γλαύκου κρανίων ἀλλὰ καὶ τῆς ἀειζώου βοτάνης, ἧς ὁ
Ἀνθηδόνιος ἐκεῖνος δαίμων ἐμφορηθεὶς ἀθάνατος
πάλιν † ητις † γέγονε, λέγε ἡμῖν περὶ τοῦ προκειμένου, ἵνα μὴ κατὰ τὸν θεῖον Πλάτωνα ὑπολάβωμέν
σε ἀποθανόντα μεταμορφωθῆναι·[31] τοὺς μὲν γὰρ τὰς
b   γαστριμαργίας | τε καὶ ὕβρεις καὶ φιλοποσίας μεμε-
λετηκότας καὶ μὴ διευλαβουμένους εἰς τὰ τῶν ὄνων
γένη καὶ τῶν τοιούτων θηρίων εἰκὸς ἐνδύεσθαι. ἀπο-
ροῦντος δ᾽ αὐτοῦ, ἐπὶ ἕτερον, φησί, στέφανον μεταβή-
σομαι, ὁ Οὐλπιανός, τὸν στρούθινον καλούμενον, οὗ
μέμνηται μὲν ὁ Ἀσκληπιάδης παρατιθέμενος τὰ ἐκ
τῶν Εὐβούλου Στεφανοπωλίδων ταῦτα·

[29] ἀνορύττων Kassel: διορύττων ACE   [30] Συνδείπνοις
Musurus: Συνδείπνοι A: Συνδείπνῳ Casaubon
[31] μεταμορφωθῆναι ἐν τῷ Περὶ Ψυχῆς A: ἐν τῷ Περὶ
Ψυχῆς del. Schweighäuser

[101] For the image, cf. 15.671c with n.

like; and do not tell me that I should take this as a reference to large garlands. For you are the person who not only collects the obscure passages in his books but actively roots them up,[101] precisely like the philosophers in the comic poet Bato's *The Partner in Deception* (fr. 6). Sophocles in *The Dinner Guests* (fr. 564) also discusses them, and they closely resemble you:

> It's not right that, when you've got such a nicely-oiled
>   chin, and aren't a boy any longer, and come from a
>   distinguished family,
> that you're called the child of someone's stomach,
>   when you could be called by your father's name.

Since, therefore, you are now full not just of *glaukos*-heads[102] but also of the herb that brings eternal life, with which the well-known Anthedonian deity stuffed himself and became immortal [corrupt] again[103]—tell us about the matter before us, so that we do not conclude that you have, as the divine Plato (*Phd.* 81e–2a) puts it, died and been transformed. For individuals who are interested in gluttony, ugly behavior, and drinking, and who are not careful, are likely to turn into donkeys or similar creatures. When Cynulcus had no answer, Ulpian said: I will move on to a different garland, the one known as a *strouthinos*, which Asclepiades refers to,[104] citing the following passage from Eubulus' *Female Garland-Vendors* (fr. 102):

---

102 The *glaukos* is an unidentified fish; cf. 7.295b–f.

103 Apparently a reference to one of the many stories told about the sea-divinity Glaucus; cf. 7.296a–7c.

104 Presumably in the work entitled *Wreaths* referred to at 15.676f.

ὦ μάκαρ ἥτις ἔχουσ᾽ ἐν δωματίῳ
στρουθίον ἀεροφόρητον
λεπτότατον περὶ σῶμα συνίλλεται
† ἡδυπότατον † περὶ νυμφίον εὔτριχα,
κισσὸς ὅπως καλάμῳ περιφύεται
† αὐξόμενος ἔαρος † ὀλολυγόνος |
c   ἔρωτι κατατετηκώς.

πλέκεται δ᾽ οὗτος ἐκ τοῦ στρουθίου καλουμένου ἄνθους, οὗ μνημονεύει Θεόφραστος ἐν ἕκτῳ Φυτικῆς
Ἱστορίας ἐν τούτοις· ἀνθεῖ δὲ καὶ ἡ ἶρις τοῦ θέρους
καὶ τὸ στρούθιον καλούμενον, ὃ τῇ μὲν ὄψει καλὸν
ἄνθος, ἄοσμον δέ. Γαλήνη δ᾽ ἡ Σμυρναία στρούθιον
αὐτὸν ὀνομάζει.

Πόθος. οὕτως τις στέφανος ὀνομάζεται, ὡς Νίκανδρός φησιν ὁ Κολοφώνιος ἐν Γλώσσαις· καὶ ἴσως ὁ
ἀπὸ τοῦ οὕτω καλουμένου ἄνθους[32] πλεκόμενος, οὗ
d μνημονεύει ὁ αὐτὸς Θεόφραστος | ἐν τῷ ἕκτῳ τῶν
Φυτικῶν γράφων ὧδε· τὰ δὲ θερινὰ μᾶλλον, ἥ τε
λυχνὶς καὶ τὸ Διὸς ⟨ἄνθος⟩[33] καὶ τὸ κρίνον καὶ ⟨τὸ⟩[34]
ἴφυον καὶ ἀμάρακος ὁ Φρύγιος, ἔτι δὲ ὁ πόθος καλούμενος. οὗτος δέ ἐστι διττός, ὁ μὲν ἔχων τὸ ἄνθος
ὅμοιον ὑακίνθῳ, ὁ δ᾽ ἕτερος ἄχρως, ἔκλευκος, ᾧ χρῶν-
ται πρὸς τοὺς τάφους.

[32] καλουμένου πόθου ἄνθους A: πόθου ἄνθους tantum CE:
πόθου del. Kaibel
[33] add. Kaibel ex Theophrasto; cf. 15.680f
[34] add. Kaibel ex Theophrasto; cf. 15.680f

Happy girl! In your bedroom you've got
a *strouthios* that's blown about by the breezes,
and you twine your slender body
[corrupt] about your bridegroom with his fine head of
    hair,
just as ivy clings to a reed
† growing larger in the spring †, melting
with love for the *ololugôn*.[105]

This garland is woven from the flower known as a
strouthios, which Theophrastus mentions in Book VI (8.3)
of the *Inquiry into Plants*, in the following passage: The iris
blooms in the summer, as does the so-called *strouthion*;
the latter flower looks attractive, but lacks a scent. Galene
of Smyrna refers to it as a *strouthios*.[106]

Pothos.[107] This is a term for a type of garland, according
to Nicander of Colophon in the *Glossary* (fr. 144 Schneider). Perhaps (it is) the garland woven from the flower
by this name, which the same Theophrastus mentions in
Book VI of the *Botany* (*HP* 6.8.3), writing as follows:[108]
Those that are instead summer flowers, such as rose campion, carnation, lily, spike-lavender, and Phrygian marjoram, as well as what is known as *pothos*. There are two
varieties of the latter; one has a flower that resembles a hyacinth, while the other is colorless and whitish, and is used
in funerary rites.

105 Perhaps "the nightingale," although "the tree-frog" seems
just as likely; see Oliphant, *TAPA* 47 (1916) 85–106; Hunter, *Eubulus*, pp. 197–8.　　　106 I.e., apparently, as a masculine rather
than a neuter noun (as above).
107 Literally "longing."
108 The first portion of the passage is quoted again at 15.680f.

Καταλέγει δὲ Εὔβουλος καὶ ἄλλους στεφάνους·

Αἰγίδιον, σὺ δὲ τόνδε φορήσεις
στέφανον πολυποίκιλον ἀνθέων
γρυπότατον, χαριέστατον, ὦ Ζεῦ.
e   † τίς γὰρ αὐτὸν | ἔχουσα φιλήσει; †

κἂν τοῖς ἑξῆς τάδε φησί·

(Α.) στεφάνους ἴσως βούλεσθε· πότερ᾽
    ἑρπυλλίνους
ἢ μυρτίνους ἢ τῶν † διηνθημένων †;
(Β.) τῶν μυρτίνων βουλόμεθα τουτωνί· σὺ ⟨δὲ⟩
τά ⟨γ᾽⟩ ἄλλα πώλει πάντα πλὴν τῶν μυρτίνων.

Φιλύρινος. Ξέναρχος Στρατιώτῃ·

               φιλύρας εἶχε γὰρ
ὁ παῖς ἀφύλλου στέφανον ἀμφικείμενον.

Καλοῦνται δέ τινες καὶ ἑλικτοὶ στέφανοι, ὥσπερ
f παρὰ | Ἀλεξανδρεῦσι μέχρι καὶ νῦν. μνημονεύει δ᾽
αὐτῶν Χαιρήμων ὁ τραγῳδιοποιὸς ἐν Διονύσῳ διὰ
τούτων·

κισσῷ τε ναρκίσσῳ τε τριέλικας κύκλῳ
στεφάνων ἑλικτῶν.

Περὶ δὲ τῶν ἐν Αἰγύπτῳ αἰεὶ ἀνθούντων στεφάνων
Ἑλλάνικος ἐν τοῖς Αἰγυπτιακοῖς οὕτως γράφει· πόλις

Eubulus (fr. 103)[109] lists other types of garlands as well:

Aegidion, you're going to wear this
garland that's made of all kinds of flowers,
and that's curved and really lovely, by Zeus.
† Because who'll kiss when she's wearing it? †

And immediately after this he says the following (fr. 104):

(A.) Maybe you want garlands; the type made from
thyme,
or from myrtle, or some of the [corrupt]?
(B.) We want some of the myrtle wreaths here. Sell
all the rest, except the ones made from myrtle.

Philurinos ("[a garland] made of lime-wood"). Xenarchus in *The Soldier* (fr. 13):

Because the boy had
a garland of lime-wood (*philura*) with no leaves
around his head.

Certain garlands are known as *heliktoi* ("twisted"), as in Alexandria even today. The tragic poet Chaeremon refers to them in *Dionysus* (*TrGF* 71 F 7), in the following passage:

triple coils of *heliktoi* garlands, with ivy
and narcissus round about.

Hellanicus in his *History of Egypt* (*FGrH* 4 F 54) writes as follows on the subject of the ever-flowering garlands in

109 Most likely another fragment of *Female Garland-Vendors* (cf. 15.679b–c), like fr. 104 below.

ἐπιποταμίη, Τίνδιον ὄνομα αὐτῇ, θεῶν ὁμήγυρις, καὶ
ἱερὸν μέγα καὶ ἁγνὸν ἐν μέσῃ τῇ πόλει λίθινον καὶ
θύρετρα λίθινα. ἔσω τοῦ ἱεροῦ ἄκανθαι πεφύκασι ‖
680   λευκαὶ καὶ μέλαιναι. ἐπ' αὐτῇσι στέφανοι ἐπιβέβλην-
ται ἄνω τῆς ἀκάνθου τοῦ ἄνθεος καὶ ῥοιῆς[35] καὶ
ἀμπέλου πεπλεγμένοι. καὶ οὗτοι αἰεὶ ἀνθέουσι· τοὺς[36]
ἀπέθεντο οἱ θεοὶ ἐν Αἰγύπτῳ πυθόμενοι βασιλεύειν
τὸν Βάβυν, ὅς ἐστι Τυφῶν. Δημήτριος δ' ἐν τῷ Περὶ
τῶν Κατ' Αἴγυπτον περὶ Ἄβυδον πόλιν τὰς ἀκάνθας
ταύτας εἶναί φησιν γράφων οὕτως· ἔχει δὲ ὁ κάτω
τόπος καὶ ἄκανθάν τινα δένδρον, ὃ τὸν καρπὸν φέρει
στρογγύλον ἐπί τινων κλωνίων περιφερῶν. ἀνθεῖ δ' |
b   οὗτος ὅταν ὥρα ᾖ, καὶ ἐστὶ τῷ χρώματι τὸ ἄνθος ‹ . . . ›
καὶ εὐφεγγές. λέγεται δέ τις μῦθος ὑπὸ τῶν Αἰγυπτίων
ὅτι οἱ Αἰθίοπες στελλόμενοι εἰς Τροίαν ὑπὸ τοῦ
Τιθωνοῦ, ἐπεὶ ἤκουσαν τὸν Μέμνονα τετελευτηκέναι,
ἐν τούτῳ ‹τῷ›[37] τόπῳ τοὺς στεφάνους ἀνέβαλον ἐπὶ
τὰς ἀκάνθας. ἐστὶ δὲ παραπλήσια τὰ κλωνία
στεφάνοις, ἐφ' ὧν τὸ ἄνθος φύεται. ὁ δὲ προειρημένος
Ἑλλάνικος καὶ Ἄμασιν Αἰγύπτου βασιλεῦσαι, ἰδι-
ώτην ὄντα καὶ τῶν τυχόντων κατὰ τὸν πρῶτον βίον,
διὰ στεφάνου δωρεάν, ὃν ἔπεμψεν ἀνθέων πλεξάμενος |
c   τῇ ὥρᾳ περικαλλεστάτων γενέθλια ἐπιτελοῦντι Πα-
τάρμιδι τῷ τῆς Αἰγύπτου τότε βασιλεύοντι. τούτου
γὰρ ἡσθέντα τῷ κάλλει τοῦ στεφάνου καὶ ἐπὶ δεῖπνον

_____

[35] ῥοιῆς ἄνθος A: ἄνθος del. Meineke   [36] τοὺς στεφάνους A: στεφάνους del. Kaibel   [37] add. edd.

Egypt: There is a city on the river-bank, known as Tindion; the gods gather in this spot, and there is a large, holy temple made of stone, as well as a set of stone gateways, in the center of the city. White and black thorn-trees grow inside the temple. Garlands woven out of acanthus-, pomegranate-, and grape-flowers have been set on top of them. These plants are always in bloom; the gods deposited them in Egypt when they heard that Babys—that is, Typhon—was king.[110] Demetrius in his *On the Sights in Egypt* (*FHG* iv.383) reports that these thorn-trees are found around the city of Abydus. He writes as follows: The region below this features a type of thorn-tree that produces a round fruit on some of its branches, which are curved. This tree flowers in the spring; its flowers are colored . . . and are shiny. The Egyptians tell a story, to the effect that when the Ethiopians who were sent to Troy by Tithonus heard that Memnon was dead,[111] they threw their garlands up into the thorn-trees in that spot. The twigs on which the flowers appear resemble garlands. The Hellanicus (*FGrH* 4 F 55) referred to above (also claims) that Amasis, who was originally an ordinary private citizen, got the throne as a result of the gift of a garland, which he wove out of the most beautiful flowers of the season and sent to Patarmis, who was the king of Egypt at that time and was celebrating his birthday. Patarmis was delighted at how beautiful the garland was, and he invited Amasis to dinner; afterward he

110 For the gods' flight to Egypt, cf. [Apollod.] *Bib*. 1.6.3. Plu. *Mor*. 371b–c gives Typhon's alternative (Egyptian) name as Bebôn.

111 Memnon was the son of Tithonus and Eos ("Dawn") and was killed by Achilleus.

καλέσαι τὸν Ἄμασιν καὶ μετὰ ταῦτα τῶν φίλων ἕνα
αὐτὸν ἔχοντα ἐκπέμψαι ποτὲ καὶ στρατηγόν, Αἰγυπτίων αὐτῷ πολεμούντων· ὑφ' ὧν διὰ τὸ τοῦ Πατάρ-
μιδος μῖσος ἀποφανθῆναι βασιλέα.

Συνθηματιαῖοι στέφανοι· ἠργολαβημένοι καὶ ἐκ-
δόσιμοι. Ἀριστοφάνης ἐν Θεσμοφοριαζούσαις·

πλέξαι στεφάνους συνθηματιαίους εἴκοσιν. |

d   Χορωνόν. Ἀπίων ἐν τῷ Περὶ τῆς Ῥωμαϊκῆς Δια-
λέκτου φησὶν τὸν στέφανον πάλαι χορωνὸν καλούμενον ἀπὸ τοῦ τοὺς χορευτὰς ἐν τοῖς θεάτροις αὐτῷ
χρῆσθαι, αὐτούς τε περικειμένους καὶ ἐπὶ τὸν στέφανον ἀγωνιζομένους, καθὼς ἐν τοῖς Σιμωνίδου Ἐπι-
γράμμασιν ἰδεῖν ἔστιν οὕτως καλουμένου·

Φοῖβον, ὃς ἁγεῖται <τοῖς> Τυνδαρίδησιν ἀοιδᾶς,
ἁμέτεροι τέττιγες ἐπεστέψαντο χορωνῷ.

Ἀκίνοι. στέφανοί τινες καλοῦνται οὕτως οἱ ἐκ τῆς
ἀκίνου τοῦ φυτοῦ πλεκόμενοι, ὥς φησιν Ἄνδρων ὁ
ἰατρός. παρέθετο δ' αὐτοῦ τὴν λέξιν Παρθένιος ὁ τοῦ
e   Διονυσίου ἐν τῷ | πρώτῳ τῶν Παρὰ τοῖς Ἱστορικοῖς
Λέξεων.

Στεφανωματικὰ δὲ ἄνθη καταλέγει Θεόφραστος

---

112 Amasis became pharaoh c.570 BCE. The king before him
(more often called Aprias or Apriês) was overthrown in a popular
revolt that followed a disastrous expedition against Cyrene; cf.
13.560e.

made him a member of his inner circle, and sent him off at one point as a general, when the Egyptians were attempting to revolt from him. Because they hated Patarmis, they made Amasis king.[112]

Bespoke garlands: those that have been contracted for or farmed out. Aristophanes in *Women Celebrating the Thesmophoria* (458):

to weave 20 bespoke garlands.

Chorônon. Apion in his *On the Roman Dialect* (*FGrH* 616 F 25)[113] reports that garlands were referred to in the past as *chorôna* because the dancers (*choreutai*) in the theaters used them, not only wearing them on their heads but competing for the victory garland. The term can be found used this way in Simonides' *Epigrams* (fr. 176 Bergk):

Our cicadas[114] garlanded Phoebus, who leads
the sons of Tyndareus in song, with a *chorônon*.

Akininoi. Certain garlands woven from the *akinos* plant were referred to this way, according to the physician Andron;[115] Dionysius' student Parthenius cited this statement by him in Book I of his *Vocabulary in the Historians*.

Theophrastus[116] lists the following flowers used to

[112] Presumably discussing the Latin word *corona*. For Latin understood to be a dialect of Greek, see 14.632a n.

[114] Also used of Spartan choruses in Pratin. *PMG* 709 (quoted at 14.633a). Tyndareus was a mythical early king of Sparta and was also the father of Helen, Clytemestra, and the Dioscuri.

[115] Perhaps to be identified with the equally obscure medical writer Andreas mentioned at 15.675c–d.

[116] Cf. *HP* 6.6.11 (a list of flowers grown from seed).

τάδε· ἴον, Διὸς ἄνθος, ἴφυον, φλόγα, ἡμεροκαλλές.
πρῶτόν τε τῶν ἀνθέων ἐκφαίνεσθαί φησιν τὸ λευ-
κόιον, ἅμα δὲ αὐτῷ καὶ τὸ φλόγινον καλούμενον τὸ
ἄγριον, ἔπειτα νάρκισσον καὶ λείριον καὶ τῶν ἀγρίων
ἀνεμώνης γένος τὸ καλούμενον ὄρειον καὶ τὸ τοῦ
βολβοῦ κώδυον· συμπλέκουσι γὰρ καὶ τοῦτ᾽ ἔνιοι εἰς
τοὺς στεφάνους. ἐπὶ τούτοις ἥ τε οἰνάνθη καὶ τὸ μέλαν
ἴον καὶ τῶν ἀγρίων ὅ τε ἐλίχρυσος καὶ τῆς ἀνεμώνης ἡ
λειμωνία καλουμένη καὶ ξίφιον καὶ ὑάκινθος. τὸ δὲ
ῥόδον ὑστερεῖ τούτων καὶ τελευταῖον μὲν φαίνεται, |
f   πρῶτον δὲ παύεται. τὰ δὲ θερινὰ μᾶλλον, ἥ τε λυχνὶς
καὶ τὸ Διὸς ἄνθος καὶ τὸ κρίνον καὶ τὸ ἴφυον καὶ
ἀμάρακος <ὁ>³⁸ Φρύγιος, ἔτι δὲ ὁ πόθος καλούμενος.
ἐν δὲ τῷ ἐνάτῃ ὁ αὐτὸς Θεόφραστός φησιν· ἐάν τις τοῦ
ἐλιχρύσου τῷ ἄνθει στεφανῶται, εὔκλειαν ἴσχει μύρῳ
ῥαίνων. μνημονεύει αὐτοῦ Ἀλκμὰν ἐν τούτοις· ‖

681   καὶ τὶν εὔχομαι φέροισα
τόνδ᾽ ἐλιχρύσω πυλεῶνα
κἠρατῶ κυπαίρω.

καὶ Ἴβυκος·

μύρτα τε καὶ ἴα καὶ ἐλίχρυσος,
μᾶλά τε καὶ ῥόδα καὶ τέρεινα δάφνα.

³⁸ add. Kaibel ex Theophrasto; cf. 15.679d

---

[117] Abbreviated and adapted, but nonetheless representing a
better version of the text than is preserved elsewhere. The final
section is quoted also at 15.679d.

produce garlands: violet, carnation, spike-lavender, wall-flower, and daylily. The first flower to appear, he claims (*HP* 6.8.1–3),[117] is the gillyflower; what is known as wild wallflower comes out at the same time, followed by pheasant's eye and polyanthus narcissus, and among the wild-flowers by the type of anemone known as mountain-anemone, and the upper portion of the purse-tassel hyacinth; for some people weave this as well into their garlands. After these come dropwart, black violet, and among the wild-flowers gold-flower, what is known as meadow-anemone, corn-flag, and hyacinth. The rose appears later than all of these, and is both the last flower to appear and the first to cease blooming. Those that are instead summer flowers include rose campion, carnation, lily, spike-lavender, and Phrygian marjoram, as well as what is known as *pothos*. In Book IX (19.3)[118] the same Theophrastus says: If someone wears a garland made of gold-flower blossoms, he gets a good reputation if he sprinkles it with perfume. Alcman mentions the flower in the following passage (*PMG* 60):

> And I pray to you, as I offer
> this *puleôn*[119] made of gold-flower
> and lovely *kupairos*.

Also Ibycus (*PMG* 315):

> myrtle and violets and gold-flower,
> and apples and roses and delicate laurel.

---

[118] Heavily adapted.

[119] See 15.678a–b; Alcman was from Sparta. The speaker is female and is thus presumably a member of one of Alcman's choruses of young women.

Κρατῖνος δὲ ἐν Μαλθακοῖς φησιν·

ἑρπύλλῳ, κρόκοις, ὑακίνθοις, ἑλιχρύσου κλάδοις.

ἐστὶ δὲ τὸ ἄνθος ὅμοιον λωτῷ. Θεμισταγόρας δ᾿ ὁ Ἐφέσιος ἐν τῇ ἐπιγραφομένῃ Χρυσέῃ Βύβλῳ ἀπὸ |

b τῆς πρώτης δρεψαμένης νύμφης Ἑλιχρύσης ὄνομα τὸ ἄνθος ὀνομασθῆναι. τὰ δὲ κρίνα φησὶν ὁ Θεόφραστος εἶναι καὶ πορφυρανθῆ.

Φιλῖνος δὲ τὸ κρίνον ὑφ᾿ ὧν μὲν λείριον, ὑφ᾿ ὧν δὲ ἴον καλεῖσθαι. Κορίνθιοι δ᾿ αὐτὸ ἀμβροσίαν καλοῦσιν, ὥς φησι Νίκανδρος ἐν Γλώσσαις.

Διοκλῆς δ᾿ ἐν τῷ Περὶ Θανασίμων Φαρμάκων, ἀμάρακον, φησίν, ὃν σάμψουχόν τινες καλοῦσιν.

Κοσμοσανδάλων δὲ μνημονεύει Κρατῖνος ἐν Μαλθακοῖς διὰ τούτων·

κεφαλὴν ἀνθέμοις ἐρέπτομαι·
λειρίοις, ῥόδοις, κρίνεσιν, κοσμοσανδάλοις. |

c Κλέαρχος δ᾿ ἐν δευτέρῳ Βίων, ὅρα, φησίν, τοὺς τὸ κοσμοσάνδαλον ἀνείροντας Λακεδαιμονίους, οἳ τὸν παλαιότατον τῆς πολιτικῆς κόσμον συμπατήσαντες ἐξετραχηλίσθησαν. διόπερ καλῶς περὶ αὐτῶν εἴρηκεν ὁ κωμῳδιοποιὸς Ἀντιφάνης ἐν Κιθαριστῇ·

---

120 Quoted at greater length at 15.685b–c; cf. 15.681b, e, 685f.
121 Cf. Nic. fr. 74.27–8 Schneider (quoted at 15.683d).
122 Cf. 15.676d–e with n.

And Cratinus says in *Soft Men* (fr. 105.4):[120]

> with tufted thyme, crocuses, hyacinths, and gold-
> flower stalks.

The flower resembles a *lôtos*. Themistagoras of Ephesus in his work entitled *The Golden Book* (fr. 2, *FHG* iv.512) (claims) that the flower got its name from Helichrusê, who was the first nymph to pick it. Theophrastus (cf. *HP* 6.6.3) reports that lilies have purple flowers.

Philinus claims that some authorities refer to a lily as a *leirion*, others as an *ion*. The Corinthians refer to it as an *ambrosia*, according to Nicander in his *Glossary* (fr. 126 Schneider).[121]

Diocles says in his *On Deadly Drugs* (fr. 206a van der Eijk): marjoram, referred to by some authorities as *sampsouchos*.[122]

Cratinus in *Soft Men* (fr. 105.1–2)[123] mentions *kosmosandala* in the following passage:

> I crown my head with flowers:
> with polyanthus narcissus, roses, lilies, *kosmosandala*.

Clearchus says in Book II of the *Lives* (fr. 39 Wehrli): Look at the Spartans, who make garlands of *kosmosandalon*, and who trampled on[124] their most ancient political arrangements (*kosmos*) and were wrecked. This is why the comic poet Antiphanes in *The Cithara-Player* (fr. 115) was right to say about them:

---

[123] Quoted at greater length at 15.685b–c; cf. 15.681a, e, 685f.

[124] As if the second element in the flower's name was *sandalon* ("sandal").

οὐκ ἐφύσων οἱ Λάκωνες ὡς ἀπόρθητοί ποτε;
νῦν δ᾽ ὁμηρεύουσ᾽ ἔχοντες πορφυροῦς
κεκρυφάλους.

Ἰκέσιος δ᾽ ἐν δευτέρῳ Περὶ Ὕλης τὸ λευκόιόν φησι
μεσότητά τινα ἔχειν ἐν τῷ στύφειν, πολὺ δ᾽ ἀρίστην |
d   εὐωδίαν καὶ δυναμένην τέρπειν, ἀλλὰ πρὸς ὀλίγιστον.
τὸ δὲ μέλαν, φησί, τὴν μὲν αὐτὴν θεωρίαν ἔχει, εὐῶδες
δ᾽ ἐστὶ πολὺ μᾶλλον. Ἀπολλόδωρος δὲ ἐν τῷ Περὶ
Θηρίων φησί· χαμαίπιτυν, οἱ δὲ ὁλόκυρον, οἱ δὲ Ἀθήνησιν ἰωνιάν, οἱ δὲ κατ᾽ Εὔβοιαν σιδηρῖτιν. Νίκανδρος δ᾽ ἐν δευτέρῳ Γεωργικῶν (τὰ δὲ ἔπη ὀλίγον
ὕστερον παραθήσομαι, ὅταν περὶ πάντων τῶν στεφα-
νωματικῶν ἀνθῶν διεξέρχωμαι), τὸ ἴον, φησίν, Ἰωνι-
άδες τινὲς νύμφαι Ἴωνι ἐχαρίσαντο πρώτῳ. τὸν δὲ
e   νάρκισσον ἐν τῷ ἕκτῳ Περὶ | Φυτῶν Ἱστορίας ὁ
Θεόφραστος καλεῖσθαί φησι καὶ λείριον. εἶθ᾽ ὑποβὰς
ὡς διαλλάσσοντα τίθησιν νάρκισσον καὶ λείριον.
Εὔμαχος δ᾽ ὁ Κορκυραῖος ἐν Ῥιζοτομικῷ καὶ ἀκακαλ-
λίδα φησὶ καλεῖσθαι τὸν νάρκισσον καὶ κρόταλον.
τοῦ δὲ ἡμεροκαλλοῦς καλουμένου ἄνθους, ὃ τὴν μὲν
νύκτα μαραίνεται, ἅμα δὲ τῷ ἡλίῳ ἀνατέλλοντι θάλ-
λει, μνημονεύει Κρατῖνος ἐν Μαλθακοῖς λέγων οὕτως·

⟨ . . . ⟩ ἡμεροκαλλεῖ τε τῷ φιλουμένῳ.

---

125 Sc. as a sign of their addiction to luxury (and thus, presumably, of an unwillingness or inability to continue to live in their tra-
ditionally harsh, militaristic style).

Didn't the Spartans brag at one point that their land
  was never ravaged?
But nowadays they wear purple head-scarves[125] and
  give hostages.

Hicesius in Book II of *On Raw Materials* claims that gillyflower is moderately astringent but has far and away the
best fragrance, which is quite pleasant, although only for a
very short time. The black variety, he says, looks identical
but smells much better. Apollodorus says in his *On Wild
Animals*: *chamaipitus*,[126] which some people call *holoku-
ros*, although the Athenians call it *iônia* and the Euboeans
call it *sidêritis*. Nicander in Book II of the *Georgics*—I will
cite the verses a little later, after I complete my account
of all the flowers used to make garlands—says: Certain
Ioniad nymphs gave the violet (*ion*) to Ion first.[127] Theophrastus in Book VI (6.9) of *Research on Plants* reports
that the narcissus is also referred to as a *leirion;*[128] but then
later on (*HP* 6.8.1) he refers to the narcissus and the *leirion*
as different plants. Eumachus of Corcyra in *The Art of
Root-Gathering* reports that the narcissus is also referred
to as an *akakallis* or *krotalos*. The flower of the so-called
daylily, which closes at night but opens up when the sun
rises, is mentioned by Cratinus in *Soft Men* (fr. 105.5),[129]
where he says the following:

and with the beloved daylily.

[126] Literally "ground-pine."
[127] A rough prose summary of Nic. fr. 74.4 Schneider, quoted
at 15.683a.
[128] Normally "lily"; cf. 15.681b.
[129] Quoted at greater length at 15.685b–c; cf. 15.681a, b, 685f.

τῆς δ᾽ ἑρπύλλου, φησὶ Θεόφραστος, τὴν ἄγριον κομί-
f ζοντες | ἐκ τῶν ὀρῶν φυτεύουσιν ἐν Σικυῶνι καὶ
Ἀθήνησιν ἐκ τοῦ Ὑμηττοῦ. παρ᾽ ἄλλοις δὲ ὄρη πλήρη
ἐστὶ τοῦ ἄνθους, καθάπερ ἐν Θράκῃ. Φιλῖνος δέ φησιν
αὐτὴν ζυγίδα καλεῖσθαι. περὶ δὲ τῆς λυχνίδος λέγων
Ἀμερίας ὁ Μακεδὼν ἐν τῷ Ῥιζοτομικῷ φησιν ἀναφῦ-
ναι αὐτὴν ἐκ τῶν Ἀφροδίτης λουτρῶν, ὅτε Ἡφαίστῳ
συγκοιμηθεῖσα ἡ Ἀφροδίτη ἐλούσατο· εἶναι δ᾽ ἀρί-
στην ἐν Κύπρῳ καὶ Λήμνῳ, ἔτι δὲ Στρογγύλῃ καὶ
Ἔρυκι καὶ Κυθήροις. ἡ δ᾽ ἶρις, φησὶ Θεόφραστος,
ἀνθεῖ τοῦ θέρους μόνη τε τῶν Εὐρωπαίων ἀνθέων
682 εὔοσμος ἐστίν. ἀρίστη δ᾽ ἐστὶν ἐν Ἰλλυριοῖς || τοῖς
ἀνῳκισμένοις τῆς θαλάσσης. Φιλῖνος δέ φησι τὰ
ἄνθη τῆς ἴριδος λέγεσθαι λύκους διὰ τὸ ἐμφερῆ εἶναι
λύκου χείλεσι. Νικόλαος δ᾽ ὁ Δαμασκηνὸς ἐν τῇ
ὀγδόῃ τῶν Ἱστοριῶν πρὸς ταῖς ἑκατὸν περὶ τὰς Ἄλ-
πεις λίμνην τινά φησιν εἶναι πολλῶν σταδίων οὖσαν,
ἧς περὶ τὸν κύκλον πεφυκέναι δι᾽ ἔτους ἄνθη ἥδιστα
καὶ εὐχρούστατα, ὅμοια ταῖς καλουμέναις καλχαίς.
τῶν δὲ καλχῶν μέμνηται καὶ Ἀλκμὰν ἐν τούτοις·

χρύσιον ὅρμον ἔχων ῥαδινᾶν πετάλοισι καλχᾶν. |

b μνημονεύει αὐτῶν καὶ Ἐπίχαρμος ἐν Ἀγρωστίνῳ.

---

130 As a blacksmith, Hephaestus was covered with soot; cf.
Macho 349–75 Gow (quoted at 13.581c–f).

131 Cyprus, Eryx, and Cythera were major sites of Aphrodite
worship, and Strongule and Lemnos were closely associated with
Hephaestus.

According to Theophrastus (*HP* 6.7.2), people gather wild thyme in the mountains and plant it in Sicyon, as they also do in Athens, where they get it from Mt. Hymettus. Elsewhere as well the mountains are full of the flower, as for example in Thrace. Philinus reports that wild thyme is also referred to as *zugis*. In his discussion of rose-campion in his *Art of Root-Gathering*, Amerias of Macedon (p. 5 Hoffmann) claims that it grows in the places where Aphrodite bathed, when she washed herself after sleeping with Hephaestus;[130] it is best in Cyprus and Lemnos, as well as in Strongule, Eryx, and Cythera.[131] According to Theophrastus (*HP* 6.8.3; 9.7.3), the iris flowers in the summer and is the only European flower with a good fragrance;[132] it is best in the parts of Illyria that are far from the coast. Philinus claims that iris-flowers are referred to as *lukoi*[133] because they resemble a wolf's lips. Nicolaus of Damascus in Book CVIII of his *History* (*FGrH* 90 F 76) reports the existence of a lake near the Alps that is several miles[134] across, and says that lovely, beautifully-colored flowers, which resemble what are known as *kalchai*, grow along its edge all year long. Alcman (*PMG* 91) too mentions *kalchai* in the following passage:

> holding a golden chain made of the petals of soft
>   *kalchai*.

Epicharmus also refers to them in *The Rustic* (fr. 2).

---

[132] I.e. good enough to be used to produce perfume.
[133] Literally "wolves."
[134] Literally "many stades," a stade being roughly 200 yards.

Τῶν δὲ ῥοδωνρόδων, φησὶ Θεόφραστος ἐν τῷ ἕκτῳ, πολλαί εἰσι διαφοραί. τὰ μὲν γὰρ πλεῖστα αὐτῶν[39] πεντάφυλλα, τὰ δὲ δωδεκάφυλλα, ἔνια δ' ἐστὶ καὶ ἑκατοντάφυλλα περὶ Φιλίππους. λαμβάνοντες γὰρ ἐκ τοῦ Παγγαίου φυτεύουσιν· ἐκεῖ γὰρ γίγνεται πολλά. μικρὰ δὲ σφόδρα τὰ ἐντὸς φύλλα· ἡ γὰρ ἔκφυσις αὐτῶν οὕτως ἐστὶν ὥστ' εἶναι τὰ μὲν ἐντός, τὰ δὲ ἐκτός· οὐκ εὔοσμα δὲ οὐδὲ μεγάλα τοῖς μεγέθεσιν. τὰ
c δὲ πεντάφυλλα εὐώδη μᾶλλον ὧν τραχὺ τὸ | κάτω. εὐοσμότατα δὲ τὰ ἐν Κυρήνῃ, διὸ καὶ τὸ μύρον ἥδιστον. καὶ τῶν ἴων δὲ καὶ τῶν ἄλλων ἀνθέων ἄκρατοι μάλιστα καὶ θεῖαι αἱ ὀσμαί· διαφερόντως δὲ ἡ τοῦ κρόκου. Τιμαχίδας δὲ ἐν τοῖς Δείπνοις τὸ ῥόδον φησὶ τοὺς Ἀρκάδας καλεῖν εὔομφον[40] ἀντὶ τοῦ εὔοσμον. Ἀπολλόδωρος δ' ἐν τετάρτῃ Παρθικῶν ἄνθος τι ἀναγράφει καλούμενον φιλάδελφον κατὰ τὴν Παρθικὴν χώραν, περὶ οὗ τάδε φησίν· καὶ μυρσίνης γένη ποικίλα μῖλάξ τε καὶ τὸ καλούμενον φιλάδελφον, ὃ τὴν
d ἐπωνυμίαν ἔλαβε τῇ φύσει | πρόσφορον· ἐπειδὰν γὰρ ἐκ διαστήματος αὐτομάτως κράδαι συμπέσωσι, ἐμψύχων περιπλοκὴν ἐν τῷ < . . . > μένουσιν ἡνωμέναι <καὶ>[41] καθάπερ ἀπὸ ῥίζης μιᾶς[42] τὸ λοιπὸν ἀνατρέ-

39 αὐτῶν εἰσὶν A: corr. Kaibel ex Theophrasto
40 εὔομφον Nauck: εὐόμφαλον ACE
41 add. Kaibel
42 μιᾶς καὶ ACE: καὶ del. Kaibel

According to Theophrastus in Book VI (*HP* 6.6.4–5, condensed), there are many different types of roses. The majority have five petals, but others have 12, and near Philippi there are some that have 100; people transplant them from Mt. Pangaeus, since large quantities of them grow there. The inner petals are extremely small—the way they grow is that some are on the inside, others on the outside—and they lack a strong scent and are not very large. The five-petalled varieties that have a rough lower portion are more fragrant. The varieties found in Cyrene have the best fragrance, which is why the sweetest-smelling perfume is produced there; their violets and their other flowers also have a marvellously strong scent, and the smell of their crocus is exceptional. Timachidas in his *Dinner Parties* (fr. 4 Blinkenberg = *SH* 773) claims that the Arcadians refer to roses as *euompha*[135] rather than *euosma* ("fragrant"). Apollodorus in Book IV of the *History of Parthia* (*FGrH* 779 F 1) lists a flower known as a *philadelphon*[136] that is found in Parthian territory, and says the following about it: Also numerous varieties of myrtle, including milax and what is referred to as *philadelphon*. The name of the latter reflects its growth-habit; when separate branches accidentally come into contact, an embrace of living creatures in the . . . they remain united, and thereafter they grow and produce shoots are if they were from a

---

[135] Cf. Hsch. o 834 "*ompha*: an odor, (according to the) Spartans"; *euompha* is attested elsewhere only at Hsch. ε 7045 (perhaps incomplete) "*euompha*: names." The manuscripts of Athenaeus, however, have *euomphalon* ("with a good navel," i.e. "a substantial hip"?), which may be right.

[136] Literally "brother-loving."

χουσιν καὶ ζωοφυτοῦσιν. διὸ καὶ τοῖς ἡμέροις φυλα-
κὴν ἀπ᾽ αὐτῶν κατασκευάζουσιν· ἀφαιροῦντες γὰρ
τῶν ῥάβδων τὰς λεπτοτάτας καὶ διαπλέξαντες[43] δικτύ-
ου τρόπῳ φυτεύουσιν κύκλῳ τῶν κηπευμάτων, καὶ
ταῦτα συμπλεκόμενα περιβόλου παρέχεται δυσπάρο-
δον ἀσφάλειαν.

e   Ἀνθῶν δὲ στεφανωτικῶν μέμνηται | ὁ μὲν τὰ Κύ-
πρια Ἔπη πεποιηκὼς Ἡγησίας ἢ Στασῖνος· Δημο-
δάμας γὰρ ὁ Ἁλικαρνασσεὺς ἢ Μιλήσιος ἐν τῷ Περὶ
Ἁλικαρνασσοῦ Κυπρία Ἁλικαρνασσέως αὐτὰ[44] εἶναί
φησι ποιήματα· λέγει δ᾽ οὖν ὅστις ἐστὶν ὁ ποιήσας
αὐτὰ ἐν τῷ πρώτῳ οὑτωσί·

> εἵματα μὲν χροΐ ἕστο, τά οἱ Χάριτές τε καὶ
>   Ὧραι
> ποίησαν καὶ ἔβαψαν ἐν ἄνθεσιν εἰαρινοῖσιν,
> οἷα φέρουσ᾽ ὧραι, ἔν τε κρόκῳ, ἔν θ᾽ ὑακίνθῳ,
> ἔν τε ἴῳ θαλέθοντι ῥόδου τ᾽ ἐνὶ ἄνθεϊ καλῷ,
> ἡδέι νεκταρέῳ, ἔν τ᾽ ἀμβροσίαις καλύκεσσιν
> αἰθέσι ναρκίσσου καλλιπνόου. ὧδ᾽ Ἀφροδίτη
> ὥραις παντοίαις τεθυωμένα εἵματα ἕστο.

οὗτος ὁ ποιητὴς καὶ τὴν τῶν στεφάνων χρῆσιν εἰδὼς
φαίνεται δι᾽ ὧν λέγει·

> ἡ δὲ σὺν ἀμφιπόλοισι φιλομμειδὴς Ἀφροδίτη |
f   πλεξάμεναι στεφάνους εὐώδεας ἄνθεα ποίης

---

43 διαπλέξαντες τε A: "τε del. nescio quis" Kaibel
44 δ᾽ αὐτὰ A: δ᾽ del. Hecker

single root. This is why people use them to protect their domesticated plants; for they remove the thinnest shoots, weave them together as if they were making a net, and plant them around their garden-plots. Once woven together, they produce a secure border that it difficult to penetrate.

Flowers used to produce garlands are mentioned by the author of the epic poem *The Cypria* (test. 8 Bernabé), who is either Hegesias or Stasinus, although Demodamas of Halicarnassus or Miletus in his *On Halicarnassus* (*FGrH* 428 F 1) claims that it was composed by Cyprias of Halicarnassus.[137] Whoever the author is, he says the following in his first Book (*Cypr.* fr. 4 Bernabé):

> She clothed her skin in the garments the Graces and
>   the Seasons
> made for her and dyed with spring flowers
> of the sort the changing seasons produce—with
>   crocus, and hyacinth,
> and flourishing violet, and lovely rose-petals,
> sweet as nectar, and with the bright, immortal
> blossoms of fragrant narcissus. Thus Aphrodite
> clothed herself in garments that bore the scent of
>   every season.

This poet also makes his familiarity with the use of garlands apparent by what he says (*Cypr.* fr. 5 Bernabé):

> Smile-loving Aphrodite and her attendant
> goddesses, wearing silky head-scarves, wove fragrant
>   garlands

[137] Cf. 8.334b–c with n.

ἂν κεφαλαῖσιν ἔθεντο θεαὶ λιπαροκρήδεμνοι,
νύμφαι καὶ Χάριτες, ἅμα δὲ χρυσέη Ἀφροδίτη,
καλὸν ἀείδουσαι κατ᾽ ὄρος πολυπιδάκου Ἴδης. ‖

683   Νίκανδρος δ᾽ ἐν δευτέρῳ Γεωργικῶν καταλέγων καὶ
      αὐτὸς στεφανωτικὰ ἄνθη καὶ περὶ Ἰωνιάδων νυμφῶν
      καὶ περὶ ῥόδων τάδε λέγει·

      ἀλλὰ τὰ μὲν σπείροις τε καὶ ὅσσ᾽ ὡραῖα
          φυτεύοις
      ἄνθε᾽ Ἰαονίηθε. γένη γε μὲν ἰάσι δισσά,
      ὠχρόν τε χρυσῷ τε φυὴν εἰς ὦπα προσεικές,
      ἅσσα τ᾽ Ἰωνιάδες νύμφαι στέφος ἁγνὸν Ἴωνι
      Πισαίοις ποθέσασαι ἐνὶ κλήροισιν ὄρεξαν.
      ἤνυσε γὰρ χλούνηνδε μετεσσύμενος
          σκυλάκεσσιν, |

b   Ἀλφειῷ καὶ λύθρον ἑῶν ἐπλύνατο γυίων
     ἑσπέριος, νύμφαισιν Ἰαονίδεσσι νυχεύσων.
     αὐτὰρ ἀκανθοβόλοιο ῥόδου κατατέμνεο βλάστας
     τάφροις τ᾽ ἐμπήξειας, ὅσον διπάλαιστα
         τελέσκων.
     πρῶτα μὲν Ὠδονίηθε Μίδης ἅπερ Ἀσίδος ἀρχὴν
     λείπων ἐν κλήροισιν ἀνέτρεφεν Ἠμαθίοισιν
     αἰὲν ἐς ἑξήκοντα πέριξ κομόωντα πετήλοις·

---

138 Cf. 15.681d with n.
139 For Midas' rose-gardens in Macedon, see Hdt. 8.138.2–3.

from the meadow flowers and placed them on their
    heads,
nymphs and Graces, and golden Aphrodite together
    with them,
singing beautifully upon the slopes of Mt. Ida with its
    many springs.

Nicander in Book II of the *Georgics* (fr. 74 Schneider) also
offers a list of flowers used to make garlands, and says the
following about Ioniad nymphs and roses:

But sow the flowers that come from Ionia, and
    transplant
those that reach full size. There are two varieties of
    gillyflower:
one is pale and looks like gold when you see it,
while the others are those the Ioniad nymphs, in their
    longing, offered
Ion as a sacred garland in the land of Pisa.[138]
For he had pursued and taken a wild boar with his
    hounds,
and was washing the gore from his limbs in the
    Alpheus
in the evening, intending to pass the night with the
    Ioniad nymphs.
But cut shoots of the thorn-producing rose
and plant them in furrows, digging them two palms
    deep.
Begin with those that Midas of Odonia, when he
    abandoned his Asian
throne, raised in the land of Emathia,[139]
which always have a fringe of 60 petals around them.

δεύτερα Νισαίης Μεγαρηίδος· οὐδὲ Φάσηλις |

c   οὐδ' αὐτὴ Λεύκοφρυν ἀγασσαμένη ἐπιμεμφής,
Ληθαίου Μάγνητος ἐφ' ὕδασιν εὐθαλέουσα.
κισσοῦ δ' ἄλλοτε κλῶνας ἐυρρίζου καπέτοισι,
πολλάκι δὲ στέφος αὐτὸ κορυμβήλοιο φυτεύσαις
Θράσκιον ἢ ἀργωπὸν ἠὲ κλαδέεσσι πλανήτην·
βλαστοδρεπῆ δ' ἐχυροῖο καὶ εἰς μίαν ὄρσεο
      κόρσην
σπεῖραν ὑπὸ σπυρίδεσσι νεοπλέκτοισι καθάπτων
ὄφρα δύο κροκόωντες ἐπιζυγέοντε κόρυμβοι |

d   μέσφα συνωρίζωσιν ὑπερφιάλοιο μετώπου,
χλωροῖς ἀμφοτέρωθεν ἐπηρεφέες πετάλοισιν.
σπέρματι μὴν κάλυκες κεφαληγόνοι ἀντέλλουσιν,
ἀργήεις πετάλοισι, κρόκῳ μέσα χροισθεῖσαι,
ἃ κρίνα, λείρια δ' ἄλλοι ἐπιφθέγγονται ἀοιδῶν,
οἳ δὲ καὶ ἀμβροσίην, πολέες δέ τε χάρμ'
    Ἀφροδίτης·
ἤρισε γὰρ χροιῇ· τὸ δέ που ἐπὶ μέσσον ὄνειδος |

e   ὅπλον βρωμήταο διεκτέλλον πεφάτισται.
ἶρις δ' ἐν ῥίζῃσιν ἀγαλλιὰς ἤ θ' ὑακίνθῳ

---

140 On the roses in Phaselis, cf. 15.688e.

141 Magnesia on the Maeander, where Artemis was worshipped under the cult-title Leucophryênê. Lethaeus is another city in the region, into which the Maeander flows.

142 Cf. 15.681b, citing Nicander' *Glossary*.

143 A reference to the flower's pistil, which is taken to resemble an erect donkey-penis.

Second should be those from Nisaea in the Megarid;
    nor does Phaselis[140]
or the city[141] that reveres Leucophrys deserve your
    contempt,
a flourishing settlement beside the waters of
    Magnesian Lethaeus.
At times plant shoots of well-rooted ivy
in trenches, or on occasion a spray of the white-
    berried ivy
that grows in Thrace, or the white variety, or the one
    whose tendrils wander.
Pluck them when they are young shoots, and
    strengthen them by forcing them to form a single
    head,
fastening the plaited ends in freshly-woven baskets
so that two saffron-colored clusters can be joined
    together,
and can merge as far as their bold crown
and be covered over with pale foliage on both sides.
From seeds arise the bud-producing lily-cups,
which have white petals but whose centers are
    stained with saffron;
some poets refer to them as *krina*, others as *leiria*,
yet others as *ambrosiê*,[142] and many as "Aphrodite's
    triumph";
for the flower is as white as her skin. But the
    disgraceful object
that grows in its middle has come to be called
    "donkey-equipment."[143]
The dwarf iris is grown from roots, as is the variety
    that resembles

αἰαστῇ προσέοικε, χελιδονίοισι δὲ τέλλει
ἄνθεσιν ἰσοδρομεῦσα χελιδόσιν, αἵ τ' ἀνὰ κόλπῳ
φυλλάδα νηλείην ἐκχεύετον, ἀρτίγονοι δὲ
εἶδοντ' ἠμύουσαι ἀεὶ κάλυκες στομίοισιν.
σὺν καὶ ἅπερ τ' ὀξεῖα χροῇ, λυχνὶς ἠδὲ
    θρυαλλίς,
οὐδὲ μὲν ἀνθεμίδων κενεὴ γηρύσεται ἀκμὴ
οὐδὲ βοάνθεμα κεῖνα τά τ' αἰπύτατον κάρη ὑψοῖ,
φλόξ τε θεοῦ αὐγῇσιν ἀνερχομένης ἰσάουσα. |

f   ἔρπυλλον δὲ † φριαλευσοτεν βώλοισι †
    φυτεύσεις,
ὄφρα κλάδοις μακροῖσιν ἐφερπύζων διάηται
ἠὲ κατακρεμάγησιν ἐφιμείρων ποτὰ νυμφέων.
καὶ δ' αὐτῆς μήκωνος ‹   . . .   ›
‹   . . .   › ἄπο πλαταγώνια βάλλοις,
ἄβρωτον κώδειαν ὄφρα κνώπεσσι φυλάξῃ·
φυλλάσιν ἦ γὰρ πάντα διοιγομένησιν ἐφίζει
ἑρπετά, τὴν δὲ δρόσοισιν εἰσκομένην βοτέονται ‖

684   κώδειαν καρποῖο μελιχροτέρου πλήθουσαν.
θρίων δ' οἰχομένων ῥέα μὲν φλόγες, ἄλλοτε
    ῥιπαὶ
πῆξαν σάρκα τυπῇσι· τὰ δ' οὐ βάσιν
    ἐστήριξαν[45]

[45] This verse is followed in A by an intrusive gloss: θρῖα δ' οὐ
λέγει τὰ τῆς συκῆς, ἀλλὰ τὰ τῆς μήκωνος ("by thria he does
not mean fig-leaves, but poppy-petals").

---

[144] I.e. leaves that resemble swords.   [145] The sun.

the mournful hyacinth, which flourishes when the
    swallows appear,
and sends up swallow-colored flowers; both produce
    pitiless
leaves[144] in their folds, and when their flowers
first emerge, they always resemble drooping lips.
So too those that have a brilliant hue, rose-campion
    and plantain;
nor shall chamomile's blossoms be proclaimed
    worthless,
nor the well-known ox-eyes, which lift their heads so
    high,
nor the wall-flower, which rivals the beams of the
    rising god.[145]
But you shall plant tufted thyme [corrupt],
so that the breeze blows through its long stems as it
    creeps forward,
or so that it may hang down, longing for the nymphs'
    water.
But of the poppy itself . . .
. . . discard the petals,
in order to preserve its seed-pod undevoured by
    caterpillars;
for in fact insects of all sorts settle on the foliage
as it opens, and they feed on the seed-pods, which
    resemble
drops of dew, in that they are full of fruit sweeter
    than honey.
When the petals vanish, the heat or at other times the
    winds with their gusts
easily harden the flesh. Then these creatures find no
    firm footing

† οὔτε τι παι † βρώμην ποτιδεγμένα· πολλάκι δ᾽
ἴχνη
στιφροῖς ὠλίσθηναν ἐνιχρίμψαντα καρείοις.

*   *   *

ἁδρύνει δὲ βλαστὰ βαθεῖ ἐν τεύχεϊ κόπρος |
b   σαμψύχου λιβάνου τε νέας κλάδας ἠδ᾽ ὅσα
κῆποι
ἀνδράσιν ἐργοπόνοις στεφάνους ἔπι
πορσαίνουσιν.

*   *   *

ἦ γὰρ καὶ λεπταὶ πτερίδες καὶ παιδὸς ἔρωτες
λεύκη ἰσαιόμενοι, ἐν καὶ κρόκος εἴαρι μύων,
κύπρος τ᾽ ὀσμηρόν τε σισύμβριον ὅσσα τε
κοίλοις
ἄσπορα ναιομένοισι τόποις ἀνεθρέψατο λειμὼν
κάλλεα, βούφθαλμόν τε καὶ εὐῶδες Διὸς ἄνθος, |
c   χάλκας, σὺν δ᾽ ὑάκινθον ἰωνιάδας τε χαμηλὰς
ὀρφνοτέρας, ἃς στύξε μετ᾽ ἄνθεσι Περσεφόνεια.
σὺν δὲ καὶ ὑψῆέν τε πανόσμεον, ὅσσα τε τύμβοι
φάσγανα παρθενικαῖς νεοδουπέσιν ἀμφιχέονται,
αὐτάς τ᾽ ἠιθέας ἀνεμωνίδες ἀστράπτουσαι
τηλόθεν ὀξυτέρῃσιν ἐφελκόμεναι χροιῇσι.[46] |
d   πᾶς δέ τις ἢ ἑλένειον ἢ ἀστέρα φωτίζοντα
δρέψας εἰνοδίοισι θεῶν παρακάββαλε σηκοῖς

---

[46] After this verse, A preserves the intrusive marginal comment ἐν ἐνίοις δὲ γράφεται ἐφελκόμεναι φιλοχροιαῖς ("some copies read 'lure with love-colors'").

[corrupt] as they search for food, and often their
    footsteps
slip as they attack the solid heads.

*   *   *

Deep manure in the pot encourages the growth of
    shoots
of marjoram,[146] of young shoots of the frankincense-
    bush, and of all the plants that gardens
furnish to produce garlands for the men who labor in
    them.

*   *   *

Indeed, delicate ferns and acanthus,
which resembles white poplar, and crocus, which
    closes in the spring,
as well as henna and fragrant bergamot-mint and all
    the other beautiful
unsown plants the meadows produce in hollow, well-
    watered
spots: ox-eye, fragrant carnation,
and chrysanthemum, along with hyacinth and dark,
    low-growing
violets, which Persephone abhors more than any
    other flower.
To this same group belong lofty all-scent, and the
    corn-flags that
encircle the tombs of girls who have recently died,
and sparkling anemones, whose brilliant colors
lure from a distance young women still alive.
And everyone picks calamint or gleaming
aster, and sets it by the roadside shrines of the gods,

146 *sampsuchos*; see 15.676d–e with n.

ἢ αὐτοῖς βρετάεσσιν, ὅτε πρώτιστον ἴδωνται·
πολλάκι θερμία καλά, τοτὲ χρυσανθὲς ἀμέργων
λείριά τε στήλῃσιν ἐπιφθίνοντα καμόντων
καὶ γεραὸν πώγωνα καὶ ἐντραπέας κυκλαμίνους
σαύρην θ᾽ ἢ χθονίου πέφαται στέφος
   Ἡγεσιλάου.

e ἐκ τούτων τῶν ἐπῶν δῆλον γίνεται ὅτι ἕτερόν ἐστιν | τὸ
χελιδόνιον τῆς ἀνεμώνης· τινὲς γὰρ ταὐτὸ εἶναί φασι.
Θεόφραστος δέ φησι· τὰς δ᾽ ἀνθήσεις λαμβάνειν δεῖ
συνακολουθοῦντα τοῖς ἄστροις τὸ ἡλιοτρόπιον καλούμενον καὶ τὸ χελιδόνιον· καὶ γὰρ τοῦτο ἅμα τῇ χελι-
δόνι[47] ἀνθεῖ. καὶ ἀμβροσίαν δὲ ἄνθος τι ἀναγράφει ὁ
Καρύστιος ἐν Ἱστορικοῖς Ὑπομνήμασι λέγων οὕτως·
Νίκανδρός φησιν ἐξ ἀνδριάντος τῆς κεφαλῆς Ἀλεξάν-
δρου τὴν καλουμένην ἀμβροσίαν φύεσθαι ἐν Κῷ.
προείρηται δ᾽ ἄνω περὶ αὐτῆς ὅτι τὸ κρίνον οὕτω
λέγουσι. Τιμαχίδας δ᾽ ἐν τετάρτῳ Δείπνου καὶ Θήσει-
όν τι ἀναγράφει καλούμενον ἄνθος· |

f Θήσειόν θ᾽ ἁπαλὸν μήλῳ ἐναλίγκιον ἄνθος,
Λευκερέης ἱερὸν περικαλλέος, ὅ ῥα μάλιστα
φίλατο.

ἀπὸ τούτου δέ φησι τοῦ ἄνθους καὶ τὸν τῆς Ἀριάδνης

---

[47] τῇ χελιδονίᾳ Thphr.: τῷ χελιδονίᾳ Schweighäuser ("when
the Swallow-wind blows")

[147] I.e. at the very beginning of spring.

> or beside the statues themselves, as soon as they
>   see it.
> Often they gather lovely lupines as well, or
>   sometimes gold-flower
> or lilies, which wither on the tombstones of the dead,
> or gray-bearded salsify, or modest cyclamens,
> or cress, referred to as the garland of the chthonic
>   Lord of Hosts.

It is apparent from these verses that a *chelidonion* is different from an anemone; for some authorities claim that they are identical. Theophrastus (*HP* 7.15.1, condensed and with a number of variant readings) says: What are referred to as *hêliotropion* and *chelidonion* must depend on heavenly objects to set their flowering-times; the latter blooms when the swallow appears.[147] Carystius in the *Historical Commentaries* (fr. 6, *FHG* iv.357) records a flower known as *ambrosia*, saying the following: Nicander (fr. 127 Schneider) claims that what is known as *ambrosia* grows from the head of Alexander's statue on Cos. Mention was made above of the fact that some authorities use this term to refer to the lily.[148] Timachidas in Book IV of the *Dinner Party* (fr. 1 Blinkenberg = *SH* 770) records a flower known as a *Thêseion*:

> and the delicate, apple-like *Thêseion*-flower,
> sacred to lovely Leucereê,[149] which she loved
> more than any other.

He also says that what is referred to as "Ariadne's garland"

[148] 15.681b, citing Nicander's *Glossary*.
[149] An unidentified female deity.

καλούμενον στέφανον πεπλέχθαι. καὶ ὁ Φερεκράτης ‖
δὲ ἢ ὁ πεποιηκὼς τὸ δρᾶμα τοὺς Πέρσας μνημονεύων
καὶ αὐτὸς ἀνθῶν τινων στεφανωτικῶν φησιν·

ὦ μαλάχας μὲν ἐξερῶν, ἀναπνέων δ᾽ ὑάκινθον,
καὶ μελιλώτινον λαλῶν καὶ ῥόδα προσσεσηρώς·
ὦ φιλῶν μὲν ἀμάρακον, προσκινῶν δὲ σέλινα,
γελῶν δ᾽ ἱπποσέλινα καὶ κοσμοσάνδαλα βαίνων,
ἔγχει κἀπιβόα τρίτον παιῶν᾽, ὡς νόμος ἐστίν.

ὁ δὲ πεποιηκὼς τοὺς εἰς αὐτὸν ἀναφερομένους Μεταλ-
λεῖς φησιν·

ὑπ᾽ ἀναδενδράδων ἁπαλὰς ἀσπαλάθους
πατοῦντες
b ἐν λειμῶνι λωτοφόρῳ κύπειρόν | τε δροσώδη
κἀνθρύσκου μαλακῶν τ᾽ ἴων λείμακα καὶ
τριφύλλου.

ἐν τούτοις ζητῶ τί τὸ τρίφυλλον· καὶ γὰρ εἰς Δημα-
ρέτην ἀναφέρεταί τι ποιημάτιον ὃ ἐπιγράφεται Τρί-
φυλλον. κἀν τοῖς ἐπιγραφομένοις δὲ Ἀγαθοῖς ὁ Φερεκράτης ἢ Στράττις φησίν·

---

150 Presumably because Ariadne was seduced and carried
away from Crete by Theseus.

151 Athenaeus also expresses doubts about the authorship of
Persians at 3.78d, where see n.; 11.502a.

152 According to Harpocration and Photius (*Miners* test. i and
ii), doubts were expressed about the authorship of the play by the
Hellenistic scholar Eratosthenes of Cyrene.

is produced from this flower.[150] So too Pherecrates (fr. 138)—or whoever wrote the play *Persians*[151]—mentions various flowers used to produce garlands, saying:

> O you whose vomit is mallows, whose breath is
>   hyacinth,
> whose chatter is *melilôt*, and whose grins are roses;
> O you whose kisses are marjoram, whose screwing is
>   celery,
> who laughter is horse-celery, and whose walk is
>   *kosmosandala*—
> pour me a drink, and sing a third paean, as custom
>   demands!

The author of the *Miners* (test. iii) attributed to the same author (Pherecr. fr. 114)[152] says:

> treading on delicate *aspalathoi* beneath climbing
>   grape-vines
> in a meadow full of *lôtos*, and on dewy galingale
> and a field of chervil, tender violets, and *triphullion*.

I am interested in the question of what the *triphullion*[153] mentioned in this passage might be; for a short poem entitled *Triphullon* is in fact attributed to Demarete (*SH* 372). So too in the play entitled *Good Men* Pherecrates (fr. 2) or Strattis[154] says:

---

[153] Literally "three-leaf."

[154] Athenaeus (or his source) also expresses doubts about the play's authorship at 6.248c; 10.415c. But Pollux twice attributes it unambiguously to Pherecrates.

λουσάμενοι δὲ πρὸ λαμπρᾶς ἡμέρας
  ἐν τοῖς στεφανώμασιν, οἱ δ᾽ ἐν τῷ μύρῳ
λαλεῖτε περὶ σισυμβρίων κοσμοσανδάλων τε.

καὶ Κρατῖνος ἐν Μαλθακοῖς·

παντοίοις γε μὴν κεφαλὴν ἀνθέμοις ἐρέπτομαι·
λειρίοις, ῥόδοις, κρίνεσιν, κοσμοσανδάλοις, |
c   ἴοις,
καὶ σισυμβρίοις ἀνεμωνῶν κάλυξί τ᾽ ἠριναῖς,
ἑρπύλλῳ, κρόκοις, ὑακίνθοις, ἑλιχρύσου κλάδοις,
οἰνάνθῃσιν, ἡμεροκαλλεῖ τε τῷ φιλουμένῳ,
† ανθρυσκισσου φόβῃ †
τῷ τ᾽ ἀειφρούρῳ μελιλώτῳ κάρα πυκάζομαι
καὶ < . . . > κύτισος αὐτόματος παρὰ Μέδοντος
  ἔρχεται.

ἡ δὲ τῶν στεφάνων καὶ μύρων πρότερον εἴσοδος εἰς τὰ
συμπόσια ἡγεῖτο τῆς δευτέρας τραπέζης, ὡς παρ-
ίστησι Νικόστρατος ἐν Ψευδοστιγματίᾳ διὰ τούτων· |

d   καὶ σὺ μὲν
τὴν δευτέραν τράπεζαν εὐτρεπῆ πόει,
κόσμησον αὐτὴν παντοδαποῖς τραγήμασιν,
μύρον, στεφάνους, λιβανωτόν, αὐλητρίδα λαβέ.

Φιλόξενος δ᾽ ὁ διθυραμβοποιὸς ἐν τῷ ἐπιγραφομένῳ

---

[155] Scattered verses from this fragment are quoted also at
15.681a, b, e, 685f.

after they take a bath, before the sun is fully up,
>   in the garland-market, while others of you chatter
>   away
in the perfume-market, surrounded by bergamot-
>   mint and *kosmosandala*.

Also Cratinus in *Soft Men* (fr. 105):[155]

I crown my head with flowers of every sort:
with polyanthus narcissus, roses, lilies, *kosmosandala*,
>   violets,
and with bergamot-mint and springtime anemone
>   blossoms,
with tufted thyme, crocuses, hyacinth, gold-flower
>   stalks,
dropwort, and the beloved daylily,
[corrupt]
and I wrap my head close with ever-watching *melilôt*,
and tree-medick comes of its own accord from
>   Medon.[156]

Garlands and perfume used to be brought into the party
just before the second table, as Nicostratus establishes in
Falsely Tattooed (fr. 27), in the following passage:

>   You!
Get the second table ready!
Put all kinds of snacks on it!
And get perfume, garlands, frankincense, and a pipe-
>   girl!

The dithyrambic poet Philoxenus in his work entitled *The*

---

156 *PAA* 637005; otherwise unknown.

Δείπνῳ ἀρχὴν ποιεῖται τὸν στέφανον τῆς εὐωχίας οὑτωσὶ λέγων·

κατὰ χειρὸς δ᾿
ἤλιθ᾿ ὕδωρ ἁπαλὸς
παιδίσκος ἐν ἀργυρέᾳ
πρόχῳ φορέων ἐπέχευεν,
εἶτ᾿ ἔφερε στέφανον
λεπτᾶς ἀπὸ μυρτίδος εὐ-
γνήτων κλαδέων δισύναπτον. |

e   Εὔβουλος Τιτθαῖς·

ὡς γὰρ εἰσῆλθε τὰ γερόντια τότ᾿ εἰς δόμους,
εὐθὺς ἀνεκλίνετο· παρῆν στέφανος ἐν τάχει,
ᾔρετο τράπεζα, παρέκειθ᾿ ἅμα τετριμμένη
μᾶζα χαριτοβλέφαρος.

τοῦτο δ᾿ ἦν ἔθος καὶ παρ᾿ Αἰγυπτίοις, ὡς Νικόστρατός φησιν ἐν Τοκιστῇ. Αἰγύπτιον γὰρ ὑποστησάμενος τὸν τοκιστήν φησιν·

καταλαμβάνομεν τὸν πορνοβοσκὸν καὶ δύο
ἑτέρους κατὰ χειρὸς ἀρτίως εἰληφότας
f   καὶ στέφανον. εἶέν· καλὸς ὁ καιρός, | Χαιρεφῶν.

Dinner Party (*PMG* 836(a)) represents the garland as the very beginning of the feast, saying the following:

> A dainty
> little slaveboy fetched
>   a lot of water in a silver pitcher
>   and poured it over our hands;
> then he brought a double-plaited
>   garland made of lush sprays
>   of delicate myrtle.

Eubulus in *Wet-Nurses* (fr. 111):

> Because the minute the old codgers entered the
>   house,
> they immediately lay down. A garland rapidly
>   appeared;
> a table was fetched; and at once a kneaded barley-
>   cake
> with a sweet expression on its face was served.

This was also standard procedure in Egypt, according to Nicostratus in *The Loan-Shark* (fr. 26). For he presents the loan-shark as an Egyptian and then says:

> We found the pimp there, along with two
> other guys who had just had water poured over their
>   hands
> and got a garland. Well! Nice timing, Chaerephon![157]

---

[157] Presumably a reference to the notorious parasite (*PAA* 975770) mentioned repeatedly in late 4th-century sources; cf. 4.134e n.

σὺ δὲ γαστρίζου, Κύνουλκε· καὶ μετὰ ταῦτα ἡμῖν εἰπὲ
διὰ τί Κρατῖνος εἴρηκε τὸν μελίλωτον·

τῷ τ᾽ ἀειφρούρῳ μελιλώτῳ.

ἐπεὶ δέ σε ὁρῶ ἔξοινον ἤδη γεγενημένον – οὕτως δ᾽
εἴρηκε τὸν μεθύσην Ἄλεξις ἐν Εἰσοικιζομένῳ – παύ-
σομαί σε ἐρεσχηλῶν καὶ τοῖς παισὶ παρακελεύομαι,
κατὰ τὸν Σοφοκλέα, ὃς ἐν Συνδείπνοις φησί· ‖

686   φορεῖτε, μασσέτω τις, ἐγχείτω βαθὺν
          κρατῆρ᾽· ὅδ᾽ ἀνὴρ οὐ πρὶν ἂν φάγῃ καλῶς
          ὅμοια καὶ βοῦς ἐργάτης ἐργάζεται.

καὶ κατὰ τὸν Φλιάσιον δὲ Ἀριστίαν· καὶ γὰρ οὗτος ἐν
ταῖς ἐπιγραφομέναις Κηρσὶν ἔφη·

      σύνδειπνος ἢ ᾽πίκωμος ἢ μαζαγρέτας,
      Ἅιδου τραπεζεύς, ἀκρατέα νηδὺν ἔχων.

ἐπεὶ δὲ τοσούτων λεχθέντων μηδὲν ἀποκρίνεται, κε-
λεύω αὐτὸν κατὰ τοὺς Ἀλέξιδος Διδύμους χυδαίοις
b   στεφανωθέντα στεφάνοις ἐξάγεσθαι τοῦ ǀ συμποσίου.
τῶν δὲ χυδαίων στεφάνων μνημονεύων ὁ κωμῳδιο-
ποιός φησιν·

      στεφάνων τε τούτων ⟨τῶν⟩ χύδην πεπλεγμένων.

---

158 From *Soft Men*; quoted at greater length at 15.685b–c, cf.
15.681a, b, e.

Go on stuffing your belly, Cynulcus! But afterward, tell us why Cratinus (fr. 105.7)[158] refers to *melilôt* as:

> ever-watching *melilôt*.

Since I see, however, that you are already *exoinos*—this is how Alexis in *The Man Who Was Moving In* (fr. 64)[159] refers to a drunk—I will stop teasing you, and I now order the slaves, to quote Sophocles, who says in *The Dinner Guests* (fr. 563):

> Fetch (what we need)! Someone ought to knead a
>   barley-cake and fill a deep
> mixing-bowl! This guy's just like a plow-ox; he doesn't
> do any work until he's had a good meal!

And to quote Aristias of Phlius; for he in fact said in his play entitled *Goddesses of Doom* (*TrGF* 9 F 3):

> a dinner guest, a reveler, or a barley-cake-beggar;
> Hades' parasite, a man with an uncontrollable
>   appetite.

But since he[160] offers no response to anything I have said, I order him to be crowned with garlands of confusion, as Alexis puts it in *Twins* (fr. 54, quoted below), and removed from the party! When he refers to garlands of confusion, the comic poet says:

> and of these garlands that have been confusedly
>   woven.

---

[159] Quoted at 14.613c, again in connection with the question of the sense of *exoinos*.
[160] Cynulcus.

κἀγὼ δ' ἐπὶ τούτοις τοῦ λέγειν ἤδη παύσομαι τὸ
τήμερον, παραχωρῶν τε τὸν περὶ τῶν μύρων λόγον
τοῖς βουλομένοις διεξέρχεσθαι τῷ τε παιδὶ προστάτ-
των ἐπὶ τῇ στεφανηφόρῳ ταύτῃ μου διαλέξει κατὰ τὸν
Ἀντιφάνους ‹ . . . ›·

‹στεφάνους› ἐνεγκεῖν δεῦρο τῶν χρηστῶν δύο |
c   καὶ δᾷδα χρηστὴν ἡμμένην χρηστῷ πυρί.

οὕτω γὰρ τὴν τῶν λόγων ἔξοδον ὥσπερ δράματος
ποιήσομαι. καὶ μετ' οὐ πολλὰς ἡμέρας ὥσπερ ‹αὐτὸς›⁴⁸ αὑτοῦ σιωπὴν καταμαντευσάμενος ἀπέθανεν
εὐτυχῶς, οὐδένα καιρὸν νόσῳ παραδούς, πολλὰ δὲ
λυπήσας ἡμᾶς τοὺς ἑταίρους.

   Περιενεγκόντων δὲ τῶν παίδων ἐν ἀλαβάστοις καὶ
ἄλλοις χρυσοῖς σκεύεσιν μύρα, ‹νυστάζοντα›⁴⁹ τὸν
Κύνουλκον θεασάμενός τις πολλῷ τῷ μύρῳ τὸ πρόσωπον ἐπέχρισεν. ὁ δὲ διεγερθεὶς καὶ μόλις ἑαυτὸν
d   ἀναλαβών, τί τοῦτ', | εἶπεν, Ἡράκλεις; οὐ σπογγιᾷ τίς
μου παρελθὼν τὸ πρόσωπον ἐκκαθαρίσει μεμολυ-
σμένον μαγγανείαις πολλαῖς; ἢ οὐκ οἴδατε καὶ τὸν
καλὸν Ξενοφῶντα ἐν τῷ Συμποσίῳ ποιοῦντα τὸν Σω-
κράτην τοιαυτὶ λέγοντα· "νὴ Δί', ὦ Καλλία, τελέως
ἡμᾶς ἑστιᾷς· οὐ γὰρ μόνον δεῖπνον ἄμεμπτον παρ-
έθηκας, ἀλλὰ καὶ ἀκροάματα καὶ θεάματα ἥδιστα
παρέχεις." "τί οὖν εἰ καὶ μύρον ἐνέγκαι τις ἡμῖν, ἵνα
καὶ εὐωδίᾳ ἑστιώμεθα;" "μηδαμῶς," ἔφη ὁ Σωκράτης·

⁴⁸ add. Kaibel   ⁴⁹ add. Schweighäuser

114

With that, I will put an end to my own remarks for today, and I yield the floor to anyone willing to offer a systematic discussion of perfumes; and I command the slave, at the conclusion of this prize-winning[161] speech of mine, to quote Antiphanes' . . . [162] (fr. 269):

> to bring two of the good garlands here,
> and a good torch burning with a good flame.

For this will allow me to conclude my speech as if it were a play. And a few days later, as if he[163] himself had foreseen the silence that settled over him, he died an easy death, having wasted no time on sickness, but bringing considerable grief to those of us who were his friends.

The slaves brought perfumes around in *alabasta* and gold containers of other sorts; when someone saw Cynulcus nodding off, he smeared a large amount of perfume on his face. Cynulcus woke up, and before he had fully recovered consciousness, he said: Heracles! What is this? Someone get over here and use a sponge to clean my face, which has been defiled with a lot of dirty tricks! Or are you unaware that the noble Xenophon in his *Symposium* (2.2–4) represents Socrates as saying the following: "By Zeus, Callias, this is a perfect feast you're offering us! For not only did you serve us a meal no one could criticize, but you're providing us with wonderful music and entertainment!" "Well, what if someone were to bring us perfume, so that we could smell nice as we feasted?" "Absolutely

---

161 Literally "garland-wearing," matching the topic of the preceding discussion.
162 The title of the play has been lost.
163 Ulpian.

e "ὥσπερ γάρ τοι ἐσθὴς ἄλλη μὲν γυναικεία, | ἄλλη δὲ
ἀνδρεία,[50] οὕτω καὶ ὀσμὴ ἄλλη μὲν γυναικί, ἄλλη δὲ
ἀνδρὶ πρέπει. καὶ γὰρ ἀνδρὸς μὲν δή που ἕνεκεν
ἀνδρῶν οὐδεὶς μύρῳ χρίεται. αἵ γε μὴν γυναῖκες
ἄλλως τε καὶ ἂν νύμφαι τύχωσιν οὖσαι, ὥσπερ ἡ
Νικηράτου τε τούτου καὶ ἡ Κριτοβούλου, μύρου μὲν τί
καὶ προσδέονται; αὐταὶ γὰρ τούτου ὄζουσιν. ἐλαίου δὲ
τοῦ ἐν γυμνασίοις ὀσμὴ καὶ παροῦσα ἡδίων ἢ μύρου
γυναιξὶν[51] καὶ ἀποῦσα ποθεινοτέρα. καὶ γὰρ δὴ μύρῳ
μὲν ἀλειψάμενος δοῦλος καὶ ἐλεύθερος εὐθὺς ἅπας
f ὅμοιον ὄζει· αἱ δ᾽ | ἀπὸ τῶν ἐλευθερίων μόχθων ὀσμαὶ
ἐπιτηδευμάτων τε πρῶτον χρηστῶν καὶ χρόνου πολλοῦ δέονται, εἰ μέλλουσιν ἡδεῖαί τε καὶ ἐλευθέριαι
ἔσεσθαι." καὶ ὁ θαυμασιώτατος δὲ Χρύσιππος τὴν
ὀνομασίαν φησὶ λαβεῖν τὰ μύρα ἀπὸ τοῦ μετὰ πολλοῦ
μόρου καὶ πόνου ματαίου γίνεσθαι. Λακεδαιμόνιοί τε
ἐξελαύνουσι τῆς Σπάρτης τοὺς τὰ μύρα κατασκευά-
ζοντας ὡς διαφθείροντας τοὔλαιον, καὶ τοὺς τὰ ἔρια
δὲ βάπτοντας ὡς ἀφανίζοντας τὴν λευκότητα τῶν
687 ἐρίων. ‖ Σόλων τε ὁ σοφὸς διὰ τῶν νόμων κεκώλυκε
τοὺς ἄνδρας μυροπωλεῖν. νῦν δὲ τῶν ἀνθρώπων οὐχ αἱ
ὀσμαὶ μόνον, ὥς φησιν Κλέαρχος ἐν τρίτῳ Περὶ Βίων,
ἀλλὰ καὶ αἱ χροιαὶ τρυφερὸν ἔχουσαί τι συνεκθη-

---

[50] ἀνδρεία κάλλη A: κάλλη del. Kaibel
[51] γυναιξὶν ἡδίων A: ἡδίων del. Kaibel

not!" said Socrates; "Just as women's clothing is different
from men's, so too a woman ought to smell one way, and a
man another. For no man wears perfume in order to ap-
peal to another man. As for married women—and in particular recent brides, like the wives of Niceratus here and
Critobulus—what do they need perfume for? They already smell like it! But when the fragrance of the olive oil
used in the gymnasium is on your skin, it's more pleasant
than perfume is on a woman; and when that fragrance is
absent, it's missed more. The fact is that the minute someone puts on perfume, he smells the same, regardless of
whether he's a slave or free. But if the odors derived from
the exercise engaged in by free men are going to be pleasant and appropriate to a free man's status, they require,
first of all, noble pursuits engaged in for an extended period of time." The remarkable Chrysippus (xxviii fr. 12,
SVF iii.200) as well claims that perfume (*muron*) got its
name from the fact that producing it requires a great deal
of hard work (*moros*) and wasted labor.[164] The Spartans
ban perfume-makers from their country, on the ground
that they corrupt the olive oil; they do the same with wool-
dyers, on the ground that they ruin the whiteness of the
wool. The wise Solon (fr. 73a Ruschenbusch)[165] too used
his laws to prevent men from selling perfume. But nowadays it is not just the fragrances people use, according to
Clearchus in Book III of *On Lives* (fr. 41 Wehrli), but also
their complexions[166] whose luxurious elements help ef-

[164] A false etymology. For *moros* in this sense, see Hsch. μ
1681, 1683.   [165] Cited also at 13.612a.
[166] I.e., presumably, "(the substances they apply to their skin
to alter) their complexions."

λύνουσι τοὺς μεταχειριζομένους. ὑμεῖς δὲ οἴεσθε τὴν
ἁβρότητα χωρὶς ἀρετῆς ἔχειν τι τρυφερόν; καίτοι
Σαπφώ, γυνὴ μὲν πρὸς ἀλήθειαν οὖσα καὶ ποιήτρια,
ὅμως ᾐδέσθη τὸ καλὸν τῆς ἁβρότητος ἀφελεῖν λέγουσα ὧδε·

> ἔγω δὲ φίλημμ' ἀβροσύναν, < . . . > καί μοι
b > τὸ λάμπρον ἔρως ἀελίω | καὶ τὸ κάλον λέλογχε,

φανερὸν ποιοῦσα πᾶσιν ὡς ἡ τοῦ ζῆν ἐπιθυμία τὸ
λαμπρὸν καὶ τὸ καλὸν εἶχεν αὐτῇ· ταῦτα δ' ἐστὶν
οἰκεῖα τῆς ἀρετῆς. Παρράσιος δὲ ὁ ζωγράφος, καίπερ
παρὰ μέλος ὑπὲρ τὴν ἑαυτοῦ τέχνην τρυφήσας καὶ τὸ
λεγόμενον ἐλευθέριον ἐκ ῥαβδίων[52] ἑλκύσας, λόγῳ
γοῦν ἀντελάβετο τῆς ἀρετῆς, ἐπιγραψάμενος τοῖς ἐν
Λίνδῳ πᾶσιν αὐτοῦ ἔργοις·

> ἁβροδίαιτος ἀνὴρ ἀρετήν τε σέβων τάδ' ἔγραψεν
> Παρράσιος.

c ᾧ κομψός τις, ὡς ἐμοὶ δοκεῖ, ὑπεραλγήσας | ῥυπαί-
νοντι τὸ τῆς ἀρετῆς ἁβρὸν καὶ καλόν, ἅτε φορτικῶς
μετακαλεσαμένῳ εἰς τρυφὴν τὴν δοθεῖσαν ὑπὸ τῆς
τύχης χορηγίαν, παρέγραψε τὸ "ῥαβδοδίαιτος ἀνήρ."

---

[52] ἐκ ῥαβδίων ἔκ τινων ποτηρίων A: ἔκ τινων ποτηρίων
del. Kaibel

---

[167] The characterization of the author of the comment as clever does not appear in the version of the anecdote preserved in
Book 12 (see next n.), and the interjection may thus be designed to
mark this as an addition to Clearchus' account.

feminize those who employ them. Do you believe that daintiness, if divorced from virtue, contains anything resembling luxury? Yet Sappho, who was certainly a woman as well as a poetess, was nonetheless reluctant to distinguish beauty from daintiness, putting it thus (fr. 58.25–6):

> But I love daintiness, . . . and in my opinion
> a longing for the sun implies what is bright and
>   beautiful,

making it apparent to everyone that her lust for life involved the bright and beautiful; these qualities are closely associated with virtue. Although the painter Parrhasius led a life that was inappropriately more luxurious than a painter should, and used his brushes to obtain what is referred to as "the life of a free man," in conversation he laid claim to being a decent person, and he inscribed on all the works he completed on Lindos (*FGE* 279–80):

> This was painted by Parrhasius, a man who led a
>   dainty life (*anêr habrodiaitos*) but respected
> decent behavior.

Someone clever—or so it seems to me[167]—who was quite upset with him for debasing the daintiness and beauty associated with virtue, inasmuch as he had vulgarly recruited the opportunities his good fortune had given him to the service of luxury, wrote *anêr rhabdodiaitos* ("a man who lived off his paintbrush") on the side.[168] But since he

---

[168] The anecdote, along with a longer version of the epigram attributed to Parrhasius, is preserved also at 12.543c–d, where the connection to Clearchus is somewhat more loosely drawn.

ἀλλ' ὅμως διὰ τὸ τὴν ἀρετὴν φῆσαι τιμᾶν ἀνεκτέον. ταῦτα μὲν ὁ Κλέαρχος. Σοφοκλῆς δ' ὁ ποιητὴς ἐν Κρίσει τῷ δράματι τὴν μὲν Ἀφροδίτην Ἡδονήν τινα οὖσαν δαίμονα μύρῳ τε ἀλειφομένην παράγει καὶ κατοπτριζομένην, τὴν δὲ Ἀθηνᾶν Φρόνησιν οὖσαν καὶ d Νοῦν, ἔτι δ' Ἀρετήν, ἐλαίῳ χριομένην[53] καὶ | γυμναζομένην. τούτοις ἀπαντήσας ὁ Μασούριος ἔφη· ὦ δαιμόνιε ἀνδρῶν, οὐκ οἶδας ὅτι αἱ ἐν τῷ ἐγκεφάλῳ ἡμῶν αἰσθήσεις ὀδμαῖς ἡδείαις παρηγοροῦνται προσέτι τε θεραπεύονται, καθὰ καὶ Ἄλεξίς φησιν ἐν Πονήρᾳ οὕτως·

> ὑγιείας μέρος
> μέγιστον ὀσμὰς ἐγκεφάλῳ χρηστὰς ποεῖν.

καὶ ὁ ἀνδρειότατος δέ, προσέτι δὲ καὶ πολεμικὸς ποιητὴς Ἀλκαῖος ἔφη· |

e
> κὰδ δὲ χευάτω μύρον ἆδυ κὰτ τὼ
> στήθεος ἄμμι.

καὶ ὁ σοφὸς δὲ Ἀνακρέων λέγει που·

> τί μὲν πέτεαι
> συρίγγων κοϊλώτερα
> στήθεα χρισάμενος μύρῳ;,

[53] χριομένην Nauck: χρωμένην ACE

120

claims to honor virtue, we must nonetheless put up with
him. Thus Clearchus. The poet Sophocles, on the other
hand, in his play *The Judgment*[169] (fr. *361.I), brings Aphrodite onstage in the guise of a deity named Pleasure, putting perfume on herself and looking at herself in a mirror,
but brings on Athena, who represents Insight and Intel-
ligence, as well as Virtue, rubbing olive oil on her skin
and exercising. Masurius responded to these remarks by
saying: You strange man—you seem unaware that the sen-
sations in our brains are soothed and even cared for by
pleasant smells, precisely as Alexis says in *The Miserable
Woman* (fr. 195.2–3),[170] putting it as follows:

> producing smells
> the brain likes is the most significant contribution to
> good health.

So too the extremely courageous, as well as warlike poet
Alcaeus (fr. 362.3–4)[171] said:

> and let delicious perfume be poured down over
> our chest.

The wise Anacreon (*PMG* 363) as well says somewhere:

> Why are you excited,
> after anointing your chest, which is hollower
> than a Pan-pipe, with perfume?,

[169] Sc. *of Paris*, hence the presence of Aphrodite and Athena
(and doubtless Hera as well).

[170] Quoted at slightly greater length at 2.46a.

[171] Two other verses seemingly from the same fragment are
quoted at 15.674c–d (where note also an observation about the
chest, the heart, and perfume very similar to the one below).

τὰ στήθη παρακελευόμενος μυροῦν, ἐν οἷς ἐστιν ἡ
καρδία, ὡς καὶ ταύτης δηλονότι παρηγορουμένης τοῖς
εὐώδεσι. τοῦτο δ' ἔπρασσον οὐ μόνον τῆς εὐωδίας ἀπὸ
τοῦ στήθους κατὰ φύσιν ἀναφερομένης ἐπὶ τὴν
ὄσφρησιν, ἀλλὰ καὶ διὰ τὸ νομίζειν ἐν τῇ καρδίᾳ τὴν
ψυχὴν καθιδρῦσθαι, ὡς Πραξαγόρας καὶ Φυλότιμος
f   οἱ ἰατροὶ παραδεδώκασιν. | καὶ Ὅμηρος δέ φησιν·

στῆθος δὲ πλήξας κραδίην ἠνίπαπε μύθῳ.

καί·

⟨ . . . ⟩ κραδίη δέ οἱ ἔνδον ὑλάκτει.

καί·

Ἕκτορι δ'[54] αὐτῷ θυμὸς ἐνὶ στήθεσσι πάτασσε.

ὃ δὴ καὶ σημεῖον φέρουσι τοῦ τὸ κυριώτερον τῆς
ψυχῆς ἐνταῦθα κεῖσθαι· κατὰ γὰρ τὰς ἐν τοῖς φόβοις
γινομένας ἀγωνίας πάλλεσθαι τὴν καρδίαν ἐπιδηλό-
688 τατα συμβαίνει. ‖ καὶ ὁ Ἀγαμέμνων δέ φησιν ὁ
Ὁμηρικός·

αἰνῶς γὰρ Δαναῶν περιδείδια, οὐδέ μοι ἦτορ
ἔμπεδον, ἀλλ' ἀλαλύκτημαι, κραδίη δέ μοι ἔξω
στηθέων ἐκθρῴσκει, τρομέει δ' ὑπὸ φαίδιμα
    γυῖα.

καὶ ὁ Σοφοκλῆς δὲ τὰς ἀπολελυμένας τοῦ φόβου
πεποίηκε λεγούσας·

[54] The traditional text of Homer has Ἕκτορί τ'.

thus encouraging us to pour perfume on our chests, which contains our heart, as if our heart as well were, obviously, soothed by fragrant substances. They used to do this not only because the fragrance naturally moves upward from the chest to where the sense is perceived,[172] but also because they believed that the soul was located in the heart, as the physicians Praxagoras (fr. 30 Steckerl) and Phylotimus teach. Homer as well says (*Od.* 20.17):

> He struck his chest and rebuked his heart with a
>> word.

And (*Od.* 20.13):

> His heart within him was barking.

And (*Il.* 7.216):

> Hector's heart was pounding inside his chest.

They treat this as evidence that the most important part of the soul is located there; for the fact is that the heart's beating becomes most pronounced when we suffer the agony associated with terror. So too the Homeric Agamemnon says (*Il.* 10.93–5):

> Because I am terribly afraid for the Danaans, and my
>> heart does not
> stay in its place, but is in anguish; it leaps out
> of my chest, and my glorious limbs tremble beneath
>> me.

Sophocles (fr. 766) as well represents women who have been released from fear as saying:

[172] I.e. the nose.

θυμῷ δ᾽ οὔτις φαιδρὰ χορεύει
τάρβους θυγάτηρ.

Ἀναξανδρίδης δὲ τὸν ἀγωνιῶντα παράγει λέγοντα· |

b   ὦ πονηρὰ καρδία,
ἐπιχαιρέκακον ὡς εἶ μόνον τοῦ σώματος·
ὀρχεῖ γὰρ εὐθύς, ἄν ‹μ᾽› ἴδῃς δεδοικότα.

Πλάτων δέ φησι τὸν τῶν ὅλων δημιουργὸν καὶ τὴν
τοῦ πλεύμονος αὐτῇ φύσιν περιθεῖναι, πρῶτον μὲν
μαλακὴν καὶ ἄναιμον, εἶτα σήραγγας ἔχουσαν οἷον
σπόγγου κατατετρημένας, ἵν᾽ ἐν τῇ τῶν δεινῶν προσ-
δοκίᾳ πολλάκις ἀλλομένη τὸν παλμὸν εἰς ὑπεῖκον καὶ
μαλακὸν ποιῆται. ἀλλὰ μὴν καὶ τοὺς στεφάνους τοὺς
c περικειμένους τῷ στήθει ὑποθυμιάδας | οἱ ποιηταὶ
κεκλήκασιν ἀπὸ τῆς τῶν ἀνθῶν ἀναθυμιάσεως, οὐκ
ἀπὸ τοῦ τὴν ψυχὴν θυμὸν καλεῖσθαι, ὥς τινες ἀξιοῦ-
σιν. τῷ δὲ τοῦ μύρου ὀνόματι πρῶτος Ἀρχίλοχος
κέχρηται λέγων·

οὐκ ἂν μύροισι γρηῦς ἐοῦσ᾽ ἠλείφεο.

καὶ ἀλλαχοῦ δ᾽ ἔφη·

              ἐσμυριχμένας κόμην
καὶ στῆθος, ὡς ἂν καὶ γέρων ἠράσσατο.

μύρρα γὰρ ἡ σμύρνα παρ᾽ Αἰολεῦσιν, ἐπειδὴ τὰ πολ-

---

173 Cf. 15.674c–d, citing Alcaeus, Sappho, and Anacreon.

No brilliant daughter of terror
dances in our chest.

Anaxandrides (fr. 60) brings a worried man onstage saying:

Miserable heart—
you're the only part of my body that's happy when
there's trouble!
Because you immediately start dancing, if you see I'm
frightened.

Plato (*Ti.* 70c) claims that the creator of the universe wrapped the heart in the structure consisting of the lungs, which is first of all soft and bloodless, and also contains pores that run through it, as if it were a sponge, so that when the heart leaps in anticipation of terrible events, as it often does, it can collide with something yielding and soft. The poets, moreover, refer to the garlands we wrap around our chests as *hupothumides*[173] because of the exhalation (*anathumiasis*) of vapors from the flowers, rather than from the fact that the soul is referred to as the *thumos*, as some authorities argue. Archilochus (fr. 205 West[2]) was the first to use the word *muron* ("perfume"), when he said:

Since you're an old woman, you wouldn't be putting
perfumes (*mura*) on yourself.

He also said elsewhere (fr. 48.5–6 West[2]):

her hair and chest
covered with perfume (*esmurichmenai*), so that even
an old man would have fallen in love with her.

The Aeolians refer to *smurna* ("myrrh") as *murra*, since

λὰ τῶν μύρων διὰ σμύρνης ἐσκευάζετο καὶ ἥ γε στακτὴ καλουμένη διὰ μόνης ταύτης. ὁ δὲ Ὅμηρος d τὴν μὲν χρῆσιν οἶδε τῶν μύρων, ἔλαιον δ᾽ αὐτὰ | καλεῖ μετ᾽ ἐπιθέτου·

< . . . > ῥοδόεντι δὲ χρῖεν ἐλαίῳ.

καὶ ἀλλαχοῦ δὲ λέγει τι τεθυωμένον. καὶ ἡ Ἀφροδίτη δὲ παρ᾽ αὐτῷ τὸν Ἕκτορος νεκρὸν ῥοδόεντι ἔχριεν ἐλαίῳ ἀμβροσίῳ· καὶ τοῦτο μὲν ἐξ ἀνθέων. περὶ δὲ τοῦ ἐκ τῶν ἀρωμάτων σκευαζομένου, ἃ δὴ θυώματα ἐκά-λουν, ἐπὶ τῆς Ἥρας λέγει·

ἀμβροσίη μὲν πρῶτον ἀπὸ χροὸς ἱμερόεντος
λύματα πάντα κάθηρεν, ἀλείψατο δὲ χρόα
λευκὸν[55]
ἀμβροσίῳ ἑανῷ,[56] τό ῥά οἱ τεθυωμένον ἦεν· |
e τοῦ καὶ † κινυμένοιο † Διὸς ποτὶ[57] χαλκοβατὲς
δῶ
ἔμπης ἐς γαῖάν τε καὶ οὐρανὸν ἵκετ᾽ αὐτμή.

γίνεται δὲ μύρα κάλλιστα κατὰ τόπους, ὡς Ἀπολ-λώνιός φησιν ὁ Ἡροφίλειος ἐν τῷ Περὶ Μύρων γρά-φων οὕτως· ἶρις μὲν ἐν Ἤλιδι χρηστοτάτη καὶ ἐν Κυζίκῳ· ῥόδινον δὲ κράτιστον ἐν Φασήλιδι, καὶ τὸ ἐκ Νέας δὲ πόλεως καὶ Καπύης· κρόκινον δ᾽ ἐν Σόλοις

---

[55] The traditional text of Homer has λίπ᾽ ἐλαίῳ.
[56] Most witnesses have ἑδανῷ, but there is support elsewhere for Athenaeus' ἑανῷ.
[57] Better κατὰ; but Athenaeus' ποτὶ is the majority reading.

many perfumes (*mura*) are made with myrrh and what is known as *staktê* contains nothing else. Homer is familiar with the use of perfumes, but refers to them as *elaion* ("oil") accompanied by an adjective:

> She anointed (him) with rose-scented *elaion*. (*Il.* 23.186)

So too elsewhere he refers to something as "fragrant" (*Il.* 14.172, quoted below), and his Aphrodite likewise anointed Hector's corpse with rose-scented ambrosial *elaion* (cf. *Il.* 23.186–7). This variety is made from flowers; as for the type made with spices, which they referred to as *thuômata*, he says in reference to Hera (*Il.* 14.170–4):[174]

> First she used ambrosia to wipe away every stain
> from her lovely skin; and she anointed her white flesh
> with fine ambrosial (oil), which had been scented
> (*tethuômenon*) for her,
> the smell of which, when it was † shaken † in the bronze-floored
> house of Zeus, went out over earth and heaven alike.

The finest perfumes are associated with specific places, according to Herophilus' student Apollonius in his *On Perfumes* (fr. 8 von Staden), where he writes as follows:[175] The best iris-root is found in Elis and Cyzicus, whereas the finest rose-perfume is found in Phaselis—so too the type from Neapolis and Capua—and (the finest) saffron-per-

---

[174] The final two verses are quoted also at 1.17b (where see n.) and may be drawn from the same source-document, which argued that the Homeric lifestyle was one of considerable luxury.

[175] Very similar material is preserved at Plin. *Nat.* 13.5–6.

τῆς Κιλικίας καὶ ἐν Ῥόδῳ· νάρδινον δὲ τὸ ἐν Τάρσῳ·
οἰνάνθη δὲ ἡ Κυπρία καὶ Ἀδραμυττηνή· ἀμαράκινον
Κῷον καὶ μήλινον. κύπρινον δὲ προκέκριται τὸ ἐν
f Αἰγύπτῳ, δευτερεῦον δ' ἐστὶ τὸ Κυπριακὸν | καὶ τὸ ἐν
Φοινίκῃ καὶ ταύτης τὸ ἀπὸ Σιδῶνος. τὸ δὲ Παναθη-
ναϊκὸν λεγόμενον ἐν Ἀθήναις· τὸ δὲ μετώπιον καὶ
Μενδήσιον κάλλιστα ἐν Αἰγύπτῳ σκευάζεται· σκευ-
άζεται δὲ τὸ μετώπιον ἐξ ἐλαίου τοῦ ἀπὸ τῶν πικρῶν
καρύων. οἱ δὲ χορηγοῦντες, φησί, καὶ ἡ ὕλη καὶ οἱ
τεχνῖται τὸ χρηστότατον ποιοῦσι μύρον, ἀλλ' οὐχ οἱ
τόποι. Ἔφεσός γέ τοι πρότερον, φησί, τοῖς μύροις ‖
689 διέφερεν καὶ μάλιστα τῷ[58] Μεγαλλείῳ, νῦν δὲ οὔ.
ἤκμαζε δὲ καὶ τὰ ἐν Ἀλεξανδρείᾳ διὰ πλοῦτον καὶ διὰ
τὴν Ἀρσινόης καὶ Βερενίκης σπουδήν. ἐγίνετο δὲ καὶ
ἐν Κυρήνῃ ῥόδινον χρηστότατον καθ' ὃν χρόνον ἔζη
Βερενίκη ἡ μεγάλη.[59] οἰνάνθινον δὲ ἐν Ἀδραμυττίῳ
πάλαι μὲν μέτριον, ὕστερον δὲ πρῶτον διὰ Στρατο-
νίκην τὴν Εὐμένους. ἡ δὲ Συρία τὸ παλαιὸν χρηστὰ
πάντα παρείχετο, μάλιστα δὲ τὸ τήλινον, νῦν δὲ οὔ. ἐν
b δὲ Περγάμῳ πρότερον μὲν | ἐξόχως, νῦν δὲ οὔ, μυρε-

58 ἐν τῷ ACE: ἐν del. Kaibel
59 ἡ Μάγα Schweighäuser

176 Cf. 15.690f–1a.
177 Presumably referring to Arsinoe II Philadelphus, who became the wife of Ptolemy II Philadelphus c.270 BCE, and Berenice I, who was the wife of Ptolemy I Soter and the mother of
Arsinoe II and Ptolemy II.

fume is found in Cilician Soli and Rhodes; (the finest)
nard-perfume comes from Tarsus; the (finest) dropwort-
perfume comes from Cyprus and Adramyttium; and (the
finest) marjoram- and quince-perfumes come from Cos.
Egyptian henna-perfume is considered the best, while the
Cyprian and Phoenician (especially the Sidonian) varieties
come in second. What is known as Panathenaic perfume
(is best) in Athens, and *metôpion* and Mendesian perfumes
are best when produced in Egypt. *Metôpion* is made with
the oil extracted from bitter almonds. But what makes the
best perfume, he claims, is the people who supply the raw
materials, the materials themselves, and the workers, not
the locales. In the past, in fact, he says, Ephesus produced
excellent perfumes, in particular Megalleian,[176] but it no
longer does so today. The varieties made in Alexandria
were also outstanding, because of the city's wealth and because Arsinoe and Berenice[177] took an interest in them. In
addition, excellent rose-perfume was produced in Cyrene
during the period when Berenice the Great was alive.[178] In
ancient times the dropwort-perfume produced in Adramyttium was of indifferent quality, but later it became the
top variety due to Eumenes' wife Stratonice.[179] In the past
Syria was a source of excellent perfumes of all types, and in
particular fenugreek-perfume, whereas nowadays it is not.
Pergamum was previously—but is no longer—an impor-

[178] Berenice II of Cyrene, the daughter of King Magas (hence
Schweighäuser's conjecture, recorded in the critical apparatus),
who married Ptolemy III Euergetes in 246 BCE and died in 221.

[179] Eumenes II of Pergamum reigned 197–159 BCE.

ψοῦ τινος ἐκπονήσαντος τὸ παρ᾽ οὐδενί πω γεγονὸς
ἐσκευάζετο λιβανώτινον μύρον. μύρον δὲ χρηστὸν
μύρῳ εὐτελεῖ ἐπιχεόμενον ἐπιπολῆς μένει, μέλι δὲ
χρηστὸν χείρονι ἐπιχεόμενον εἰς τὸ κάτω βιάζεται·
λαμβάνει γὰρ αὐτοῦ καθύπερθεν τὸ ἧττον.

Τοῦ δὲ Αἰγυπτίου μύρου μνημονεύων Ἀχαιὸς ἐν
Ἄθλοις φησίν·

isάργυρόν τ᾽ εἰς χεῖρα Κυπρίου λίθου
δώσουσι κόσμον χριμάτων τ᾽ Αἰγυπτίων.

μήποτε, φησὶν ὁ Δίδυμος, τὴν καλουμένην στακτὴν |
c λέγει, διὰ τὴν σμύρναν ἣν εἰς Αἴγυπτον καταγομένην
κομίζεσθαι πρὸς τοὺς Ἕλληνας. Ἰκέσιος δ᾽ ἐν δευτέρῳ Περὶ Ὕλης, τῶν μύρων, φησίν, ἃ μέν ἐστι
χρίματα, ἃ δ᾽ ἀλείμματα. καὶ ῥόδινον μὲν πρὸς πότον
ἐπιτήδειον, ἔτι δὲ μύρσινον, μήλινον· τοῦτο δ᾽ ἐστὶν
καὶ εὐστόμαχον καὶ ληθαργικοῖς χρήσιμον. τὸ δ᾽
οἰνάνθινον εὐστόμαχον ὂν καὶ τὴν διάνοιαν ἀπαραπό-
διστον φυλάσσει. καὶ τὸ σαμψούχινον δὲ καὶ ἑρπύλλινον ἐπιτήδεια πρὸς πότον καὶ κρόκινον τὸ χωρὶς
d σμύρνης πολλῆς. καὶ ἡ | στακτὴ δὲ ἐπιτήδειος πρὸς
πότον, ἔτι δὲ νάρδος. τὸ δὲ τήλινον καὶ γλυκύ ἐστι καὶ
ἁπαλόν. τὸ δὲ λευκόινον καὶ εὐῶδες καὶ σφόδρα πεπτι-
κόν. Θεόφραστος δὲ ἐν τῷ Περὶ Ὀδμῶν συντίθεσθαί
φησι μύρα ἀπ᾽ ἀνθέων μὲν ῥόδινον καὶ λευκόινον καὶ

---

180 Perhaps an emerald; cf. Plin. *Nat.* 37.66.
181 *sampsouchinos*; cf. 15.676d–e with n.

tant site for the manufacture of frankincense-perfume of a sort that had never been seen before; some perfume-maker worked hard to invent it. If good perfume is poured over cheap perfume, it remains on top, whereas if good honey is poured over inferior honey, it is forced downward; for it allows itself to be overwhelmed by the inferior variety.

Achaeus refers to Egyptian perfume in *The Games* (*TrGF* 20 F 5), saying:

> In your hand they will place an ornament worth its
>   weight in silver,
> consisting of Cyprian stone[180] and Egyptian
>   ointments.

It may be, says Didymus (pp. 305–6 Schmidt), that he is referring to what is known as *staktê*, given that the myrrh imported into Egypt is then shipped to the Greeks. Hicesius says in Book II of *On Raw Materials*: Some perfumes are poured on a person, while others are rubbed on. Rose-perfume is appropriate for a drinking party, as are myrtle- and quince-perfumes; the latter is easy on the stomach and is useful for individuals suffering from lethargy. Dropwort-perfume is easy on the stomach and also keeps the mind clear. Marjoram-[181] and tufted-thyme-perfumes are appropriate for drinking parties, as is saffron-perfume, provided it does not contain too much myrrh. *Staktê* is also appropriate for a drinking party, as is nard-perfume. Fenugreek-perfume is sweet and delicate. Gillyflower-perfume is fragrant and extremely good for the digestion. Theophrastus in his *On Odors* (27–8, condensed) reports that the perfumes made from flowers include rose-, gillyflower-,

σούσινον (καὶ γὰρ τοῦτο ἐκ τῶν κρίνων), ἔτι δὲ τὸ
σισύμβρινον καὶ ἑρπύλλινον, ἐν δὲ Κύπρῳ[60] καὶ τὸ
κρ<όκ>ινον·[61] βέλτιστον δ᾽ ἐν Αἰγίνῃ καὶ Κιλικίᾳ. ἀπὸ
δὲ φύλλων τὸ μύρρινον καὶ τὸ οἰνάνθινον· αὕτη δ᾽ ἐν
Κύπρῳ φύεται ὀρεινὴ καὶ πολύγονος· ἐν δὲ Ἑλλάδι οὐ
e γίνεται διὰ τὸ ἄοσμον. | ἀπὸ δὲ ῥιζῶν τό τ᾽ ἴρινον καὶ
τὸ νάρδινον καὶ τὸ ἀμαράκινον ἐκ τοῦ κόστου.

Ὅτι δὲ διὰ σπουδῆς ἦν τοῖς παλαιοτέροις ἡ τῶν
μύρων χρῆσις δῆλον ἐκ τοῦ καὶ ἐπίστασθαι ποῖόν τι
ἑκάστῳ τῶν μελῶν ἡμῶν ἐστιν ἐπιτήδειον. Ἀντιφάνης
γοῦν ἐν Θορικίοις ἢ Διορύττοντί φησιν·

(Α.) λοῦται δ᾽ † ου ο † ἀληθῶς (Β.) ἀλλὰ τί;
(Α.) ἐκ χρυσοκολλήτου γε κάλπιδος μύρῳ
Αἰγυπτίῳ μὲν τοὺς πόδας καὶ τὰ σκέλη,
φοινικίνῳ δὲ τὰς γνάθους καὶ τιτθία, |
f σισυμβρίνῳ δὲ τὸν ἕτερον βραχίονα,
ἀμαρακίνῳ δὲ τὰς ὀφρῦς καὶ τὴν κόμην,
ἑρπυλλίνῳ δὲ τὸ γόνυ καὶ τὸν αὐχένα.

καὶ Κηφισόδωρος ἐν Τροφωνίῳ·

(Α.) ἔπειτ᾽ ἀλείφεσθαι τὸ σῶμά μοι πρίω
μύρον ἴρινον καὶ ῥόδινον, ἄγαμαι, Ξανθία·
καὶ τοῖς ποσὶν χωρὶς πρίω μοι βάκχαριν.

[60] καὶ ἡ κύπρος Thphr.   [61] suppl. Kaibel

---

[182] Sc. to produce perfume.
[183] Quoted also at 12.553d, where see nn.

132

and *sousinon*- (the latter is made from lilies), as well as the
bergamot-mint- and tufted-thyme-varieties, and on Cyprus the saffron-variety, although it is best on Aegina and
in Cilicia. Myrtle- and dropwort-perfumes, on the other
hand, are made from leaves; dropwort grows in large quantities in the mountains on Cyprus, but is not used[182] in
Greece, because it lacks a fragrance. Iris- and nard-perfumes, and the marjoram-perfume made from *kostos*, are
produced from roots.

That people in previous times were interested in using
perfume is apparent from the fact that they knew which
type is appropriate for all the various parts of our bodies.
Antiphanes, for example, says in *Men from Thoricus or The
Man Who Was Digging a Trench* (fr. 105):[183]

> (A.) She's actually washing [corrupt]
>   (B.) What? what?
> (A.) her feet and her legs with Egyptian
> perfume she took from a container inlaid with gold,
> and her cheeks and titties with palm-perfume,
> and one arm with mint-perfume,
> and her eyebrows and her hair with marjoram-
>   perfume,
> and her knees and her neck with tufted-thyme-
>   perfume.

Also Cephisodorus in *Trophonius* (fr. 3):[184]

> (A.) Then buy me iris- or rose-perfume
> to rub on my body, please, Xanthias;
> and on top of that, buy me *bakcharis* for my feet!

[184] The first three verses are quoted also at 12.553a.

(Ξα.) ὦ λακκόπρωκτε, βάκχαριν τοῖς σοῖς ποσὶν
ἐγὼ πρίωμαι; λαικάσομ' ἄρα. βάκχαριν;

Ἀναξανδρίδης Πρωτεσιλάῳ·

μύρον τε παρὰ Πέρωνος, οὗπερ ἀπέδοτο ‖
690   ἐχθὲς Μελανώπῳ, πολυτελοῦς Αἰγυπτίου,
ᾧ νῦν ἀλείφει τοὺς πόδας Καλλιστράτου.

μνημονεύει τοῦ μυροπώλου τούτου τοῦ Πέρωνος καὶ
Θεόπομπος ἐν Ἀδμήτῳ καὶ Ἡδυχάρει. Ἀντιφάνης δ᾽
ἐν Ἀντείᾳ·

πρὸς τῷ Πέρ⟨ων⟩ι γευόμενον κατελίμπανον
αὐτὸν μύρων μέλλει τε συνθείς σοι φέρειν
τὰ κινναμώμινα ταῦτα καὶ τὰ νάρδινα.

παρὰ πολλοῖς δὲ τῶν κωμῳδιοποιῶν ὀνομάζεταί τι
μύρον βακκαρίς· οὗ μνημονεύει καὶ Ἱππῶναξ διὰ ‖
b   τούτων·

βακκάρι δὲ τὰς ῥῖνας
ἤλειφον † ἐστι δ᾽ † οἵηνπερ Κροῖσος.

Ἀχαιὸς δ᾽ ἐν Αἴθωνι σατυρικῷ·

βακκάρει χρισθέντα καὶ ψυκτηρίοις
πτεροῖς ἀναστήσαντα προσθίαν τρίχα.

---

185 Quoted also, with some minor variants, at 12.553d–e.
186 PAA 772900. Melanopus (mentioned in the next verse) is
PAA 638765, while Callistratus is PAA 561575; both were promi-
nent politicians.

(Xanthias) You pervert—I'm supposed to buy you
bakcharis for your feet? Suck me! *Bakcharis*?

Anaxandrides in *Protesilaus* (fr. 41):[185]

and perfume from Peron,[186] some of which he sold
yesterday to Melanopus—an expensive Egyptian
variety,
which he's now using to anoint Callistratus' feet.

This perfume-maker Peron is also mentioned by Theopompus in *Admetus* (fr. 1) and *The Hedonist* (fr. 17). Antiphanes in *Anteia* (fr. 37):

I left him at Peron's place, sampling
the perfumes; after he makes a deal, he's going to
bring you
these types made from cinnamon and nard.

Many comic poets refer to a variety of perfume known as
bakkaris.[187] Hipponax (fr. 107.21–2 Degani) also mentions
it, in the following passage:

I smeared *bakkaris* on my
nostrils † but is † the type Croesus (uses).

Achaeus in the satyr play *Aethon* (*TrGF* 20 F 10):

anointed with *bakkaris* and using cooling
wings[188] to make his hair stand up in front.

[187] Hsch. β 107 offers various descriptions of *bakkaris* (also
spelled *bakcharis*, as in Cephisodorus fr. 3 [above]), including "a
dry powder made from the root (sc. of the plant in question)."
[188] I.e. fans made of feathers.

Ἴων Ὀμφάλῃ·

> βακκάρις δὲ καὶ μύρα
> καὶ Σαρδιανὸν κόσμον εἰδέναι χροὸς
> ἄμεινον ἢ τὸν Πέλοπος ἐν νήσῳ τρόπον.

ἐν τούτοις Σαρδιανὸν κόσμον εἴρηκε τὸ μύρον, ἐπεὶ διαβόητοι ἐπὶ ἡδυπαθείᾳ οἱ Λυδοί· καὶ τὸ παρὰ |

c Ἀνακρέοντι

> Λυδοπαθὴς[62]

ἀκούουσιν ἀντὶ τοῦ ἡδυπαθής. μνημονεύει τῆς βακκάριδος καὶ Σοφοκλῆς. Μάγνης δ᾽ ἐν Λυδοῖς·

> λούσαντα χρὴ καὶ βακκάριδι κεχριμένον.

καὶ μήποτε οὔκ ἐστι μύρον ἡ βάκκαρις. Αἰσχύλος γὰρ ἐν Ἀμυμώνῃ ἀντιδιαστέλλων φησίν·

> κἄγωγε τὰς σὰς βακκάρεις τε καὶ μύρα.

καὶ Σιμωνίδης·

> κἠλειφόμην μύροισι καὶ θυώμασι
> καὶ βακκάρι.

Ἀριστοφάνης δ᾽ ἐν Θεσμοφοριαζούσαις· |

[62] Cited by the Scholiast to Aeschylus in the form λυδοπαθεῖς.

Ion in *Omphale* (*TrGF* 19 F 24):

> It's better to know about
> *bakkaris* and perfumes and Sardian cosmetics
> than about how they live in the Peloponnese.[189]

He refers in this passage to perfume as a Sardian cosmetic because the Lydians were notorious for their luxurious lifestyle; thus the word

Lydian-style

in Anacreon (*PMG* 481) is taken to mean "living in luxury." Sophocles also mentions *bakkaris* (fr. 1032). Magnes in *Lydians* (fr. 3):

> After he bathes and anoints himself with *bakkaris*, he
>   has to . . .

But perhaps *bakkaris* is not a type of perfume, given that Aeschylus in *Amymone* (fr. 14) distinguishes between the two, saying:

> And as for me, your *bakkareis* and perfumes . . .

Also Simonides (Semon. fr. 16.1–2 West[2]):

> And I used to anoint myself with perfumes, scented
>   oils,
> and *bakkaris*.

Aristophanes in *Women Celebrating the Thesmophoria* (fr. 336):[190]

---

[189] I.e. in Sparta, where such luxuries were frowned upon (cf. 15.686f).   [190] From the lost play by that title, rather than the preserved one of 411 BCE.

d   ὦ Ζεῦ πολυτίμηθ᾽, οἷον ἐνέπνευσ᾽ ὁ μιαρὸς
φάσκωλος εὐθὺς λυόμενός μοι τοῦ μύρου
καὶ βακκάριδος.

βρενθείου δὲ μύρου μνημονεύει Φερεκράτης ἐν Λήροις
οὕτως·

    ἔστην δὲ κἀκέλευον † ἐγχέασθαι νῷν μύρον †
βρένθειον, ἵνα τοῖς εἰσιοῦσιν ἐγχέῃ.

βασιλείου δὲ μύρου μνημονεύει Κράτης ἐν Γείτοσιν
λέγων οὕτως·

    < . . . > γλυκύτατον δ᾽ ὦζε βασιλείου μύρου. |

e   Σαπφὼ δ᾽ ὁμοῦ μέμνηται τοῦ τε βασιλείου καὶ τοῦ
βρενθείου, λέγουσα οὕτως·

    βρενθείῳ < . . . >
    <   . . .   > βασιληίῳ.

ψάγδης Ἀριστοφάνης ἐν Δαιταλεῦσιν·

    φέρ᾽ ἴδω, τί σοι δῶ τῶν μύρων; ψάγδαν φιλεῖς;

Εὔπολις δ᾽ ἐν Μαρικᾷ·

    < . . . > ψάγδαν ἐρυγγάνοντα.

Εὔβουλος δ᾽ ἐν Στεφανοπώλισιν·

    Αἰγυπτίῳ ψαγδάνι τρὶς λελουμένη.

---

[191] Cited also, at slightly less length, at 15.691c, where see nn.

O much-honored Zeus! What a smell the vile
bag breathed out at me the moment I opened it—
    perfume
and *bakkaris*!

Pherecrates in *Frills* (fr. 105) refers to *brentheios* perfume,
as follows:

I stood there and told him † to pour the two of us
    perfume †
brentheios, so he could pour it for them as they
    came in.

Crates in *Neighbors* (fr. 2) refers to royal perfume, saying
the following:

She gave off the sweet, sweet smell of royal perfume.

Sappho (fr. 94.19–20) refers to royal perfume and *brentheios* perfume together, saying the following:

with *brentheios* . . .
. . . with royal.

Aristophanes in *Banqueters* (fr. 213)[191] (mentions) *psagdê*:

Alright—what kind of perfume should I give you? Do
    you like *psagdas*?

Eupolis in *Marikas* (fr. 204.1):[192]

belching *psagdas*.

Eubulus in *Female Garland-Vendors* (fr. 100):

washed three times in Egyptian *psagdas*.

---

[192] Quoted again, in a slightly different form, at 15.691c,
where see n.

Πολέμων δ' ἐν τοῖς Πρὸς Ἀδαῖον παρὰ Ἠλείοις φησὶ
μύρον τι Πλαγγόνιον καλεῖσθαι, εὑρεθὲν ὑπό τινος
Πλαγγόνος. ὁμοίως ἱστορεῖ καὶ Σωσίβιος ἐν Ὁμοι-
f ότησιν. | ὡς καὶ τὸ Μεγάλλειον· ὠνομάσθη γὰρ καὶ
τοῦτο ἀπὸ Μεγάλλου τοῦ Σικελιώτου· οἱ δ' Ἀθηναῖόν
φασιν εἶναι τὸν Μέγαλλον. μνημονεύει δ' αὐτοῦ Ἀριστοφάνης ἐν Τελμησσεῦσι καὶ Φερεκράτης ἐν Πετά-
λῃ, Στράττις δ' ἐν Μηδείᾳ οὕτως·

> καὶ λέγ' ὅτι φέρεις αὐτῇ μύρον
> τοιοῦτον, οἷον οὐ Μέγαλλος πώποτε
> ἥψησεν, οὐδὲ Δεινίας Αἰγύπτιος
> οὔτ' εἶδεν οὔτ' ἐκτήσατο. ‖

691   τοῦ Μεγαλλείου δὲ μύρου μνημονεύει καὶ Ἄμφις ἐν
Ὀδυσσεῖ διὰ τούτων·

> (Α.) ἐρίοισι τοὺς τοίχους κύκλῳ Μιλησίοις,
> ἔπειτ' ἀλείφειν τῷ Μεγαλλείῳ μύρῳ,
> καὶ τὴν βασιλικὴν θυμιᾶτε μίνδακα.
> (Β.) ἀκήκοας σύ, δέσποτ', ἤδη πώποτε
> τὸ θυμίαμα τοῦτο;

Ἀναξανδρίδης Τηρεῖ·

> ἀλλ' οἷα νύμφη βασιλὶς ὠνομασμένη
> μύροις Μεγαλλείοισι σῶμ' ἀλείφεται.

ναρδίνου δὲ μύρου μέμνηται Μένανδρος ἐν Κεκρυ-
φάλῳ οὕτως· |

140

Polemon in his *Response to Adaeus* (fr. 74 Preller) claims that the inhabitants of Elis have a type of perfume known as Plangonion, which was invented by a certain Plangon. Sosibius in *Similarities* (*FGrH* 595 F 9) offers similar information. So too in the case of Megalleian; it got its name from Megallus of Sicily, although other authorities claim that Megallus was an Athenian.[193] Aristophanes refers to him in *Telmessians* (fr. 549),[194] as do Pherecrates in *Petale* (fr. 149) and Strattis in *Medea*, as follows (fr. 34):

> And say you're bringing her perfume
> of a type Megallus never
> produced, and Deinias the Egyptian
> never saw or owned.

Amphis in *Odysseus* (fr. 27) also refers to Megalleian perfume, in the following passage:

> (A.) the walls all around with Milesian wool;
> then to anoint them with Megalleian perfume,
> and burn the royal *mindax*-incense.
> (B.) Master—have you ever heard of this kind of
> incense before?

Anaxandrides in *Tereus* (fr. 47):

> But just like someone referred to as a royal bride,
> she covers her body with Megalleian perfumes.

Menander in *The Headdress* (fr. 210) refers to nard-perfume, as follows:

---

[193] *PAA* 636610.
[194] The verse is quoted by Hsch. μ 1011.

b   (A.) ἡδὺ τὸ μύρον, παιδάριον. (B.) ἡδύ; πῶς γὰρ
       οὔ;
       νάρδινον.

       Τὸ δὲ χρίσασθαι τῷ τοιούτῳ ἀλείμματι μυρίσα-
σθαι εἴρηκεν Ἀλκαῖος ἐν Παλαίστραις διὰ τούτων·

       μυρίσασα συγκατέκλεισεν ἀνθ᾽ αὑτῆς λάθρᾳ.

       μυρώμασιν μέντοι, οὐ μυρίσμασιν ἔλεγεν Ἀριστο-
φάνης ἐν Ἐκκλησιαζούσαις·

       ἥτις μεμύρισμαι τὴν κεφαλὴν μυρώμασιν.

c   τῆς δὲ λεγομένης σάγδας (μύρον δ᾽ ἐστὶ καὶ | τοῦτο)
      Ἐπίλυκος ἐν Κωραλίσκῳ·

       < . . . > βάκκαρίς τε καὶ σάγδας ὁμοῦ.

       καὶ Ἀριστοφάνης ἐν Δαιταλεῦσιν· < . . . > καὶ ἐν
Μαρικᾷ Εὔπολις

       < . . . > σάγδαν ἐρυγγάνοντα

---

195 Manuscript A gives the title (perhaps a courtesan's name)
in the plural here, but elsewhere in Athenaeus it appears in the
singular (3.107f; 9.370f, 396c).

196 "to apply *muron* (perfume) to oneself"; but the verb is used
in the active rather than the middle in the quotation that follows.

197 Sc. despite the fact that *murismata* (< *murizô*, whence the
aorist infinitive *murisasthai* noted above) might be expected as
the common form of the noun.

198 The entire verse is cited by Photius (Tsantsanoglou p. 117),

(A.) This is wonderful perfume, slave! (B.) It's
    wonderful? Of course—
it's made with nard!

Alcaeus in *The Wrestling-Schools*[195] (fr. 23) uses the
verb *murisasthai*[196] to refer to smearing oneself with a substance of this sort, in the following passage:

After she smeared the girl with perfume (*murisasa*),
    she secretly locked (her), rather than herself, up
    with (him).

Aristophanes in *Ecclesiazusae* (1117), moreover, uses *mu-
rômata* rather than *murismata:*[197]

I who have had my head anointed (*memurismai*) with
    murômata.

Epilycus in *Coraliscus* (fr. 1.1)[198] (mentions) what is
known as *sagda*—this is also a type of perfume:

bakkaris and *sagdas* together.

Also Aristophanes in *Banqueters* (fr. 213):[199] . . . And
Eupolis in *Marikas* (fr. 204.1),[200] saying:

belching *sagdas*.

although he refers to the substance in question as *psagdas* rather
than *sagdas*; cf. below.

[199] The quotation (for which, see 15.690e—where all the material cited here would seem to belong) has apparently fallen out
of the text.

[200] Quoted also at 15.690e, as well as by Photius (Tsantsanoglou pp. 119–20), but in both cases with the substance in question
referred to as *psagda* rather than *sagda*.

λέγων. ὅπερ ὁ Θυατειρηνὸς Νίκανδρος ἐπὶ τοῦ ἄγαν
χλιδῶντος εἰρῆσθαι ἀκούει, Θεόδωρος δὲ θυμίαμά τί
φησιν αὐτὸ εἶναι.

Παμπόλλου δ᾿ ἐπιπράσκετο Ἀθήνησιν ἡ τοῦ μύρου
κοτύλη, καὶ ὡς μὲν Ἵππαρχός φησιν ἐν Παννυχίδι,
πέντε μνῶν, ὡς δὲ Μένανδρος ἐν Μισογύνῃ, δέκα.
d Ἀντιφάνης δ᾿ ἐν Φρεαρρίῳ | στακτῆς τοῦ μύρου μνη-
μονεύων φησίν·

στακτὴ δυοῖν μναῖν οὐκ ἀρέσκει μ᾿ οὐδαμῶς.

οὐ μόνον δὲ τὸ τῶν Σαρδιανῶν γένος φιλόμυρον ἦν, ὡς
Ἄλεξίς φησιν ἐν Ἐκπωματοποιῷ·

ἀεὶ φιλόμυρον πᾶν τὸ Σάρδεων γένος,

ἀλλὰ καὶ αὐτοὶ οἱ Ἀθηναῖοι οἱ πάντων τῶν καλλίστων
εἰσηγηταὶ τῷ τῶν ἀνθρώπων βίῳ γενόμενοι, παρ᾿ οἷς
ἀνυπερβλήτου τιμῆς, ὡς προείρηται, τῶν μύρων
e ὑπαρχούσης οὐκ ἀπείχοντο τῆς χρήσεως, | ὥσπερ
οὐδὲ ἡμεῖς νῦν οὕτω πολυτίμων τῶν καλλίστων ὑπαρ-
χόντων, ὡς λῆρον εἶναι τὰ ἐν τῷ Εἰσοικιζομένῳ
Ἀλέξιδος ταυτί·

οὐ γὰρ ἐμυρίζετ᾿ ἐξ ἀλαβάστου, πρᾶγμά τι
γιγνόμενον ἀεί, Κρονικόν, ἀλλὰ τέτταρας
περιστερὰς ἀφῆκεν ἀποβεβαμμένας

---

[201] Approximately one cup.
[202] 1 *mina* = 100 drachmas.

144

Nicander of Thyateira (*FGrH* 343 F 18) takes this as a reference to someone who lives in excessive luxury, while Theodorus (*FGrH* 346 F 5) claims that (*sagdas*) is a type of incense.

A *kotulê*[201] of perfume sold for a substantial amount of money in Athens: for five *minas*,[202] according to Hipparchus in *The All-Night Festival* (fr. 4), and for ten, according to Menander in *The Misogynist* (fr. 243). Antiphanes in *The Man from the Deme Phrearrhoi* (fr. 222) refers to the perfume known as *staktê*, saying:

> *Staktê* that costs two *minas* will definitely not
> satisfy me.

It was not just the people of Sardis who liked perfume, as Alexis says in *The Goblet-Maker* (fr. 67):

> All the people in Sardis always like perfume,

but also the Athenians themselves, who introduced everything that is best into all aspects of human existence. Nor did they refuse to use perfumes, despite the fact that they cost an exorbitant amount in their country, as was noted above, just as we today do not, even though the best varieties are so extremely expensive that they make nonsense of the following passage from Alexis' *The Man Who Was Moving In* (fr. 63):

> Since he didn't get perfume out of a jar, which is
> the usual procedure and totally old-fashioned.
>   Instead, he released
> four pigeons that had been dipped—

145

εἰς οὐχὶ ταὐτὸν μὰ Δία τὴν αὐτὴν μύρον,
ἰδίῳ δ' ἑκάστην. πετόμεναι δ' αὗται κύκλῳ
ἔρραινον ἡμῶν θαἰμάτια καὶ στρώματα.
μή μοι φθονήσητ', ἄνδρες Ἑλλήνων ἄκροι· |
f   ἠλειφόμην ὑόμενος ἰρίνῳ μύρῳ.

πρὸς θεῶν, φίλοι, ποία ἡδονή, μᾶλλον δ' ὑοσαλακωνία
θαἰμάτια μολύνεσθαι, ἐξὸν ταῖς χερσίν, ὥσπερ ἡμεῖς
νῦν ποιοῦμεν, ἀρυσαμένους ἀλείφεσθαι πᾶν τὸ σῶμα
καὶ μάλιστα τὴν κεφαλήν. φησὶν γὰρ ὁ Φιλωνίδης ἐν
τῷ Περὶ Μύρων καὶ Στεφάνων τὴν ἀφορμὴν τοῦ τὴν
692   κεφαλὴν ἐν τοῖς πότοις λιπαίνειν ἐντεῦθεν ‖ γενέσθαι·
τοῖς αὐχμῶσι γὰρ τὰς κεφαλὰς εἰς τὸ μετέωρον ἕλ-
κεσθαι τὸ λαμβανόμενον. καὶ διὰ τοῦτο τῶν πυρετῶν
διακαιόντων τὰ σώματα τέγγουσι τὴν κεφαλὴν ἐπι-
βρέγμασιν, ἵνα μὴ πρὸς τὸ ξηρόν, ταύτῃ δὲ καὶ
πολύκενον, ὁρμὴν τὰ παρακείμενα⁶³ λαμβάνῃ. τοῦτο
δὴ λογισάμενοι καὶ ἐπὶ τῶν πότων τὴν εἰς τὸ μετέωρον
τῶν οἴνων φορὰν ὑποπτεύσαντες ἐπεσπάσθησαν κεφαλὴν λιπαίνειν, ὡς ἐλάσσονος <τῆς>⁶⁴ βίας γενησο-
μένης, εἰ ταύτην προτέγξαιεν. προστιθεὶς δ' ὁ βίος ἀεὶ
b   τοῖς χρειώδεσιν | καὶ τῶν εἰς ἀπόλαυσιν καὶ τρυφὴν
ἀγόντων ἐπὶ τὴν τῶν μύρων χρῆσιν ὥρμησεν. χρη-
στέον οὖν, ὦ Κύνουλκε Θεόδωρε, μύροις παρὰ πότον

---

⁶³ παρακαιόμενα Dalechamp
⁶⁴ add. Wilamowitz

---

²⁰³ A quotation of E. *Telephus* fr. 703.1 (the disguised Tele-

and not all into the same perfume, by Zeus,
but each into a different one! They flew around in a
    circle
and sprinkled our robes and our bedding.
Do not resent me, foremost men of Greece;[203]
I was anointed with a shower of iris-perfume.

By the gods, my friends, how pleasant—or rather, how
boorishly pretentious!—to get your clothing dirty, when
you could just as easily use your hands, as we are doing
now, to dip (the perfume) out and rub it over your entire
body, and in particular your head. For Philonides in his *On
Perfumes and Garlands*[204] claims that the practice of ap-
plying oily substances to one's head at drinking parties began as follows: When people's heads are dry, whatever they
consume is drawn upward. As a consequence, when fevers
are consuming their bodies, they protect their heads by
sprinkling liquids on them, to keep the neighboring parts
from attacking their dry, as well as porous parts. On the ba-
sis of this theory, since they expected that at their drinking
parties the wine's movement would be upward, they were
induced to apply oily substances to their heads, in the be-
lief that the wine's force would be reduced if they moist-
ened their heads in advance. And since human existence
continually adds practices that increase enjoyment and
luxury to those that are merely necessary, it moved in the
direction of using perfumes. When we drink, Cynulcus-
Theodorus,[205] we ought therefore to use the perfumes that

phus addresses the leaders of the Achaean expedition against
Troy).   [204] Cf. 15.675a–e (patently part of the same discussion).   [205] Cf. 15.669e.

τοῖς ἐλάχιστα καροῦν δυναμένοις, τοῖς στύφουσιν δὲ
καὶ ψύχουσιν ἐπ᾽ ὀλίγον. ζητεῖ δ᾽ ὁ πολυμαθέστατος
Ἀριστοτέλης ἐν τοῖς Φυσικοῖς Προβλήμασι, διὰ τί οἱ
μυριζόμενοι πολιώτεροι; ἢ ὅτι τὸ μύρον διὰ τὰ ἀρώ-
ματα ξηραντικόν ἐστι, διὸ καὶ αὐχμηροὶ οἱ μυριζόμενοι, ὁ δὲ αὐχμὸς πολιωτέρους ποιεῖ; εἴτε γὰρ
αὔανσις τριχὸς ἡ πολιὰ εἴτ᾽ ἔνδεια θερμοῦ, ἡ ξηρότης
c   μαραίνει. | διὸ καὶ τὰ πιλία θᾶττον ποιεῖ πολιούς·
ἐκπίνεται γὰρ ἡ οἰκεία τῆς τριχὸς ὑγρότης. ἥδιστον
δέ, ἄνδρες φίλοι, ἀναγινώσκων τὴν ὀγδόην καὶ εἰκο-
στὴν τῶν Ποσειδωνίου Ἱστοριῶν περὶ μύρων τι λεγόμενον ἐτήρησα, οὐκ ἀλλότριον ἡμῶν τοῦ συμποσίου.
φησὶ γὰρ ὁ φιλόσοφος· ἐν Συρίᾳ ἐν τοῖς βασιλικοῖς
συμποσίοις ὅταν τοῖς εὐωχουμένοις δοθῶσιν οἱ στέφανοι, εἰσίασίν τινες μύρων Βαβυλωνίων ἔχοντες
ἀσκίδια καὶ πόρρωθεν ἐκ τούτων περιπορευόμενοι
τοὺς μὲν στεφάνους τῶν κατακειμένων δροσίζουσι |
d   τοῖς μύροις, ἄλλο μηδὲν ἔξωθεν παραραίνοντες. ἐπεὶ
δ᾽ ἐνταῦθα τοῦ λόγου ἐσμέν,

συμβαλοῦμαί τι μέλος ὑμῖν εἰς ἔρωτα,

κατὰ τὸν Κυθήριον ποιητήν, ὅτι Ἰανὸς ὁ παρ᾽ ἡμῖν
θεός, ὃν καὶ πατέρα προσαγορεύομεν, πρῶτος εὗρεν
στέφανον. ἱστορεῖ δὲ τοῦτο Δράκων ὁ Κερκυραῖος ἐν
τῷ Περὶ Λίθων γράφων οὕτως· Ἰανὸν δὲ λόγος ἔχει
διπρόσωπον γεγονέναι, τὸ μὲν ὀπίσω, τὸ δ᾽ ἔμπροσθεν ἔχοντα πρόσωπον. ἀπὸ τούτου καὶ τὸν Ἰανὸν

are the least stupefying, but that are astringent and cool us
temporarily. The profoundly learned Aristotle in his *Physical Problems* (fr. 763) raises the question of why individuals who use perfume go gray faster. Is it because the spices
in the perfume make it parching, so that individuals who
use perfume become drier, and the dryness makes them
grayer? Because whether the grayness represents a dry-
ing-up of one's hair or a lack of warmth, the parching has a
damaging effect. This is why felt caps rapidly make people
go gray; because the cap absorbs the hair's natural moist-
ness. But as I was reading Book XXVIII of Posidonius' *History* (*FGrH* 87 F 20 = fr. 71 Edelstein–Kidd), my friends, I
noticed a very nice observation about perfumes, which will
not be out of place at our party. For the philosopher says:
At the king's drinking parties in Syria, at the point when
garlands are distributed to the individuals attending the
feast, people come in with pouches full of Babylonian perfumes and make their way around, standing at a distance
and dribbling perfumes drawn from these pouches over
the garlands of the guests who are lying there, sprinkling
them with nothing drawn from any other source. But since
we are at this point in our conversation,

I will join you in a little song about love,

to quote the poet from Cythera (Philox. Cyth. *PMG*
833),[206] since our god Janus, whom we address as "father,"
invented garlands. Draco of Corcyra in his *On Stones*
(*FHG* iv.402–3) preserves this information, writing as follows: The story goes that Janus has two faces, one of which
looks backward, the other forward. The Janus River and

[206] Alluded to (but not quoted) at 6.271b.

ποταμὸν καὶ τὸ ὄρος Ἰανὸν ὀνομάζεσθαι, κατοική-
e σαντος | αὐτοῦ ἐπὶ τοῦ ὄρους. τοῦτον δὲ καὶ στέφανον
πρῶτον εὑρεῖν καὶ σχεδίας καὶ πλοῖα καὶ νόμισμα
χαλκοῦν πρῶτον χαράξαι. διὸ καὶ τῶν κατὰ τὴν Ἑλ-
λάδα πολλὰς πόλεις καὶ τῶν κατὰ τὴν Ἰταλίαν καὶ
Σικελίαν ἐπὶ τοῦ νομίσματος ἐγχαράττειν πρόσωπον
δικέφαλον καὶ ἐκ θατέρου μέρους ἢ σχεδίαν ἢ στέφανον ἢ πλοῖον. τοῦτον δὲ τὴν ἀδελφὴν γήμαντα
Καμήσην υἱὸν μὲν Αἴθηκα, θυγατέρα δὲ Ὀλιστήνην
γεννῆσαι. καὶ αὐτὸν ὡς μειζόνων ὀρεγόμενον πραγμάτων εἰς τὴν Ἰταλίαν διαπλεῦσαι καὶ οἰκῆσαι τὸ πλη-
f σίον Ῥώμης ὄρος κείμενον | τὸ ἀπ᾽ αὐτοῦ Ἰανοῦκλον
ὀνομαζόμενον.

Τοσαῦτα καὶ περὶ μύρων ἐλέχθη. καὶ μετὰ ταῦτα
πλείστων τῶν μὲν Ἀγαθοῦ Δαίμονος αἰτούντων ποτήριον, τῶν δὲ Διὸς Σωτῆρος, ἄλλων δὲ Ὑγείας, καὶ
ἑτέρων ἕτερον ἐπιλεγόντων, τοὺς τούτων τῶν κράσεων
μεμνημένους τῶν ποιητῶν ἔδοξεν παρατίθεσθαι, ὧν
καὶ αὐτῶν μνησθήσομαι. Ἀντιφάνης μὲν γὰρ ἐν
Ἀγροικίσιν ἔφη·

Ἁρμόδιος ἐπεκαλεῖτο, παιὰν ᾔδετο,
μεγάλην Διὸς Σωτῆρος ἄκατον ᾖρέ τις.

Ἄλεξις δ᾽ ἐν Τοκιστῇ ἢ Καταψευδομένῳ·

---

207 Sc. "of wine and water," i.e. "to these bowls and their contents," and thus to the deities to whom they were dedicated.

Mt. Janus get their names from him, since he lives on the mountain. He invented garlands, as well as rafts and boats, and was the first to mint bronze coins. This is why many cities in Greece, and in Italy and Sicily as well, stamp a head with two faces on one side of their coins, and a raft, a garland, or a ship on the other. Janus married his sister Camêsê and produced a son named Aethêx and a daughter named Olistênê. And because he longed to accomplish something more significant than this, he sailed across the sea to Italy and settled on the mountain that is near to Rome and that derives its name, the Janiculum, from him.

This was the extent of our discussion of perfumes. Afterward, the majority of the guests asked for a cup dedicated to the Good Divinity, but some asked for one dedicated to Zeus the Savior, or to Hygieia ("Health"), or to another god. It accordingly seemed good to cite the poets who refer to these combinations,[207] and to whom I will refer by name. Because Antiphanes said in *Women from the Countryside*[208] (fr. 3):

Harmodius was invoked;[209] a paean was sung;
someone brought a large cup[210] dedicated to Zeus the Savior.

Alexis in *The Loan-Shark or The Liar* (fr. 234):

[208] Referred to elsewhere in the masculine as *The Rustic* or *Rustics* (e.g. 9.396b; 10.445f; 13.567d).
[209] A reference to skolia of the sort collected at 15.695a–b, where see n.
[210] *akatos*; see 11.502a with n.

151

(Α.) ἀλλ' ἔγχεον ‖

693   αὐτῷ Διός γε τήνδε Σωτῆρος, θεῶν
θνητοῖς ἁπάντων χρησιμωτάτου πολύ.
(Β.) ὁ Ζεὺς ὁ Σωτήρ, ἂν ἐγὼ διαρραγῶ,
οὐδέν μ' ὀνήσει. (Α.) πῖθι θαρρῶν.

Νικόστρατος Πανδρόσῳ·

(Α.) κἀγώ, φιλτάτη·
μετανιπτρίδ' αὐτῷ τῆς Ὑγιείας ἔγχεον.
(Β.) λαβὲ τῆς Ὑγιείας δὴ σύ. (Α.) φέρε,
    τύχἀγαθῇ.
τύχη τὰ θνητῶν πράγμαθ', ⟨ἡ⟩ πρόνοια δὲ
τυφλόν τι κἀσύντακτόν ἐστιν, ὦ πάτερ. |

b   ἐν δὲ τῷ αὐτῷ δράματι καὶ τῆς τοῦ Ἀγαθοῦ Δαίμονος
κράσεως μνημονεύει, ἧς καὶ σχεδὸν πάντες οἱ τῆς
ἀρχαίας κωμῳδίας ποιηταί. ἀλλ' ὅ γε Νικόστρατος
οὕτως φησίν·

ἀλλ' ἐγχέασα θᾶττον Ἀγαθοῦ Δαίμονος
ἀπενεγκάτω μοι τὴν τράπεζαν ἐκποδών·
ἱκανῶς κεχόρτασμαι γάρ. Ἀγαθοῦ Δαίμονος
δέχομαι. λαβοῦσ' ἀπένεγκε ταύτην ἐκποδών.

Ξέναρχος ἐν Διδύμοις·

> (A.) But pour him
> this cup dedicated to Zeus the Savior, who's
> far and away the most useful god for mortals.
> (B.) Zeus the Savior won't do me any good
> if I explode! (A.) Don't worry about that; have a
>   drink!

Nicostratus in *Pandrosus* (fr. 18):

> (A.) Me too, dearie.
> Pour him an after-washing cup dedicated to
>   Hygieia![211]
> (B.) You take some Hygieia! (A.) Alright—here's to
>   good luck!
> Mortal existence is just luck, and foresight's
> something blind and disorganized, pops!

In the same play he also refers to the bowl mixed in honor of the Good Divinity, as do nearly all the Old Comic poets. Nicostratus (fr. 19), at any rate, says the following:

> But have her hurry up and pour me some that's
>   dedicated to the Good Divinity
> and then get the table out of my way!
> Because I'm completely stuffed. I accept the cup
>   dedicated to
> the Good Divinity. Take this (table) and get it out of
>   the way!

Xenarchus in *Twins* (fr. 2):

---

[211] An identical verse is cited in isolation at 11.487b but is attributed there to Nicostratus' *The Female Rival in Love* (fr. 3) rather than to his *Pandrosus*.

ὡς ὑπό τι νυστάζειν γε καὐτὸς ἄρχομαι· |

c   ἢ τἀγαθοῦ ⟨γὰρ⟩ Δαίμονος συνέσεισέ με
   ἄκρατος ἐκποθεῖσα φιάλη παντελῶς.
   ἢ τοῦ δὲ Σωτῆρος Διὸς τάχιστά γε
   ἀπώλεσε ναύτην καὶ κατεπόντωσέν μ', ὁρᾷς.

Ἔριφος Μελιβοίᾳ·

   ἐκπεπήδηκας πρὶν Ἀγαθοῦ πρῶτα Δαίμονος
      λαβεῖν,
   πρὶν Διὸς Σωτῆρος.

Θεόφραστος δ' ἐν τῷ Περὶ Μέθης, τὸν ἄκρατον,
φησίν, οἶνον τὸν ἐπὶ τῷ δείπνῳ διδόμενον, ὃν δὴ
d λέγουσιν | Ἀγαθοῦ Δαίμονος εἶναι πρόποσιν, ὀλίγον
τε προσφέρουσιν, ὥσπερ ἀναμιμνήσκοντες μόνον τῇ
γεύσει τὴν ἰσχὺν αὐτοῦ καὶ τὴν τοῦ θεοῦ δωρεάν, καὶ
μετὰ τὴν πλήρωσιν διδόασιν, ὅπως ἐλάχιστον ᾖ τὸ
πινόμενον· καὶ τρίτον προσκυνήσαντες λαμβάνουσιν
ἀπὸ τῆς τραπέζης, ὥσπερ[65] ἱκετείαν τινὰ ποιούμενοι
τοῦ θεοῦ μηθὲν ἀσχημονεῖν μηδ' ἔχειν ἰσχυρὰν ἐπιθυ-
μίαν τοῦ πότου τούτου καὶ λαμβάνειν ἐξ αὐτοῦ τὰ
καλὰ καὶ χρήσιμα. Φιλόχορος δ' ἐν δευτέρῳ Ἀτθίδος,
e καὶ θέσμιον, φησίν, ἐτέθη τότε προσφέρεσθαι | μετὰ
τὰ σιτία πᾶσιν ἀκράτου μὲν ὅσον γεῦμα καὶ δεῖγμα
τῆς δυνάμεως τοῦ Ἀγαθοῦ Θεοῦ, τὸν δὲ λοιπὸν ἤδη

---

[65] καὶ ὥσπερ A: ὥσπερ tantum CE: καὶ del. Meineke

I'm also starting to nod off a bit myself!
Since the bowl of unmixed wine dedicated to
the Good Divinity totally staggered me when I
    emptied it,
while the one dedicated to Zeus the Savior abruptly
wrecked and drowned me as I was sailing along, you
    see.

Eriphus in *Meliboea* (fr. 4):

You raced off before you got a bowl dedicated to the
    Good Divinity,
or to Zeus the Savior.

Theophrastus says in his *On Drunkenness* (fr. 572 Fortenbaugh): As for the unmixed wine offered after dinner, which they identify as a toast in honor of the Good Divinity, they consume only a little, as if the taste was merely a reminder to them of how strong it is and of the god's generosity; and they offer it once everyone is already full, so that as little as possible of it will be drunk. After they show their respects to him three times, they remove it from the table, as if they were begging the god to guarantee that they engage in no ugly behavior and that they feel no overwhelming desire to drink this, but receive only what is good and beneficial from him. Philochorus says in Book II of the *History of Attica* (*FGrH* 328 F 5a):[212] At that point a custom was established that, after they ate, just enough unmixed wine was distributed to everyone to give them a taste of it and to put the Good Divinity's power on display,

---

[212] A more extended version of the passage is preserved at 2.38c–d, where see n.

κεκραμένον· διὸ καὶ τροφοὺς τοῦ Διονύσου τὰς νύμ-
φας ὀνομασθῆναι. ὅτι δὲ δοθείσης τῆς τοῦ Ἀγαθοῦ
Δαίμονος κράσεως ἔθος ἦν βαστάζεσθαι τὰς τρα-
πέζας ἔδειξεν διὰ τῆς αὐτοῦ ἀσεβείας ὁ Σικελιώτης
Διονύσιος· τῷ γὰρ Ἀσκληπιῷ ἐν ταῖς Συρακούσαις
ἀνακειμένης τραπέζης χρυσῆς προπιὼν αὐτῷ ἄκρατον
Ἀγαθοῦ Δαίμονος ἐκέλευσεν βασταχθῆναι τὴν τρά-
f   πεζαν. παρὰ δὲ τοῖς Ἐμεσηνοῖς | θύοντες τῷ Ἡλίῳ, ὥς
φησι Φύλαρχος ἐν τῇ δωδεκάτῃ τῶν Ἱστοριῶν, μέλι
σπένδουσιν, οἶνον οὐ φέροντες τοῖς βωμοῖς, δεῖν λέγοντες τὸν τὰ ὅλα συνέχοντα καὶ διακρατοῦντα θεὸν
καὶ ἀεὶ περιπολεύοντα τὸν κόσμον ἀλλότριον εἶναι
μέθης.

Ἐμέμνηντο δ' οἱ πολλοὶ καὶ τῶν Ἀττικῶν ἐκείνων
σκολίων· ἅπερ καὶ αὐτὰ ἄξιόν ἐστί σοι ἀπομνημο-
νεῦσαι διά τε τὴν ἀρχαιότητα καὶ ἀφέλειαν τῶν ποιησάντων, ἐπαινουμένων[66] ἐπὶ τῇ ἰδέᾳ ταύτῃ τῆς ποιητι-
κῆς Ἀλκαίου τε καὶ Ἀνακρέοντος, ὡς Ἀριστοφάνης
694   παρίστησιν ἐν Δαιταλεῦσιν ‖ λέγων οὕτως·

ᾆσον δή μοι σκόλιόν τι λαβὼν Ἀλκαίου
κἀνακρέοντος.

καὶ Πράξιλλα δ' ἡ Σικυωνία ἐθαυμάζετο ἐπὶ τῇ τῶν
σκολίων ποιήσει. σκόλια δὲ καλοῦνται οὐ κατὰ τὸν
τῆς μελοποιίας τρόπον ὅτι σκολιὸς ἦν (λέγουσιν γὰρ

---

[66] καὶ τῶν ἐπαινουμένων A: καὶ τῶν del. Kaibel

and after that they drank it mixed. This is why the nymphs are referred to as Dionysus' nurses. Dionysius of Sicily[213] made it clear through his own impiety that the normal practice was for the tables to be removed after the wine mixed in honor of the Good Divinity had been distributed. For there was a gold cult-table dedicated to Asclepius in Syracuse, and after Dionysius drank a toast of unmixed wine dedicated to the Good Divinity in Asclepius' honor, he ordered that the table be taken away.[214] When they sacrifice to the Sun in Emesa, according to Phylarchus in Book XII of his *History* (*FGrH* 81 F 25), they pour libations of honey, but they bring no wine to the altars, since they say that the god who maintains and governs the universe, and who travels constantly from one end of the world to the other, has nothing to do with drunkenness.

Many of the guests also referred to the well-known Attic skolia; these deserve to be cited for you, both because of their antiquity and because of the simplicity of the men who composed them, given that Alcaeus and Anacreon were both praised for this style of poetry, as Aristophanes establishes in *Banqueters* (fr. 235), where he says the following:

Take this and sing me a skolion by Alcaeus or
    Anacreon!

Praxilla of Sicyon was also regarded highly for the skolia she composed.[215] They are not referred to as skolia because the songs were composed in a *skolios* ("crooked")

213 I.e. Dionysius I, tyrant of Syracuse from the late 400s to 367 BCE. A similar anecdote is preserved at Ael. *VH* 1.20.
214 Sc. to his own house.   215 Cf. *PMG* 749–50.

τὰ ἐν ταῖς ἀνειμέναις εἶναι σκολιά), ἀλλὰ τριῶν γενῶν
ὄντων, ὥς φησιν Ἀρτέμων ὁ Κασσανδρεὺς ἐν δευτέρῳ
Βιβλίων Χρήσεως, ἐν οἷς τὰ περὶ τὰς συνουσίας ἦν
ᾀδόμενα, ὧν τὸ μὲν πρῶτον ἦν ὃ δὴ πάντας ᾄδειν
νόμος ἦν, τὸ δὲ δεύτερον ὃ δὴ πάντες μὲν ᾖδον, οὐ μὴν
b   ἀλλά γε | κατά τινα περίοδον ἐξ ὑποδοχῆς, ⟨τὸ⟩[67]
τρίτον δὲ καὶ τὴν ἐπὶ πᾶσι τάξιν ἔχον, οὗ μετεῖχον
οὐκέτι πάντες, ἀλλ' οἱ συνετοὶ δοκοῦντες εἶναι μόνοι,
καὶ κατὰ τόπον τινὰ εἰ τύχοιεν ὄντες· διόπερ ὡς
ἀταξίαν τινὰ μόνον παρὰ τἆλλα ἔχον τὸ μήθ' ἅμα
μήθ' ἑξῆς γινόμενον, ἀλλ' ὅπου ἔτυχον εἶναι σκόλιον
ἐκλήθη. τὸ δὲ τοιοῦτον ᾔδετο ὁπότε τὰ κοινὰ καὶ πᾶσιν
ἀναγκαῖα τέλος λάβοι· ἐνταῦθα γὰρ ἤδη τῶν σοφῶν
ἕκαστον ᾠδήν τινα καλὴν εἰς μέσον ἠξίουν προφέρειν,
c   καλὴν δὲ ταύτην ἐνόμιζον τὴν παραίνεσίν | τέ τινα καὶ
γνώμην ἔχειν δοκοῦσαν χρησίμην[68] εἰς τὸν βίον. τῶν
οὖν δειπνοσοφιστῶν ὁ μέν τις ἔλεγε τῶν σκολίων
τόδε, ὁ δέ τις τόδε· πάντα δ' ἦν τὰ λεχθέντα ταῦτα·

Παλλὰς Τριτογένει' ἄνασσ' Ἀθηνᾶ,
ὄρθου τήνδε πόλιν τε καὶ πολίτας,
ἄτερ ἀλγέων καὶ στάσεων
καὶ θανάτων ἀώρων, σύ τε καὶ πατήρ.

[67] add. Kaibel   [68] χρησίμην τε A: ἔχουσαν τῷ βίῳ
χρησίμην tantum CE: τε del. Kaibel

[216] Cf. Dicaearch. fr. 88 Wehrli = fr. 89 Mirhady; Plu. Mor.
615b–c.

lyric style, since people call songs that use a particularly free meter "crooked." Instead, according to Artemon of Cassandreia in Book II of *On the Use of Books* (fr. 10, *FHG* iv.342), the various songs performed at parties belong to three categories.[216] The first was the type that everyone customarily sang; the second was the type that everyone sang, not (in a group), however, but in rotation, one after another; and the third type came after all the others, and not everyone participated at this point, but only those regarded as intelligent, regardless of where they happened to be sitting. This is why, since singing neither all together nor in a fixed sequence, but simply wherever they happened to be located, involved a certain amount of disorder—although only in comparison to the other categories—this type was referred to as a skolion. Songs of this sort were sung when those in which everyone participated and that were obligatory were over; for they thought it appropriate that everyone wise offer the entire group a beautiful song at this point, and they regarded a beautiful song as one that contained some advice or wisdom that seemed likely to be useful in human life. Individual members of the group of learned banqueters recited different skolia; what follows is a complete collection of all those that were sung.[217]

Pallas, Tritogeneia, Queen Athena—
guide this city and its citizens,
you and your father, and allow no griefs
or internal divisions or untimely deaths! (*PMG* 884)

[217] For other skolia, see 11.783e (= *PMG* 913); 14.625c (= *PMG* 910).

Πλούτου μητέρ᾽ Ὀλυμπίαν ἀείδω
Δήμητρα στεφανηφόροις ἐν ὥραις
σέ τε παῖ Διὸς Φερσεφόνη·
χαίρετον, εὖ δὲ τάνδ᾽ ἀμφέπετον πόλιν.

d   ἐν Δήλῳ ποτ᾽ | ἔτικτε τέκνα Λατώ,
Φοῖβον χρυσοκόμαν ἄνακτ᾽ Ἀπόλλω
ἐλαφηβόλον τ᾽ ἀγροτέραν
Ἄρτεμιν, ἃ γυναικῶν μέγ᾽ ἔχει κράτος.

ὦ Πὰν Ἀρκαδίας μεδέων κλεεννᾶς,
ὀρχηστὰ Βρομίαις ὀπαδὲ νύμφαις,
γελάσειας, ὦ Πάν, ἐπ᾽ ἐμαῖς
† εὐφροσύναις ταῖσδ᾽ ἀοιδαῖς αοιδε †
    κεχαρημένος.

ἐνικήσαμεν ὡς ἐβουλόμεσθα
καὶ νίκην ἔδοσαν θεοὶ φέροντες
παρὰ Πανδρόσου † ὡς φίλην Ἀθηνᾶν †.

        *   *   *

εἶθ᾽ ἐξῆν ὁποῖός τις ἦν ἕκαστος
τὸ στῆθος διελόντ᾽, ἔπειτα τὸν νοῦν

---

218 Demeter's daughter, more often referred to as Persephone.

219 The worship of Pan was instituted in Attica after he appeared to the runner Pheidippides, just before the Battle of Mara-
thon (Hdt. 6.105; *APl.* 232 = "Simon." *FGE* 700–1; *APl.* 239), and
this skolion and the one that follow are presumably connected
with the decisive Athenian victory over the Persians there.

I sing of the Olympian mother of Wealth,
Demeter, in the seasons when garlands are worn,
and of you, Phersephone,[218] child of Zeus.
Hail to you both! Keep careful watch over this city!
  (*PMG* 885)

On Delos once upon a time Leto bore children:
Lord Phoebus Apollo of the golden hair
and the deer-shooting huntress
Artemis, who exercises great power over women.
  (*PMG* 886)

O Pan, ruler of famous Arcadia,
dancer and companion of Bacchic nymphs—
may you smile, Pan, and take pleasure
in my † festivities these songs [corrupt]! †
  (*PMG* 887)[219]

We were triumphant, as we wished to be,
and the gods granted us victory, fetching it
from Pandrosus † to beloved Athena †[220]

        *   *   * (*PMG* 888)

If only it were possible (to learn) what everyone is
    like
by opening his chest, examining

---

[220] "to beloved Athena" is perhaps a corrupt remnant of an ancient marginal comment on the song (originally "[Pandrosus is mentioned] since she was Athena's friend" *vel sim.*). Pandrosus was a daughter of the mythical Athenian king Cecrops and was entrusted with caring for the infant Erichthonius.

e   ἐσιδόντα, κλείσαντα | πάλιν,
  ἄνδρα φίλον νομίζειν ἀδόλῳ φρενί.

  ὑγιαίνειν μὲν ἄριστον ἀνδρὶ θνητῷ,
  δεύτερον δὲ καλὸν φυὰν γενέσθαι,
  τὸ τρίτον δὲ πλουτεῖν ἀδόλως,
  καὶ τὸ τέταρτον ἡβᾶν μετὰ τῶν φίλων.

ὁσθέντος δὲ τούτου καὶ πάντων ἡσθέντων ἐπ' αὐτῷ καὶ
μνημονευσάντων ὅτι καὶ ὁ καλὸς Πλάτων αὐτοῦ
μέμνηται ὡς ἄριστα εἰρημένου, ὁ Μυρτίλος ἔφη
Ἀναξανδρίδην αὐτὸ διακεχλευακέναι τὸν κωμῳδιο-
ποιὸν ἐν Θησαυρῷ λέγοντα οὕτως·

  ὁ τὸ σκόλιον εὑρὼν ἐκεῖνος, ὅστις ἦν, |
f   τὸ μὲν ὑγιαίνειν πρῶτον ὡς ἄριστον ὂν
  ὠνόμασεν ὀρθῶς· δεύτερον δ' εἶναι καλόν,
  τρίτον δὲ πλουτεῖν, τοῦθ', ὁρᾷς, ἐμαίνετο.
  μετὰ τὴν ὑγίειαν γὰρ τὸ πλουτεῖν διαφέρει·
  καλὸς δὲ πεινῶν ἐστιν αἰσχρὸν θηρίον. ||

695   ἑξῆς δ' ἐλέχθη καὶ τάδε·

    ἐκ γῆς χρὴ κατίδην πλόον,
  εἴ τις δύναιτο καὶ παλάμην ἔχοι.
  ἐπεὶ δέ κ' ἐν πόντῳ γένηται,
  τῷ παρεόντι τρέχειν ἀνάγκη.

his mind, and closing him up again,
so as to regard as a friend the man whose mind
    conceals no treachery. (*PMG* 889)

What is best for a mortal man is to be healthy;
second is to be good-looking;
third is to be rich without having cheated anyone;
and fourth is to be young and have friends.
    (*PMG* 890)

After this song had been sung, and everyone had enjoyed it and noted that the noble Plato (cf. *Grg.* 451e) refers to it as particularly well-put, Myrtilus observed that the comic poet Anaxandrides in *The Treasure* (fr. 18) makes fun of it, saying the following:

Whoever the guy was that came up with the skolion,
he got it right when he mentioned being healthy first,
as what's best. But as for how good looks are number
    two,
and being rich is number three—that, you have to
    admit, was crazy!
Because after good health, being rich is what matters;
a handsome man who's hungry is an ugly creature.

Immediately after this, the following additional skolia were recited:

        You should think carefully about your
            voyage while you're still on land,
if you can and you're cunning.
Once you're at sea,
you have to run with whatever wind appears.
    (*PMG* 891)

ὁ δὲ καρκίνος ὧδ' ἔφα
χαλᾷ τὸν ὄφιν λαβών·
"εὐθὺν χρὴ τὸν ἑταῖρον ἔμ-
μεν καὶ μὴ σκολιὰ φρονεῖν."

ἐν μύρτου κλαδὶ τὸ ξίφος φορήσω,
ὥσπερ Ἁρμόδιος καὶ Ἀριστογείτων
ὅτε τὸν τύραννον κτανέτην |
b   ἰσονόμους τ' Ἀθήνας ἐποιησάτην.

φίλταθ' Ἁρμόδι', οὔ τί πω τέθνηκας,
νήσοις δ' ἐν μακάρων σέ φασιν εἶναι,
ἵνα περ ποδώκης Ἀχιλεύς,
Τυδεΐδην τέ † φασι τὸν ἐσθλὸν † Διομήδεα.

ἐν μύρτου κλαδὶ τὸ ξίφος φορήσω,
ὥσπερ Ἁρμόδιος καὶ Ἀριστογείτων
ὅτ' Ἀθηναίης ἐν θυσίαις
ἄνδρα τύραννον Ἵππαρχον ἐκαινέτην.

αἰεὶ σφῷν κλέος ἔσσεται κατ' αἶαν,
φίλταθ' Ἁρμόδιε καὶ Ἀριστόγειτον,
ὅτι τὸν τύραννον κτάνετον
ἰσονόμους τ' Ἀθήνας ἐποιήσατον.

---

221 Cf. Aes. *fab*. 196, in which a crab—normally itself a prover-
bially "crooked" creature (Ar. *Pax* 1083 with Olson ad loc.)—at-
tempts to deal fairly with a treacherous snake but is ultimately reduced to seizing the snake in his claws and killing it, making it at
last stretch out "straight."

Thus spoke the crab,
as he held the snake in his claw:
"A friend ought to be straightforward
   and not have crooked thoughts."[221] (*PMG* 892)

I will bear my sword in a myrtle branch,
like Harmodius and Aristogiton
when the two of them killed the tyrant
and made Athens a place of political equality.[222]
   (*PMG* 893)

Beloved Harmodius, you are not dead at all;
instead, they say you are in the Isles of the Blessed,
where swift-footed Achilleus is,
and Tydeus' son † they say the noble † Diomedes.
   (*PMG* 894)

I will bear my sword in a myrtle branch,
like Harmodius and Aristogiton
when at a sacrifice in honor of Athena
the two of them killed the tyrant Hipparchus.
   (*PMG* 895)

The story of you two will always survive in our land,
beloved Harmodius and Aristogiton,
how the two of you killed the tyrant
and made Athens a place of political equality.
   (*PMG* 896)

---

[222] A reference to the assassination of the tyrant Hipparchus (*PAA* 537615) in 514 BCE. The democracy was not in fact established until 507, and the murder of Hipparchus merely led to a political crackdown by his older brother Hippias. Aristogiton is *PAA* 168195; Harmodius is *PAA* 203425.

c   Ἀδμήτου λόγον, ὦ ἑταῖρε, | μαθὼν τοὺς ἀγαθοὺς
         φίλει,
     τῶν δειλῶν δ᾽ ἀπέχου γνοὺς ὅτι δειλοῖς ὀλίγη
         χάρις.

     παῖ Τελαμῶνος, Αἶαν αἰχμητά, λέγουσί σε
     ἐς Τροίαν ἄριστον ἐλθεῖν Δαναῶν μετ᾽ Ἀχιλλέα.

     τὸν Τελαμῶνα πρῶτον, Αἴαντα δὲ δεύτερον
     ἐς Τροΐαν λέγουσιν ἐλθεῖν Δαναῶν μετ᾽ Ἀχιλλέα.

     εἴθε λύρα καλὴ γενοίμην ἐλεφαντίνη
     καί με καλοὶ παῖδες φέροιεν Διονύσιον ἐς χορόν.

     εἴθ᾽ ἄπυρον καλὸν γενοίμην μέγα χρυσίον |
d   καί με καλὴ γυνὴ φοροίη καθαρὸν θεμένη νόον.

     σύν μοι πῖνε, συνήβα, συνέρα, συστεφανηφόρει,
     σύν μοι μαινομένῳ μαίνεο, σὺν σώφρονι
         σωφρόνει.

     ὑπὸ παντὶ λίθῳ σκορπίος, ὦ ἑταῖρ᾽, ὑποδύεται.
     φράζευ μή σε βάλῃ· τῷ δ᾽ ἀφανεῖ πᾶς ἕπεται
         δόλος. |

---

223 Given the Attic context of almost all these skolia, this must
be a reference to the time Admetus spent in exile in his old age in
Athens with Theseus (ΣVΓ Ar. V. 1238).

Grasp Admetus' meaning,[223] my friend, and associate
  with brave men,
but stay away from cowards, recognizing that cowards
  rarely return favors. (*PMG* 897)

Child of Telamon, Ajax the spearsman—they say that,
  after Achilleus,
you were the best of the Danaans who went to Troy.
  (*PMG* 898)

They say that, after Achilleus, Telamon ranked
  first,[224]
Ajax second of the Danaans who went to Troy.
  (*PMG* 899)

If only I could be a beautiful ivory lyre,
and beautiful boys could carry me in a chorus
  honoring Dionysus. (*PMG* 900)

If only I could be a large, beautiful nugget of gold,
and a beautiful woman with a pure mind could wear
  me. (*PMG* 901)

Drink with me; be young with me; love with me;
  wear garlands with me!
Be crazy with me when I am crazy, and calm with me
  when I am calm! (*PMG* 902)

A scorpion lurks, my friend, under every rock.
Watch that it doesn't sting you; treachery of all kinds
  is connected with secrecy. (*PMG* 903)[225]

---

[224] For Telamon at Troy, see 11.783c with n.
[225] Cf. Ar. *Th*. 528–30 with Austin–Olson ad loc.

e   ἁ ὗς τὰν βάλανον τὰν μὲν ἔχει, τὰν δ' ἔραται
       λαβεῖν·
    κἀγὼ παῖδα καλὴν τὴν μὲν ἔχω, τὴν δ' ἔραμαι
       λαβεῖν.

    πόρνη καὶ βαλανεὺς τωὐτὸν ἔχουσ' ἐμπεδέως
       ἔθος·
    ἐν ταὐτᾷ πυέλῳ τόν τ' ἀγαθὸν τόν τε κακὸν λόει.

    ἔγχει καὶ Κήδωνι, διάκονε, μηδ' ἐπιλήθου,
    εἰ δὴ[69] χρὴ τοῖς ἀγαθοῖς ἀνδράσιν οἰνοχοεῖν.

    αἰαῖ Λειψύδριον προδωσέταιρον,
    οἵους ἄνδρας ἀπώλεσας, μάχεσθαι
    ἀγαθούς τε καὶ εὐπατρίδας,
    οἳ τότ' ἔδειξαν οἵων πατέρων κύρησαν.[70] |

f   ὅστις ἄνδρα φίλον μὴ προδίδωσιν, μεγάλην ἔχει
    τιμὴν ἔν τε βροτοῖς ἔν τε θεοῖσιν κατ' ἐμὸν νόον.

σκόλιον δέ φασί τινες καὶ τὸ ὑπὸ Ὑβρίου τοῦ Κρητὸς
ποιηθέν. ἔχει δ' οὕτως·

---

[69] Aristotle quotes the verse (correctly) without δή.
[70] Better (with the other witnesses) ἔσαν.

---

[226] This line for some reason features Doric *alphas* rather than
the expected *êtas*.
[227] Cedon (*PAA* 566795; perhaps an Alcmaeonid) led an un-
successful revolt against the Pisistratids at some point; cf. [Arist.]
Ath. 20.5, where a slightly better version of the same skolion is
quoted.

168

The sow has one acorn, but wants to get another;[226]
I have one pretty girl, but want to get another.
   (*PMG* 904)

A whore and a bathman behave in precisely the same
    way:
they wash the good man and the bad in the same tub.
   (*PMG* 905)

Pour a cup for Cedon,[227] servant, and don't forget
    him,
   if we should in fact pour wine for brave men.
   (*PMG* 906)

Alas, treacherous Lipsydrion—
the men you killed, brave
fighters from good families,
who showed on that day the sort of fathers they
    had![228] (*PMG* 907)

Anyone who refuses to betray a friend has
    tremendous
honor among both mortals and gods, in my opinion.
   (*PMG* 908)

Some authorities also refer to the poem by Hybrias of
Crete (*PMG* 909) as a skolion. It runs as follows:

---

[228] During the final phase of the Pisistratid tyranny, after
Hipparchus had been assassinated (15.695b n.), the Alcmaeonids
went into exile and fortified Lipsydrion, on the flanks of Mt.
Parnes. They were besieged there and apparently suffered serious
losses (Hdt. 5.62.2; [Arist.] *Ath.* 19.3 with Rhodes ad loc.).

ἔστι μοι πλοῦτος μέγας δόρυ καὶ ξίφος
696   καὶ τὸ καλὸν λαισήιον, ‖ πρόβλημα χρωτός·
τούτῳ γὰρ ἀρῶ, τούτῳ θερίζω,
τούτῳ πατέω τὸν ἁδὺν οἶνον ἀπ' ἀμπέλων,
τούτῳ δεσπότας μνοΐας κέκλημαι.
τοὶ δὲ μὴ τολμῶντ' ἔχειν δόρυ καὶ ξίφος
καὶ τὸ καλὸν λαισήιον, πρόβλημα χρωτός,
πάντες γόνυ πεπτηῶτες † ἐμὸν †
⟨ . . . ⟩ κυνέοντι δεσπόταν ⟨ . . . ⟩
καὶ μέγαν βασιλῆα φωνέοντες.

Τούτων λεχθέντων ὁ Δημόκριτος ἔφη· ἀλλὰ μὴν
καὶ τὸ ὑπὸ τοῦ πολυμαθεστάτου γραφὲν Ἀριστοτέλους εἰς Ἑρμείαν τὸν Ἀταρνέα οὐ παιάν ἐστιν, ὡς ὁ
τὴν τῆς ἀσεβείας κατὰ τοῦ φιλοσόφου γραφὴν ἀπ-
b ενεγκάμενος | Δημόφιλος † εἰς αἰδῶτε † παρασκευ-
ασθεὶς ὑπ' Εὐρυμέδοντος, ὡς ἀσεβοῦντος καὶ ἄδοντος
ἐν τοῖς συσσιτίοις ὁσημέραι εἰς τὸν Ἑρμείαν παιᾶνα.
ὅτι δὲ παιᾶνος οὐδεμίαν ἔμφασιν παρέχει τὸ ᾆσμα,
ἀλλὰ τῶν σκολίων ἕν τι καὶ αὐτὸ εἶδός ἐστιν ἐξ αὐτῆς
τῆς λέξεως φανερὸν ὑμῖν ποιήσω·

Ἀρετὰ πολύμοχθε γένει βροτείῳ,
    θήραμα κάλλιστον βίῳ,

---

229 Hermeias was the uncle and adoptive father of Aristotle's
wife Pythias; he was murdered by the Persians in 341 BCE. See
D.L. 5.3–11 (also quoting the poem that follows); Bowra, *CQ* 32
(1938) 182–9 (on Aristotle's poem).

A spear and a sword represent great wealth for me,
as does my fine skin-shield, which guards my skin;
with this equipment I plow, with this I harvest grain,
with this I trample the sweet wine from the vines,
and with this I am called a master of serfs.
Those who do not dare to take up a spear and a
    sword,
or a fine skin-shield, which guards their skin,
all fall to † my † knee
. . . and prostrate themselves, calling . . .
master and great king.

After these (skolia) were recited, Democritus said: The
poem the deeply learned Aristotle (*PMG* 842) wrote in
honor of Hermeias of Atarneus,[229] on the other hand, is not
a paean, as Demophilus,[230] who brought the indictment
for impiety against the philosopher [corrupt] having been
egged on by Eurymedon, (claimed), alleging that he behaved impiously by singing a paean in Hermeias' honor
every day when they all had dinner together. I will make
it clear to you from the text itself that the song lacks any
features of a paean, but is instead a variety of skolion:

Virtue, which mortals obtain only through much hard
    work,
    finest object we pursue in life—

[230] *PAA* 320885. Eurymedon (below; *PAA* 444992) was an
Eleusinian hierophant and thus had a strong interest in the main-
tenance of religious propriety.

σᾶς πέρι, παρθένε, μορφᾶς |
c   καὶ θανεῖν ζηλωτὸς ἐν Ἑλλάδι πότμος
καὶ πόνους τλῆναι μαλερούς ἀκάμαντας·
τοῖον ἐπὶ φρένα βάλλεις
    καρπὸν ἰσαθάνατον χρυσοῦ τε κρείσσω
καὶ γονέων μαλακαυγήτοιό θ᾽ ὕπνου.
σεῦ δ᾽ ἕνεκεν ὁ δῖος
    Ἡρακλέης Λήδας τε κοῦροι
πόλλ᾽ ἀνέτλασαν ἐν ἔργοις
    σὰν † ἕποντες δύναμιν †·
d   σοῖς δὲ πόθοις Ἀχιλεὺς | Αἴ-
ας τ᾽ Ἀίδαο δόμους ἦλθον·
σᾶς δ᾽ ἕνεκεν φιλίου μορφᾶς καὶ Ἀταρνέος
ἔντροφος ἀελίου χήρωσεν αὐγάς.
τοιγὰρ ἀοίδιμος ἔργοις,
    ἀθάνατόν τέ μιν αὐξήσουσι Μοῦσαι,
Μναμοσύνας θύγατρες, Δι-
ὸς Ξενίου σέβας αὔξου-
σαι φιλίας τε γέρας βεβαίου.

e ἐγὼ μὲν οὐκ οἶδα εἴ τίς τι κατιδεῖν ἐν τούτοις | δύναται
παιανικὸν ἰδίωμα, σαφῶς ὁμολογοῦντος τοῦ γεγρα-
φότος τετελευτηκέναι τὸν Ἑρμείαν δι᾽ ὧν εἴρηκεν·

    σᾶς † γὰρ † φιλίου μορφᾶς Ἀταρνέος
    ἔντροφος ἀελίου χήρωσεν αὐγάς.

---

231 The Dioscuri, Castor and Polydeuces, who *inter alia* joined
the Argonauts on their adventures.

it is an enviable fate in Greece,
    virgin, to die for the sake of your beauty
and to endure fierce, ceaseless labors.
Such is the crop you plant in
    our minds: a crop virtually immortal, and better
        than gold,
or distinguished ancestors, or languid-eyed sleep.
For your sake the brilliant
    Heracles and Leda's sons[231]
performed many painful labors
    your † following power †;
out of longing for you, Achilleus and
    Ajax went to the house of Hades;
and for the sake of your lovely form the native
    of Atarneus left the sun's rays behind.
Certainly his deeds will be remembered in song,
    and the Muses, the daughters of Memory,
will elevate him to immortal status,
    exalting the majesty of Zeus Xenios
    and the place of honor that belongs to enduring
        friendship.

I cannot imagine how anyone could claim to detect any
distinctive characteristic of a paean in this passage, given
that the author openly admits that Hermeias is dead,[232] in
the passage where he says (*PMG* 842.15–16):[233]

    † because † of your lovely form the native
        of Atarneus left the sun's rays behind.

---

[232] Sc. "and thus cannot be a god."
[233] Quoted more accurately above.

οὐκ ἔχει δ' οὐδὲ τὸ παιανικὸν ἐπίρρημα, καθάπερ ὁ εἰς
Λύσανδρον τὸν Σπαρτιάτην γραφεὶς ὄντως παιάν, ὅν
φησι Δοῦρις ἐν τοῖς Σαμίων ἐπιγραφομένοις Ὥροις
ᾄδεσθαι ἐν Σάμῳ. παιὰν δ' ἐστὶν καὶ ὁ εἰς Κρατερὸν
τὸν Μακεδόνα γραφείς, ὃν ἐτεκτήνατο Ἀλεξῖνος ὁ
f διαλεκτικός, | φησὶν Ἕρμιππος ὁ Καλλιμάχειος ἐν τῷ
πρώτῳ Περὶ Ἀριστοτέλους· ᾄδεται δὲ καὶ οὗτος ἐν
Δελφοῖς, λυρίζοντός γέ τινος παιδός. καὶ ὁ εἰς Ἀγή-
μονα δὲ τὸν Κορίνθιον Ἀλκυόνης πατέρα, ὃν ᾄδουσιν
Κορίνθιοι, ἔχει τὸ παιανικὸν ἐπίφθεγμα· παρέθετο δ'
αὐτὸν Πολέμων ὁ περιηγητὴς ἐν τῇ Πρὸς Ἀράνθιον
Ἐπιστολῇ. καὶ ὁ εἰς Πτολεμαῖον δὲ τὸν πρῶτον Αἰγύπτου βασιλεύσαντα παιάν ἐστιν, ὃν ᾄδουσιν Ῥόδι-
697 οι· ἔχει γὰρ τὸ ἰὴ παιὰν ἐπίφθεγμα, ‖ ὥς φησιν
Γόργων ἐν τῷ Περὶ τῶν Ἐν Ῥόδῳ Θυσιῶν. ἐπ' Ἀντι-
γόνῳ δὲ καὶ Δημητρίῳ φησὶ Φιλόχορος Ἀθηναίους
ᾄδειν παιᾶνας τοὺς πεποιημένους ὑπὸ Ἑρμοκλέους[71]
τοῦ Κυζικηνοῦ, ἐφαμίλλων γενομένων τῶν παιᾶνας
ποιησάντων < . . . > καὶ τοῦ Ἑρμοκλέους προκρι-
θέντος. ἀλλὰ μὴν καὶ αὐτὸς Ἀριστοτέλης ἐν τῇ Ἀπο-
λογίᾳ τῆς Ἀσεβείας, εἰ μὴ κατέψευσται ὁ λόγος,

---

[71] Ἑρμοκλέους Schweighäuser: Ἑρμίππου ACE

---

[234] iê paian (see below).
[235] Lysander (Poralla #504; d. 395 BCE) was Sparta's greatest
military commander in the final years of the Peloponnesian War
and the period that followed. The beginning of the paean in his
honor is quoted at Plu. *Lys.* 18.3 (= *PMG* 867).

Nor does the poem have the interjection typical of paeans,[234] as the actual paean written in honor of Lysander of
Sparta,[235] which Duris in his work entitled *Samian Annals*
(*FGrH* 76 F 26) claims was sung on Samos, does. The
poem written in honor of Craterus of Macedon,[236] which
the dialectician Alexinus (*SH* 40 = *SSR* II C 15) produced,
is also a paean, according to Callimachus' student Hermippus in Book I of *On Aristotle* (fr. 48 Wehrli); this song is
sung on Delphi, and a boy plays accompaniment on a lyre.
The poem written in honor of Agemon of Corinth, the father of Alcyone,[237] which the Corinthians sing, also features the interjection typical of paeans; the travel-writer
Polemon quoted it in his *Letter to Aranthius* (fr. 76
Preller). So too the poem written in honor of the first Ptolemy to become king of Egypt,[238] which the Rhodians sing,
is a paean, since it includes the interjection *iê paian*, according to Gorgo in his *On the Sacrifices in Rhodes* (*FGrH*
515 F *19). Philochorus (*FGrH* 328 F 165) claims that the
Athenians sang the paeans composed by Hermocles of
Cyzicus (*SH* 492) in honor of Antigonus and Demetrius;[239]
the poets who produced paeans participated in a competi-
tion . . . and Hermocles won. Aristotle himself, moreover, says in his *Defense Speech against a Charge of Impiety* (fr. 645 Rose)[240]—unless the speech is a forgery: Since

---

[236] Berve i #446.

[237] Agemon and Alcyone are otherwise unknown.

[238] Ptolemy I Soter (d. 282 BCE; Berve i #668).

[239] Cf. 6.252f–3f with n.

[240] Not included in Gigon's edition of the fragments. The
charge of impiety in question is that supposedly brought by
Demophilus (15.696a–b).

φησίν· οὐ γὰρ ἄν ποτε Ἑρμείᾳ θύειν ὡς ἀθανάτῳ
προαιρούμενος ὡς θνητῷ μνῆμα κατεσκεύαζον καὶ
b ἀθανατίζειν | τὴν φύσιν βουλόμενος ἐπιταφίοις ἂν
τιμαῖς ἐκόσμησα τὸ ⟨σῶμα⟩.[72]

Τοιαῦτα λέγοντος τοῦ Δημοκρίτου ὁ Κύνουλκος
ἔφη·

τί μ᾽ ἀνέμνασας κείνων κυλίκων;,

κατὰ τὸν σὸν Φίλωνα, δέον μηδὲν τῶν σπουδῆς ἀξίων
λέγειν τι τοῦ γάστρωνος παρόντος Οὐλπιανοῦ· οὗτος
γὰρ τὰς καπυρωτέρας ᾠδὰς ἀσπάζεται μᾶλλον τῶν
ἐσπουδασμένων. οἷαί εἰσιν αἱ Λοκρικαὶ καλούμεναι,
μοιχικαί τινες τὴν φύσιν ὑπάρχουσαι, ὡς καὶ ἥδε·

ὦ τί πάσχεις; μὴ προδῷς ἄμμ᾽, ἱκετεύω·
c πρὶν καὶ μολεῖν κεῖνον, | ἀνίστω,
μὴ κακόν ⟨σε⟩ μέγα ποιήσῃ
κἀμὲ τὴν δειλάκραν.
ἀμέρα καὶ ἤδη· τὸ φῶς
διὰ τᾶς θυρίδος οὐκ εἰσορῇς;

τοιούτων γὰρ ᾀσμάτων αὐτοῦ πᾶσα πλήρης ἡ Φοι-
νίκη, ἐν ᾗ καὶ αὐτὸς περιῄει καλαμίζων μετὰ τῶν τοὺς
κολάβρους καλουμένους συντιθέντων· εἴρηται γάρ, ὦ
καλὲ Οὐλπιανέ, τοὔνομα. καὶ ὅ γε Σκήψιος Δημήτριος
ἐν τῷ δεκάτῳ τοῦ Τρωικοῦ Διακόσμου φησὶν οὕτως·
Κτησιφῶν ὁ Ἀθηναῖος ποιητὴς τῶν καλουμένων

[72] add. Kaibel

176

if I preferred to sacrifice to Hermeias as an immortal, I would never have had a tomb appropriate for a mortal constructed for him; nor, if I wanted to make him immortal, would I have honored his body with funeral rites.

As Democritus was offering remarks along these lines, Cynulcus said:

Why did you mention those cups?,

to quote your Philo (*SH* 689A); for nothing that deserves serious attention ought to be discussed in the presence of the pot-bellied Ulpian, who prefers sensuous songs to serious ones. The so-called Locrian songs,[241] which have to do with illicit sex, belong in this category, for example the following (carm. pop. *PMG* 853):

Oh—what's the matter with you? Please don't get us
     in trouble!
Get up before he comes,
or he'll do something really terrible to you
     and to poor little me.
It's already day; don't you see
     the light coming through the window?

His Phoenicia is absolutely full of songs like this, and he himself used to make the rounds there, playing a reed pipe and accompanied by the people who compose what are known as *kolabroi*; for the word is in use, my good Ulpian. Demetrius of Scepsis, for example, in Book X of his *Trojan Battle-Order* (fr. 6 Gaede) says the following: Ctesiphon of Athens,[242] who composed what are known as *kolabroi*

---

241 Cf. 14.639a (citing Clearchus).
242 Stephanis #1516; *PAA* 587575.

d κολάβρων, ὃν καὶ ὁ πρῶτος μετὰ Φιλέταιρον | ἄρξας
Περγάμου Ἄτταλος δικαστὴν καθεστάκει βασιλικῶν
τῶν περὶ τὴν Αἰολίδα. ὁ δ᾽ αὐτὸς οὗτος συγγραφεὺς
κἂν τῷ ἐννεακαιδεκάτῳ τῆς αὐτῆς πραγματείας Μνη-
σιπτολέμου φησί ποτε τοῦ ἱστοριογράφου τοῦ παρὰ
Ἀντιόχῳ τῷ προσαγορευθέντι Μεγάλῳ πλεῖστον
ἰσχύσαντος υἱὸν γενέσθαι Σέλευκον τὸν τῶν ἱλαρῶν
ᾀσμάτων ποιητήν· οὗπερ συνεχῶς ᾄδειν εἰώθασιν·

κἀγὼ παιδοφιλήσω· πολύ μοι κάλλιον ἢ γαμεῖν· |
e   παῖς μὲν γὰρ παρεὼν κἢν πολέμῳ μᾶλλον
ἐπωφελεῖ.

Καὶ μετὰ ταῦτα ἀποβλέψας εἰς αὐτὸν ἔφη· ἀλλ᾽
ἐπειδή μοι ὀργίζῃ, ἔρχομαί σοι λέξων τὸν συρβηνέων
χορὸν ὅστις ἐστί. καὶ ὁ Οὐλπιανός, οἴει γάρ, ἔφη,
κάθαρμα, θυμοῦσθαί με ἐφ᾽ οἷς εἴρηκας ἢ κἀπ᾽ ὀλίγον
σου πεφροντικέναι,

< . . . > κύον ἀδδεές;

ἀλλ᾽ ἐπεὶ διδάσκειν μέ τι ἐπαγγέλλῃ, σπονδάς σοι
ποιοῦμαι οὐ τριακοντούτιδας ἀλλ᾽ ἑκατοντούτιδας. σὺ
δὲ μόνον δίδασκε τίς ὁ συρβηνέων χορός. <καὶ ὅς·>[73]
f   Κλέαρχος, | ὦ λῷστε, ἐν δευτέρῳ Περὶ Παιδείας οὕτω-

---

[73] add. Schweighäuser

[243] Attalus I Soter (reigned 241–197 BCE); his great-grandfa-
ther, grandfather, father, and son were all also named Attalus.

(*SSH* 369A) and was made a judge in charge of the royal territory around Aeolis by the first Attalus to rule Pergamum after Philetaerus.[243] This same author in Book XIX of the same work (fr. 13 Gaede) reports that the historian Mnesiptolemus (*FGrH* 164 T 1), who at one point had considerable influence with the Antiochus known as "the Great,"[244] had a son named Seleucus[245] who wrote amusing songs. They routinely sang the following song by him (p. 176 Powell):

> And I'll love a boy. That's much better, in my opinion,
>   than getting married;
> because if a boy's around, he's more useful in war.

After this, (Cynulcus) glanced at (Ulpian) and said: Well, since you are angry with me anyway, I am going to tell you what your chorus of *surbênes* is.[246] Ulpian responded: Do you think, you scum, that I am upset about what you said, or that I feel the slightest concern about you,

> you fearless dog?[247] (cf. *Il.* 21.481)

But since you claim that you can teach me something, I offer you a truce not just for 30 years but for 100;[248] all I ask is that you instruct me as to what a chorus of *surbênes* is. And (Cynulcus) replied: Clearchus, best of men, in Book II of

---

[244] Antiochus III (reigned 222–187 BCE).

[245] Stephanis #2248.   [246] Cf. 15.669b with n., 671c.

[247] Punning on the fact that Cynulcus is a Cynic (literally "doglike one").

[248] 30 years (i.e. a full generation) was the standard term for truces among Greek states in the classical period; cf. Ar. *Ach.* 194–5 with Olson ad loc.

σί φησιν· λείπεται τίς ὁ συρβηνέων χορός, ὧν ἕκαστος τὸ δοκοῦν ἑαυτῷ † κατασαιδεῖ †, προσέχων οὐδὲν
τῷ προκαθημένῳ καὶ διδάσκοντι τὸν χορόν, ἀλλ'
αὐτὸς πολὺ τούτων ἀτακτότερός ἐστιν θεατής. καὶ
κατὰ τὸν παρῳδὸν Μάτρωνα·

> οἱ μὲν γὰρ δὴ πάντες, ὅσοι πάρος ἦσαν ἄριστοι,
> Εὔβοιός τε καὶ Ἑρμογένης δῖοί τε Φίλιπποι,
> οἱ μὲν δὴ τεθνᾶσι καὶ εἰν Ἀΐδαο δόμοισιν· ‖
698 ἔστι δέ τις Κλεόνικος, ὃν ἀθάνατον λάχε γῆρυν,
> οὔτε ποιητάων ἀδαήμων οὔτε θεάτρων,
> ᾧ καὶ τεθνειῶτι λαλεῖν πόρε Φερσεφόνεια.

σὺ δὲ καὶ ζῶν, καλὲ Οὐλπιανέ, πάντα μὲν ζητεῖς,
λέγεις δὲ οὐδὲ ἕν. καὶ ὅς, τίς ἡδέως, ἔφη, τῶν ἐπῶν
< . . . >, ὦ καλέ μου ἑταῖρε, ἕως ἔτι ἐμμένομεν ταῖς
σπονδαῖς; καὶ ὁ Κύνουλκος· πολλοί τινες παρῳδιῶν
ποιηταὶ γεγόνασιν, ὦ ἑταῖρε· ἐνδοξότατος δ' ἦν Εὔβοιος ὁ Πάριος, γενόμενος τοῖς χρόνοις κατὰ Φίλιπ-
πον. οὗτός ἐστιν ὁ καὶ Ἀθηναίοις λοιδορησάμενος, |
b καὶ σῴζεται αὐτοῦ τῶν Παρῳδιῶν βιβλία τέσσαρα.
μνημονεύει δ' αὐτοῦ Τίμων ἐν τῷ πρώτῳ τῶν Σίλλων.
Πολέμων δ' ἐν τῷ δωδεκάτῳ τῶν Πρὸς Τίμαιον περὶ
τῶν τὰς παρῳδίας γεγραφότων ἱστορῶν τάδε γράφει·
καὶ τὸν Βοιωτὸν δὲ καὶ τὸν Εὔβοιον τοὺς τὰς παρῳδίας γράψαντας λογίους ἂν φήσαιμι διὰ τὸ παίζειν
ἀμφιδεξίως καὶ τῶν προγενεστέρων ποιητῶν ὑπερ-

On Education (fr. 15 Wehrli) says the following: What remains is the question of the identity of the chorus of *surbênes*, each of whom [corrupt] whatever he likes and pays no attention to the man who directs and trains the chorus, but is a far more disorderly audience than they are. To quote the parodist Matro (fr. 7 Olson–Sens = *SH* 540):

> For all those who were outstanding men of old,
> Euboeus, Hermogenes, and the brilliant Philips—
> they are dead and in the house of Hades.
> But there is a certain Cleonicus, who has got an
> immortal voice,
> a man unknown neither to poets nor to audiences,
> to whom Persephone granted the ability to chatter
> even after death.

Whereas you, my noble Ulpian, raise questions of all sorts while you are alive, but offer no answers. And (Ulpian) said: Who would enjoy . . . of verses, my noble friend, while we are still maintaining our truce? Cynulcus (replied): Many poets have produced parodies, my friend. The most famous was Euboeus of Paros (*SH* 410), who was a contemporary of Philip.[249] He is the one who made nasty remarks about the Athenians, and four Books of his *Parodies* are preserved; Timo mentions him in Book I of his *Silloi* (*SH* 776). Polemon in Book XII of his *Response to Timaeus* (fr. 45 Preller), in the course of his discussion of the authors of parodies, writes the following: I would refer to both Boeotus and Euboeus, who wrote parodies, as learned men, since they make witty remarks that can be understood several ways and are better than the poets of earlier

[249] Presumably Philip II of Macedon (382–336 BCE).

ἔχειν ἐπιγεγονότας. εὑρετὴν μὲν οὖν τοῦ γένους Ἱππώ-
νακτα φατέον τὸν ἰαμβοποιόν. λέγει γὰρ οὗτος ἐν τοῖς
ἑξαμέτροις· |

c   Μοῦσά μοι Εὐρυμεδοντιάδεω τὴν ποντοχάρυβδιν,
    τὴν ἐγγαστριμάχαιραν, ὃς ἐσθίει οὐ κατὰ
      κόσμον,
    ἔννεφ', ὅπως ψηφῖδι <κακῇ> κακὸν οἶτον ὄληται
    βουλῇ δημοσίῃ παρὰ θῖν' ἁλὸς ἀτρυγέτοιο.

κέχρηται δὲ καὶ Ἐπίχαρμος ὁ Συρακόσιος ἔν τισι τῶν
δραμάτων ἐπ' ὀλίγον καὶ Κρατῖνος ὁ τῆς ἀρχαίας
κωμῳδίας ποιητὴς ἐν Εὐνείδαις καὶ τῶν κατ' αὐτὸν
Ἡγήμων ὁ Θάσιος, ὃν ἐκάλουν Φακῆν. λέγει γὰρ
οὕτως· |

d   ἐς δὲ Θάσον μ' ἐλθόντα μετεωρίζοντες ἔβαλλον
    πολλοῖσι σπελέθοισι, καὶ ὧδέ τις εἶπε παραστάς·
    "ὦ πάντων ἀνδρῶν βδελυρώτατε, τίς σ' ἀνέπεισε
    καλὴν <ἐς> κρηπῖδα ποσὶν τοιοῖσδ' ἀναβῆναι;" |
e   τοῖσι δ' ἐγὼ πᾶσιν μικρὸν μετὰ τοῦτ' ἔπος εἶπον·
    "μνῆ μ' ἀνέπεισε γέροντα καὶ οὐκ ἐθέλοντ'
      ἀναβῆναι
    καὶ σπάνις, ἣ πολλοὺς Θασίων εἰς ὁλκάδα
      βάλλει

---

250 Cratinus' floruit is c.455–423 BCE. For Hegemon's dates,
cf. 9.407a–c with nn.
251 Most of the final four verses is quoted also at 9.406e–f,
along with additional anecdotes about Hegemon (*PAA* 480870).

generations, despite coming later. It must be acknowl-
edged, of course, that the genre was invented by the iambic poet Hipponax; for he says in his hexameters (fr. 126
Degani):

Muse, as for the son of Eurymedon, the sea-
    Charybdis,
the knife in the gut, who eats in a disorderly fashion,
tell me how the wretch will die a wretched death by
    stoning
by the popular will beside the shore of the barren
    sea.

Epicharmus of Syracuse (test. 20) also uses parody in some
of his plays, to a limited extent, as do the Old Comic poet
Cratinus in *Euneidae* (test. i) and, among his contemporar-
ies,[250] Hegemon of Thasos, who was nicknamed Lentil-
Soup. Because he says the following:[251]

When I came to Thasos, they hoisted numerous
    lumps of shit
and began to pelt me with them, and one of those
    present spoke thus:
"O foulest of all men—who convinced you
to go up onto the lovely stage with feet like these?"
But I addressed this one little word to all of them:
"A *mina* of silver[252] convinced me, old and unwilling
    though I am, to go up,
along with my poverty, which drives many Thasians
    into cargo-ships,

[252] = 100 drachmas, which must have been the prize for first
place; that Hegemon came home with only 50 drachmas (below)
makes it clear that he took second place, at best.

183

εὐκούρων βδελυρῶν, ὀλλύντων τ᾽ ὀλλυμένων τε
ἀνδρῶν, οἳ νῦν κεῖθι κακῶς κακὰ ῥαψῳδοῦσιν·
οἷς καὶ ἐγὼ σιτοῖο μέγα χρηΐζων ἐπίθησα.
αὖθις δ᾽ οὐκ ἐπὶ κέρδος ἀπείσομαι, εἰς Θασίους
δὲ
μηδένα πημαίνων κλυτὸν ἄργυρον ἐγγυαλίξων,
μή τίς μοι κατὰ οἶκον Ἀχαιιάδων νεμεσήσῃ |
f   πεσσομένης ἀλόχου τὸν ἀχαϊνὸν ἄρτον ἀεικῶς,
καί ποτέ τις εἴπῃ σμικρὸν τυροῦντ᾽ ἐσιδοῦσα,
'ὡς φίλη, ὦνὴρ μὲν παρ᾽ Ἀθηναίοισιν ἀείσας
πεντήκοντ᾽ ἔλαβε δραχμάς, σὺ δὲ μικρὸν
ἐπέψω.'"
ταῦτά μοι ὁρμαίνοντι παρίστατο Παλλὰς Ἀθήνη
χρυσῆν ῥάβδον ἔχουσα καὶ ἤλασεν εἶπέ τε
φωνῇ· ‖
699   "δεινὰ παθοῦσα, Φακῆ βδελυρά, χώρει ᾽ς τὸν
ἀγῶνα."
καὶ τότε δὴ θάρσησα καὶ ἤειδον πολὺ μᾶλλον.

πεποίηκε δὲ παρῳδίας καὶ Ἕρμιππος ὁ τῆς ἀρχαίας
κωμῳδίας ποιητής. τούτων δὲ πρῶτος εἰσῆλθεν εἰς
τοὺς ἀγῶνας τοὺς θυμελικοὺς Ἡγήμων καὶ παρ᾽ Ἀθηναίοις ἐνίκησεν ἄλλαις τε παρῳδίαις καὶ τῇ Γιγαντο-
μαχίᾳ. γέγραφε δὲ καὶ κωμῳδίαν εἰς τὸν ἀρχαῖον
τρόπον, ἣν ἐπιγράφουσιν Φιλίνην. ὁ δὲ Εὔβοιος πολ-

---

253 An echo of *Il.* 4.451.
254 An echo of *Od.* 2.101 = 19.146 = 24.136.
255 *achaïnon*; cf. 3.109e–f.

well-barbered wretches, destroying and destroyed,[253]
who now do a bad job of performing bad songs there;
this is what convinced me, in my desperate need for
    food.
But I will not go away after profit again, but will hand
    over
glorious silver to the Thasians, doing no one harm,
lest one of the Achaean women in my house express
    resentment against me[254]
when my wife bakes Demeter's bread[255] too
    meagerly,
and then one of them says, seeing the tiny cheese-
    cake,
'My dear, your husband got 50 drachmas in Athens
by his singing—but you baked something small!'"
And as I was pondering these things, Pallas Athena
    stood beside me
with a gold wand in her hand, and she struck me with
    it and made a speech:
"Although you have suffered terrible things,
    wretched Lentil-Soup, enter the contest."
And then I got my courage up and sang much louder.

The Old Comic poet Hermippus (test. 7) also composed
parodies.[256] The first of these men to enter competitions
onstage was Hegemon, who took the prize in Athens with
various parodies, including with his *Gigantomachy*.[257] He
is also (test. 2) the author of a comedy in the old style; the
title given to it is *Philinê*. Euboeus makes many witty re-

---

[256] Cf. frr. 63 (quoted at 1.27e–8a); 77 (quoted at 1.29e–f).
[257] Cf. 9.407a–b.

b λὰ μὲν εἴρηκεν ἐν τοῖς ποιήμασιν χαρίεντα, | περὶ μὲν τῆς τῶν βαλανέων μάχης·

βάλλον δ' ἀλλήλους χαλκήρεσιν ἐγχείῃσιν.

περὶ δὲ τοῦ λοιδορουμένου κουρέως τῷ κεραμεῖ τῆς γυναικὸς χάριν·

μήτε σὺ τόνδ' ἀγαθός περ ἐὼν ἀποαίρεο, κουρεῦ,
μήτε σύ, Πηλεΐδη.

ὅτι δὲ ἦν τις περὶ αὐτοὺς δόξα παρὰ τοῖς Σικελιώταις Ἀλέξανδρος ὁ Αἰτωλὸς ὁ τραγῳδοδιδάσκαλος ποιήσας ἐλεγεῖον τρόπον τοῦτον δηλοῖ· |

c ὡς Ἀγαθοκλεῖος λάσιαι φρένες ἤλασαν ἔξω
    πατρίδος. ἀρχαίων ἦν ὅδ' ἀνὴρ προγόνων,
εἰδὼς ἐκ νεότητος ἀεὶ ξείνοισιν ὁμιλεῖν
    ξεῖνος, Μιμνέρμου δ' † εἰς ἔπος ἄκρον ἰὼν
παιδομανεῖ σὺν ἔρωτι ποτὴν ἶσον †· ἔγραφε δ'
      ὡνὴρ
    εὖ παρ' Ὁμηρείην ἀγλαΐην ἐπέων
πισύγγους ἢ φῶρας ἀναιδέας ἤ τινα χλούνην
    φλύοντ' ἀνθηρῇ σὺν κακοδαιμονίῃ,

---

258 = *Il.* 18.534 = *Od.* 9.55, but with a key word to be taken in a different sense than in Homer.

259 A slightly altered version of *Il.* 1.275, 277 (Nestor intervenes in the quarrel of Agamemnon and Achilleus over Briseis). For "son of Mud" (punning on the name Peleus), cf. 11.474d–e n.

260 Tyrant of Syracuse 316–289/8 BCE.

marks in his poems; about the battle of the bathmen, for example (*SH* 411):

> They hurled bronze-edged bowls at one another.[258]

And about the barber who called the potter names on account of the woman (*SH* 412):

> Neither do you, brave man though you are, rob this fellow, barber,
> nor do you, son of Mud . . .[259]

That these authors had a reputation of some sort in Sicily is made clear by the tragic poet Alexander Aetolus, who produced an elegy along the following lines (fr. 5, p. 125 Powell):

> when Agathocles'[260] coarse mind drove (him)
>   out of
> his native land. This man traced his ancestry far
>   back,
> and even as a youth he always understood how to
>   behave as a stranger
> among strangers, and Mimnermus' † to the
>   extreme word going
> with a mad lust for boys balanced flight. † The man
>   used to write,
> in a lovely parody of the Homeric splendor of epic
>   verses,
> about shoemakers, or shameless thieves, or some
>   other robber
> babbling with flowery baseness,

οἷα Συρηκόσιος, καὶ ἔχων χάριν· ὃς δὲ Βοιωτοῦ
ἔκλυεν, Εὐβοίῳ τέρψεται οὐδ' ὀλίγον. |

d   Πολλῶν οὖν ἑκάστοτε τοιούτων λεγομένων, ἐπεί
ποτε ἑσπέρα κατελάμβανεν ἡμᾶς, ὁ μέν τις ἔλεγεν,
παῖ, λυχνεῖον, ὁ δὲ λυχνέα, ὁ δὲ λοφνίδα, οὕτω καλεῖσθαι φάσκων τὴν ἐκ τοῦ φλοιοῦ λαμπάδα, ὁ δὲ πανόν,
ἄλλος δὲ φανόν, ὁ δὲ λυχνοῦχον, ὁ δὲ λύχνον, καὶ
δίμυξον δὲ λύχνον ἕτερος, ἄλλος δὲ ἑλάνην, ὁ δέ τις
ἑλάνας, τὰς λαμπάδας οὕτω φάσκων καλεῖσθαι παρὰ
τὴν ἕλην· οὕτω δ' εἰπεῖν Νεάνθην ἐν πρώτῃ τῶν Περὶ
Ἄτταλον Ἱστοριῶν· καὶ ἄλλος ὅ τι δή ποτε, ὡς τάρα-
e χον γίνεσθαι οὐ τὸν τυχόντα τῶν | ἐπὶ τούτοις
πίστεων παρὰ πάντων λεγομένων. Σιληνὸν μὲν γάρ
τις τὸν γλωσσογράφον ἔφασκεν Ἀθηναίους λέγειν
τὰς λαμπάδας φανούς. Τιμαχίδας δὲ ὁ Ῥόδιος δέλε-
τρον τὸν φανὸν καλεῖσθαι, οἷον, φησίν, οἱ νυκτερευ-
όμενοι τῶν νέων ἔχουσιν, < . . . > οὓς οὗτοι ἑλάνας
καλοῦσιν.⁷⁴ Ἀμερίας δὲ γράβιον τὸν φανόν. Σέλευκος
δὲ οὕτως ἐξηγεῖται ταύτην τὴν λέξιν· γράβιόν ἐστιν

---

⁷⁴ Everything that follows from Ἀμερίας to πρίνι- (about 4½
lines of the text) is now missing from A. The damage has apparently occurred since Kaibel's time, and I give the text as he
prints it.

---

²⁶¹ Cf. 15.701a, citing Cleitarchus.
²⁶² Apparently to be understood as a variant form of *hela*/*heilê*
("the sun's heat").
²⁶³ Thus also Hsch. δ 589. The word is attested elsewhere only

as Syracusans do; and he got a good reception.
    Anyone who listened
      to Boeotus will take considerable pleasure in
      Euboeus.

We routinely discussed numerous topics similar to these, and when evening began to overtake us, one member of the group said, Slave! (Get me) a *luchneion*!, while others asked for a *luchneus*, a *lophnis* (insisting that this was the term for a torch made of bark),[261] or a *panos*, while yet others called for a *phanos*, a *luchnouchos*, or a *luchnos*, and someone else demanded a *dimuxos luchnos*, and yet another person requested a *helanê* or used the plural *helanai* (claiming that this was a term for torches derived from *helê*,[262] and that Neanthes used it in Book I of his *History Involving Attalus* [*FGrH* 171 F 1]). Other members of the group used various other terms, producing extraordinary confusion, as testimonia in support of all the words were cited from authors of all sorts. Someone claimed that the lexicographer Silenus argued that the Athenians referred to torches as *fanoi*. Whereas Timachidas of Rhodes (fr. 23 Blinkenberg) says that a torch (*phanos*) of the type young men carry when they are out at night is referred to as a *deletron*[263] . . . which these people call *helanai*. Amerias (p. 10 Hoffmann) (claims that) a torch (*phanos*) (is known as) a *grabion*.[264] Seleucus (fr. 46 Müller) glosses this word as follows: A *grabion* is a piece of holm oak or

---

at Numen. *SH* 570.2 (quoted at 7.287c); 574.1 (quoted at 7.306c) (both emendations), where it means "bait, a lure."

  264 Cf. Hsch. γ 757, where the word appears in the form *gobriai*.

τὸ πρίνινον ἢ δρύινον ξύλον, ὃ περιεθλασμένον καὶ
κατεσχισμένον ἐξάπτεσθαι καὶ φαίνειν τοῖς ὁδοιπο-
f ροῦσιν. Θεοδωρίδας γοῦν ὁ | Συρακόσιος ἐν Κενταύ-
ροις διθυράμβῳ φησίν·

πίσσα δ᾽ ἀπὸ γραβίων ἔσταζεν,

οἷον ἀπὸ <..⁴⁻⁶.. λαμ>πάδων.⁷⁵ μν<ημονεύει δὲ> γραβίων κα<ὶ Στράττις> ἐν Φοινίσσαις. ὅτι δὲ λυχνοῦχοι
οἱ νῦν καλούμενοι φανοὶ ὠνομάζοντο Ἀριστοφάνης ἐν
Αἰολοσίκωνι παρίστησιν·

καὶ διαστίλβονθ᾽ ὁρῶμεν,
ὥσπερ ἐν καινῷ λυχνούχῳ,
πάντα τῆς ἐξωμίδος.

ἐν δὲ τῷ δευτέρῳ Νιόβῳ προειπὼν λυχνοῦχον

οἴμοι κακόδαιμον (φησίν), ὁ λύχνος ἡμῖν
οἴχεται.

εἶτ᾽ ἐπιφέρει·

καὶ πῶς ὑπερβὰς τὸν λυχνοῦχον ἔλαθέ σε;

ἐν δὲ τοῖς ἑξῆς καὶ λυχνίδιον αὐτὸν καλεῖ διὰ τούτων·

⁷⁵ The material that follows (to the beginning of 700a) is omitted in Casaubon's edition and therefore lacks further section-
designations.

oak, which has had its bark stripped off and been split,[265] and which is then set alight and shows travelers their way. Theodoridas of Syracuse, for example, says in his dithyramb *Centaurs* (*SH* 739):

> Pitch was dripping from *grabia*,

which is to say, from . . . torches. Strattis in *Phoenician Women* (fr. 53) also refers to *grabia*. That what are known today as *phanoi* were called *luchnouxoi*[266] is established by Aristophanes in *Aeolosicon* (fr. 8):

> And we see them all
> shining through her dress,
> as if they were set in a new *luchnouchos*.

And in *Niobe II*[267] (fr. 290, encompassing both quotations) he first mentions a *luchnouchos*, and then says:

> Oh no! Damn! We're losing our *luchnos*!

Then he continues:

> How could you not have noticed that he'd got ahead
>   of the *luchnouchos*?

But in the section that comes next he refers to it as a *luchnidion*,[268] in the following passage (fr. 291):

---

[265] Allowing flammable material to be inserted between the pieces of wood, which were then bound together again.

[266] Properly "*luchnos*-holders," i.e. "lanterns."

[267] Presumably the play elsewhere referred to as *Dramas* or *Niobus* (e.g. 7.301b).

[268] Properly a diminutive form of *luchnos*, but clearly to be taken "lampstand" in the quotation that follows.

ἀλλ᾽ ὥσπερ λύχνος
ὁμοιότατα καθηῦδ᾽ ἐπὶ τοῦ λυχνιδίου.

Πλάτων δ᾽ ἐν Νυκτὶ Μακρᾷ·

ἕξουσιν οἱ πομπεῖς λυχνούχους δηλαδή.

Φερεκράτης Δουλοδιδασκάλῳ·

ἄνυσόν ποτ᾽ ἐξελθών, σκότος γὰρ γίγνεται,[76]
καὶ τὸν λυχνοῦχον ἔκφερ᾽ ἐνθεὶς τὸν λύχνον.

Ἄλεξις δ᾽ ἐν Κηρυττομένῳ·

ὥστ᾽ ἐξελὼν <ἐκ> τοῦ λυχνούχου τὸν λύχνον
μικροῦ κατακαύσας ἔλαθ᾽ ἑαυτόν, ὑπὸ μάλης
τῇ γαστρὶ μᾶλλον τοῦ δέοντος προσαγαγών.

Εὐμήδης δ᾽ ἐν Σφαττομένῳ προειπών·

ἡγουμένην[77] δὲ .υκνὸν εἰς τὸ πρόσθ᾽ ἰδὼν
[. . . . .]ατο . υμένιδι[. . . . .]ς,

ἐπιφέρει·

[. . . λυχνο]ύχῳ . . . κο[

Ἐπικράτης δ᾽ ἐν Τριόδοντι ἢ Ῥωποπώλῃ προειπών·

(Α.) λαβὲ τριόδοντα καὶ λυχνοῦχον,

---

[76] Everything that follows from καὶ to λυχνούχ- or so (about
4½ lines of the text) is now missing from A. The damage has apparently occurred since Kaibel's time, and I give the text as he
prints it.

But he was sleeping
just like a *luchnos* on its *luchnidion*.

Plato in *The Long Night* (fr. 91):

Our escorts will have *luchnouchoi*, obviously.

Pherecrates in *The Slave-Teacher* (fr. 44):

Hurry up and get out here; it's getting dark!
Put the *luchnos* in the *luchnouchos*, and bring it out!

Alexis in *The Man Who Was Named in a Proclamation* (fr. 107):

so that after he took the *luchnos* out of the
    luchnouchos,
he accidentally almost burned himself, by furtively
holding it closer to his belly than he should have.

Eumedes in *The Man Who Was Murdered* (fr. 1, encompassing both quotations) begins by saying:

When he saw . . . being led forward,
he [indecipherable],

and then continues:

with a [*luchno*]*uchos* . . .

Epicrates in *The Trident or The Frills-Vendor* (fr. 7, encompassing both quotations) begins by saying:

(A.) Take a trident and a *luchnouchos*,

---

77 K–A do not accent the word, noting that the letters might instead be divided ἡγοῦ μέν· ἦν ("Lead the way! If . . . "); thus Kaibel.

ἐπιφέρει·

(B.) ἐγὼ δὲ δεξιᾷ γε τόνδ᾽ ἔχω τινά,
σιδηρότευκτον ἐναλίων θηρῶν βέλος,
κερατίνου τε φωσφόρου λύχνου σέλας. ‖

700   Ἄλεξις Μίδωνι·

ὁ πρῶτος εὑρὼν μετὰ λυχνούχου περιπατεῖν
τῆς νυκτὸς ἦν τις κηδεμὼν τῶν δακτύλων.

ἐν δὲ Θεοφορήτῳ ὁ αὐτὸς Ἄλεξις·

οἶμαί γ᾽ ἐπιτιμᾶν τῶν ἀπαντώντων τινὰς
ἡμῖν, ὅτι τηνικαῦτα μεθύων περιπατῶ.
ποῖος γάρ ἐστιν φανός, ὦ πρὸς τῶν θεῶν,
τοιοῦτος οἷος ὁ γλυκύτατος ἥλιος;

Ἀναξανδρίδης δὲ ἐν Ὕβρει·

b   οὔκουν λαβὼν τὸν | φανὸν ἅψεις μοι λύχνον;

ἄλλοι δὲ ἔφασκον φανὸν λέγεσθαι τὴν λαμπάδα, οἱ δὲ
τὴν ἔκ τινων ξύλων τετμημένων δέσμην. Μένανδρος
Ἀνεψιοῖς·

ὁ φανός ἐστι μεστὸς ὕδατος οὑτοσί·
δεῖ τ᾽ οὐχὶ σείειν, ἀλλ᾽ ἀποσείειν αὐτόθεν.

Νικόστρατος ἐν Πατριώταις·

---

[269] This quotation and the one from Anaxandrides that follows
belong to the discussion of the word *phanos* below.

and then continues:

> (B.) I've got this in my right hand, whatever it is:
> an iron-forged missile intended for aquatic beasts,
> and the gleam of a light-bearing *luchnos* made of
>   horn.

Alexis in *Midon* (fr. 152):

> Whoever came up with the idea of wandering around
>   at night
> with a *luchnouchos* was concerned about his toes.

The same Alexis in *The Man Who Was Possessed by a God*
(fr. 91):[269]

> I imagine some people we meet will criticize
> me for wandering around drunk at this time of day.
> But what *phanos*, by the gods, is
> as good as the sun we love so much?

Anaxandrides in *Outrageous Behavior* (fr. 49):

> Won't you take the *phanos* and light it for me as a
>   *luchnos*?

But other members of the group claimed that a *lampas*
("torch") can be referred to as a *phanos*, while some in-
sisted that *phanos* is a term for a number of pieces of split
wood of some sort that have been bundled together. Menander in *Cousins* (fr. 60):

> This *phanos* here's full of water.
> It's not a matter of shaking it—you have to shake it
>   out!

Nicostratus in *Men from the Same Country* (fr. 22):

ὁ κάπηλος γὰρ οὐκ τῶν γειτόνων
ἄν τ᾽ οἶνον ἄν τε φανὸν ἀποδῶταί τινι
ἄν τ᾽ ὄξος, ἀπέπεμψ᾽ ὁ κατάρατος δοὺς ὕδωρ. |

c Φιλιππίδης Συμπλεούσαις·

(Α.) ὁ φανὸς ἡμῖν οὐκ ἔφαινεν οὐδὲ ἕν.
(Β.) ἔπειτα φυσᾶν δυστυχὴς οὐκ ἠδύνω;

Φερεκράτης δὲ ἐν Κραπατάλλοις τὴν νῦν λυχνίαν
καλουμένην λύχνειον κέκληκεν διὰ τούτων·

(Α.) τίς τῶν λυχνείων ἠργασία; (Β.) Τυρρηνική.

ποικίλαι γὰρ ἦσαν αἱ παρὰ τοῖς Τυρρηνοῖς ἐργασίαι,
φιλοτέχνων ὄντων τῶν Τυρρηνῶν. Ἀντιφάνης δ᾽ Ἱπ-
πεῦσι·

                  τῶν δ᾽ ἀκοντίων
συνδοῦντες ὀρθὰ τρία λυχνείῳ χρώμεθα.

d Δίφιλος δ᾽ ἐν | Ἀγνοίᾳ·

                  ἅψαντες λύχνον
λυχνεῖον ἐζητοῦμεν.

Εὐφορίων δ᾽ ἐν Ἱστορικοῖς Ὑπομνήμασιν Διονύσιόν
φησι τὸν νεώτερον Σικελίας τύραννον Ταραντίνοις εἰς
τὸ πρυτανεῖον ἀναθεῖναι λυχνεῖον δυνάμενον καίειν

---

270 Poll. 9.30 (citing fr. 17) calls the play The Woman Who
Sailed off with Others, and Meineke suggested that the actual title
might be Women Who Sailed off with Others.

Since whether the neighborhood bartender
sells someone wine, or a *phanos*,
or vinegar, the bastard gives him water and sends him
off.

Philippides in *Women in a Boat Together* (fr. 16):[270]

(A.) Our *phanos* wasn't shedding any light (*ephainen*)
at all.
(B.) So couldn't you blow on it, you fool?

Pherecrates in *Small Change* (fr. 90) uses the term *luchneion* ("lampstand") for what is known today as a *luchnia*, in the following passage:

(A.) Where were these *luchneia* made? (B.) They're
Etruscan.

A wide variety of goods were manufactured in Etruria, since the Etruscans were interested in crafts of all sorts. Antiphanes in *Knights* (fr. 109):

We tie three of our javelin-shafts
together, stand them up, and use them as a
luchneion.

Diphilus in *Ignorance* (fr. 2):

After we lit a *luchnos*,
we started looking for a *luchneion*.

Euphorion in the *Historical Commentaries* (fr. 5, *FHG* iii.72) says that the Sicilian tyrant Dionysius the Younger[271] dedicated a *luchneion* in the *prytaneion* ("town-hall") in

[271] Reigned 367–357 BCE.

τοσούτους λύχνους ὅσος ὁ τῶν ἡμερῶν ἐστιν ἀριθμὸς
εἰς τὸν ἐνιαυτόν. Ἕρμιππος δὲ ὁ κωμῳδιοποιὸς ἐν
Ἰάμβοις τὸ στρατιωτικὸν λυχνεῖον σύνθετον οὕτως
ὀνομάζει, ἐν δὲ Φορμοφόροις δράματι·

τῇδ᾽ ἐξιόντι † δεξιᾷ †, ὦ λυχνίδιον.

πανὸς δ᾽ ὀνομάζεται τὸ διακεκομμένον ξύλον καὶ |
e συνδεδεμένον· τούτῳ δ᾽ ἐχρῶντο λαμπάδι. Μένανδρος
Ἀνεψιοῖς·

                    εἰσιὼν
πανόν, λύχνον, λυχνοῦχον, ὅ τι πάρεστι· φῶς
μόνον πολὺ ποίει.

Δίφιλος Στρατιώτῃ·

ἀλλ᾽ ὁ πανὸς ὕδατός ἐστι μεστός.

πρότερος δὲ τούτων Αἰσχύλος ἐν Ἀγαμέμνονι μέμνηται τοῦ πανοῦ <καὶ Εὐριπίδης>[78] ἐν Ἴωνι. ἔλεγ<ον δὲ
τοῦτον οἱ>[79] πρὸ ἡμῶν κ<αὶ ξυλολυχνοῦ>χον,[80] οὗ
μνη<μονεύει Ἄλεξις>[81] ἐν Εἰσοικιζ<ομένῳ[82] οὕτως[83]>·

---

[78] add. Meineke   [79] suppl. Kaibel   [80] suppl. Kaibel
[81] suppl. Meineke   [82] suppl. Meineke
[83] add. Kaibel. Most of the right-hand column of the recto of
folio 381 of manuscript A is missing, as is therefore most of the
left-hand column of the verso. Kaibel was apparently able to read
more letters than can be seen today, and I print the text as he gives
it, with a few minor corrections. Each line in this section of the
text originally contained 17–20 letters.

Tarentum that could hold as many lighted *luchnoi* as there are days in the year. The comic poet Hermippus in the *Iambs* (fr. 8 West²) refers to the sort of *luchneion* soldiers use specifically as *suntheton* ("compound"), whereas in his play *Porters* (fr. 62) (he says):

> as one exits here † on the right †, my *luchnidion*.

Wood that has been cut up and then bound together is referred to as a *panos*; they used this as a torch (*lampas*). Menander in *Cousins* (fr. 59):

> Go inside (and get)
> a *panos*, or a *luchnos*, or a *luchnouchos*, or whatever's
>   available! Just
> generate a lot of light!

Diphilus in *The Soldier*²⁷² (fr. 6):

> But the *panos* is full of water!

Even earlier than these authors, Aeschylus mentions a *panos* in *Agamemnon* (284),²⁷³ as does Euripides in *Ion* (195). Our predecessors also referred to this as a *xuloluchnouchos*.²⁷⁴ Alexis in *The Man Who Was Moving In* (fr. 66) mentions one of these, as follows:

---

²⁷² For the title of the play, see 11.496f–497a with n.

²⁷³ Most of two columns of text has been lost from manuscript A at this point, leaving only a few letters in each line. Some of what has been lost can be restored from Pollux and the Epitome (below).

²⁷⁴ Literally "a wood-*luchnouchos*," i.e. "a lantern made of wood."

ὁ δὲ ξυλο[λυχνοῦχος . . .
πυρὸς[. . .

υἰ[
χ[
ο[
κ[. . . μνημο]νε[ύει δὲ Θεόπομπος ἐν Εἰρή]ν[ῃ λέγων
οὑτωσί·

ἡμᾶς δ᾽ ἀ]παλ[λαχθέντας ἐπ᾽ ἀγαθαῖς] τύχα[ις
ὀβελισκολυχνίου] καὶ ξ[ιφομαχαίρας πικρᾶς].[84]

επακ[
επισ[
ασελ[
ωτι[
πῶς[
μεν[
δαίν[υ
γωδ[
ὀισπ[
φη[
ενο[
νειμ[
απτ[

[84] Restored by Kaibel from Poll. 10.118. The absence of marginal carats (marking verbatim quotations of ancient authors) sug-
gests that this section was mostly a summary of grammarians'
comments and the like.

But the *xulo[luchnouchos]* . . .
of fire . . .

Theopompus in *Peace* (fr. 8) mentions (an *obeliskoluch-nion*[275]), saying the following:

we who were lucky enough to escape
the *obeliskoluchnion* and the bitter dagger.

[275] Literally "a spit-*luchnion*," i.e. presumably "a spit used as a *luchnion*"; here clearly a piece of makeshift equipment used by soldiers in the field. Cf. Antiph. fr. 109 (quoted at 15.700c).

Φιλύ[λλιος[85]
π[
δι[
λα[
φ[
φ[
τ[
ξ[
δ[
. [
. [
. [

           ]ὡς ἐβάδι
ζον δαΐδας . . .] μετὰ χερσὶν
ἔχοντες.[86] . . .] δὲ τῶν ἄλλων
        ἔμενον ἔν
        δέοι κατα
        ὅπερ ἔτι
          νι
        . ρων
          ιη

          .

          .

          .

          .
        κάν
        ῆι

[85] suppl. Schoell   [86] suppl. Kaibel

Phily[llius] (fr. 29)[276]

how they made their
way, holding torches (*daïdes*)
in their hands (adesp. com. fr. *126) . . . But of the
others

which very thing still

[276] See the text of the Epitome below.

ο φησὶ
λεί
οδω
ι εἰσ
ωλι
δ᾽ ενι
λύ
νθέ
υτί
όν
ῆσ
εκ
ου
ψη
χρυ
αφά
ει |
ον
υ
διμύ]ξου[87]
ει
ὰ
σ
αῖ

. α

.
.

says

with two oil-chambers

---

[87] suppl. Kaibel

ΕΚ ΤΟΥ ΙΕ

Ξυλολύχνου δὲ μέμνηται Ἄλεξις· καὶ τάχα τούτῳ
ὅμοιόν ἐστι τὸ παρὰ Θεοπόμπῳ ὀβελισκόλυχνον. Φι-
f λύλλιος δὲ τὰς λαμπάδας δᾷδας καλεῖ. οὐ παλαιὸν | δ᾽
εὕρημα λύχνος· φλογὶ δ᾽ οἱ παλαιοὶ τῆς τε δᾳδὸς καὶ
τῶν ἄλλων ξύλων ἐχρῶντο. † κοιμίσαι λύχνον † Φρύ-
νιχος φησί.

ΙΕ

⟨ . . . ⟩σω καὶ θρυαλλίδ᾽, ἢν δέῃ.

καὶ Πλάτων ἐν Νυκτὶ Μακρᾷ·

ἐνταῦθ᾽ ἐπ᾽ ἄκρων τῶν κροτάφων ἕξει λύχνον
δίμυξον.

μνημονεύει τοῦ διμύξου λύχνου καὶ Μεταγένης ἐν
701 Φιλοθύτῃ καὶ Φιλωνίδης ἐν Κοθόρνοις. ‖ Κλείταρχος
δ᾽ ἐν ταῖς Γλώσσαις λοφνίδα φησὶ καλεῖν Ῥοδίους
τὴν ἐκ τοῦ φλοιοῦ τῆς ἀμπέλου λαμπάδα. Ὅμηρος δὲ
τὰς λαμπάδας δετὰς ὀνομάζει·

καιόμεναί τε δεταί, τάς τε τρεῖ ἐσσύμενός περ.

---

277 The text that follows represents the—unfortunately extremely laconic—portion of the Epitome that overlaps with the
damaged portion of manuscript A.

278 A more complete and metrical version of the line is quoted
at Poll. 7.178.

FROM BOOK XV[277]

Alexis (fr. 66) mentions a *xulolouchnos*, which is perhaps to be identified with what Theopompus (fr. 8) calls an *obeliskoluchnos*. Philyllius (fr. 29) refers to *lampades* as *daides*. The *luchnos* was unknown in ancient times; instead, the ancients used flame produced by a torch or by wood of another sort. Phrynichus (fr. 25.1, unmetrical)[278] says: † to put a *luchnos* to sleep. †

BOOK XV[279]

and a wick, if necessary. (Philyll. fr. *25)

Also Plato in *The Long Night* (fr. 90):

There at the highest point of his temples he'll have a
    luchnos
with two oil-chambers.

Metagenes in *The Man Who Loved Sacrifices* (fr. 13.1) mentions a *luchnos* with two chambers,[280] as does Philonides in *High Boots* (fr. 3.1). Cleitarchus in his *Glossary* says that the Rhodians refer to a lamp made of grape-vine bark as a *lophnis*.[281] Homer (*Il.* 11.554 = 17.663) calls torches (*lampades*) *detai*:

and burning *detai*, which he fears, eager though he is.

---

[279] Two more columns of text are preserved in manuscript A at this point; but see 15.701e n.

[280] I.e. with two nozzles and thus two wicks. Poll. 6.103 quotes the verse and also offers a slightly corrupt version of it at 10.115, along with Philonid. fr. 3 (below).   [281] Cf. 15.699d.

ἐλάνη δὲ ἡ λαμπὰς καλεῖται, ὡς Ἀμερίας φησίν.
Νίκανδρος δ' ὁ Κολοφώνιος ἐλάνην τὴν τῶν καλάμων
δέσμην. λύχνα δὲ οὐδετέρως εἴρηκεν Ἡρόδοτος ἐν
b δευτέρᾳ Ἱστοριῶν. λυχνοκαυτίαν | δὲ ἦν οἱ πολλοὶ
λέγουσιν λυχναψίαν Κηφισόδωρος ἐν Ὑί.

Καὶ ὁ Κύνουλκος αἰεί ποτε τῷ Οὐλπιανῷ ἀντικορυσσόμενος ἔφη, ἐμοὶ δέ, παῖ δωρόδειπνε, ἀσσαρίου
κανδήλας πρίω, ἵνα κἀγὼ κατὰ τὸν καλὸν Ἀγάθωνα
ἀναφωνήσω τάδε τὰ τοῦ ἡδίστου Ἀριστοφάνους·

ἐκφέρετε πεύκας κατ' Ἀγάθωνα φωσφόρους.

καὶ ταῦτ' εἰπών·

οὐρὰν ὑπίλας ὑπὸ λεοντόπουν βάσιν,

ὑπεξῆλθεν τοῦ συμποσίου ὑπηλὸς κάρτα γενόμενος.

c   Τῶν δὲ πολλῶν τὸ ἰὴ παιὼν ἐπιφθεγγομένων | ὁ
Ποντιανὸς ἔφη· τὸ ἰὴ παιών, ἄνδρες φίλοι, μαθεῖν
βούλομαι εἴτε παροιμία ἐστὶν εἴτε ἐφύμνιον εἴτε τι
ἄλλο. πρὸς ὃν ὁ Δημόκριτος ἔφη· Κλέαρχος ὁ Σολεὺς
οὐδενὸς ὢν δεύτερος τῶν τοῦ σοφοῦ Ἀριστοτέλους
μαθητῶν ἐν τῷ προτέρῳ Περὶ Παροιμιῶν τὴν Λητώ

---

282 Cf. 15.699d with n.
283 I.e. the neuter plural.
284 Cf. 15.669b with n.
285 A Latin word (candela, "candle, taper"), presumably intended to irritate Ulpian, who routinely objects to the use of Latin
loan-words (cf. 3.121e–f; 8.362a; 9.376d), one final time. An assarius is a small Roman coin (an as, a fraction of a denarius).

According to Amerias (p. 10 Hoffmann), a torch (*lampas*) is referred to as a *helanê*; but Nicander of Colophon (fr. 89 Schneider) (claims that) a *helanê* is a bundle of reeds.[282] Herodotus in Book II (62) of the *History* uses the neuter form[283] *luchna*. Cephisodorus in *The Pig* (fr. 11) refers to what many authorities call *luchnapsia* ("*luchnos*-lighting") as *luchnokautia* ("*luchnos*-burning").

Cynulcus, who was constantly butting heads with Ulpian,[284] said: Waiter! Buy me an assarius' worth of *candêlai*,[285] so that I can quote the following passage from the delightful Aristophanes (fr. 592.35), who is in turn citing Agathon (*TrGF* 39 F 15):

Bring forth light-bearing pine-torches, as Agathon
     put it!

After he said this,

He wrapped his tail beneath his lion-footed stride[286]

and left the party, very eager to go to sleep.

Many of the guests were beginning to pronounce the *iê paian*, and Pontianus said: I would like to be informed, my friends, as to whether the phrase *iê paian* is a proverb, a refrain appended to hymns, or something else. Democritus replied: Clearchus of Soli, who was at least as important as any of the wise Aristotle's other students, says in Book I of *On Proverbs* (fr. 64 Wehrli) that as Leto was bringing

---

[286] Adapted from E. *Oed.* fr. 540.1.3 (referring to the Sphinx), where the participle is feminine. Ael. *NA* 12.7 quotes the first word of the next line, *kathizet(o)* (better *kathezeto*, "she sat down"), which is inappropriate here and has accordingly been omitted.

φησιν ἐκ Χαλκίδος τῆς Εὐβοίας ἀνακομίζουσαν εἰς
Δελφοὺς Ἀπόλλωνα καὶ Ἄρτεμιν γενέσθαι περὶ τὸ
τοῦ κληθέντος Πύθωνος σπήλαιον. καὶ φερομένου τοῦ
Πύθωνος ἐπ᾽ αὐτοὺς ἡ Λητὼ τῶν παίδων τὸν ἕτερον |
d ἐν ταῖς ἀγκάλαις ἔχουσα, ἐπιβᾶσα τῷ λίθῳ τῷ νῦν ἔτι
κειμένῳ ὑπὸ τῷ ποδὶ τῆς χαλκῆς εἰργασμένης Λη-
τοῦς, ὃ τῆς τότε πράξεως μίμημα γενόμενον ἀνάκειται
παρὰ τὴν πλάτανον ἐν Δελφοῖς, εἶπεν, "ἵε παῖ." τυχεῖν
δὲ τόξα μετὰ χεῖρας ἔχοντα τὸν Ἀπόλλωνα. τοῦτο δ᾽
ἐστὶν ὡς ἂν εἴποι τις, "ἄφιε παῖ" καὶ "βάλε παῖ."
διόπερ ἀπὸ τούτου λεχθῆναί φασιν τὸ ἵε παῖ καὶ ἵε
παιών. ἔνιοι δὲ παρεγκλίνοντές τε τὴν λέξιν καὶ
⟨ψιλοῦντες⟩[88] ἐπὶ τοῖς[89] δεινοῖς ἀλεξητήριόν τινα παρ-
e οιμίαν | λέγουσιν "ἰὴ παιών" καὶ οὐχὶ "ἵε παῖ." πολλοὶ
δὲ καὶ ἐπὶ τοῖς τέλος ἔχουσιν ἐπιφθεγγόμενοι οἱ μὲν
ἐν παροιμίᾳ φασὶν οὕτως τοῦτο δὴ τὸ λεγόμενον ἰὴ
παιών, διὰ δὲ τὸ λίαν ἡμῖν εἶναι σύνηθες λανθάνον ὂν
ἐν παροιμίᾳ, οἱ δὲ τὸ τοιοῦτο λέγοντες οὐχ ὡς παρ-
οιμίαν ⟨ . . . ⟩ τὸ δὲ ὑφ᾽ Ἡρακλείδου τοῦ Ποντικοῦ
λεχθὲν φανερῶς πέπλασται, ἐπὶ σπονδαῖς τοῦτο πρῶτον εἰς τρὶς εἰπεῖν τὸν θεὸν οὕτως "ἰὴ παιάν, ἰὴ παιάν,
⟨ἰὴ παιάν⟩."[90] ἐκ ταύτης γὰρ τῆς πίστεως τὸ τρί-

---

[88] add. Kaibel, cf. Σ Il. 15.365   [89] Everything that follows from δεινοῖς to Σώπα- (in Σώπατρος) in 15.702b has now
either been lost from manuscript A, or is so blotted and stained as
to be illegible. The damage has apparently occurred since Cobet's
time, and I give the text as he transcribed it.

[90] add. Kaibel, ducente Casaubone

Apollo and Artemis back to Delphi from Euboean Chalcis, she came to the cave of the creature known as Pytho.[287] When Pytho attacked them, Leto, who was holding her son in her arms, got on top of the stone that even today rests beneath the foot of the bronze statue of her—it recalls what went on then, and stands beside the plane-tree in Delphi—and said: *"Hie pai!"* ("Let it go, child!"); for Apollo happened to have a bow in his hands. This is the equivalent of saying "Send it forth, child!" or "Shoot, child!" This is the origin, they say, of the phrase *"hie pai"* or *"hie paiôn."* But some people alter the word by giving it a smooth breathing, and say *"iê paiôn,"*[288] which serves as a sort of proverb intended to evade[289] danger, rather than *"hie pai."* Many people also say this at the conclusion of a task, and some claim that the phrase *"iê paiôn"* is proverbial when used this way, but that our over-familiarity with it means that we fail to recognize it as such, whereas others say something along the following lines, that it is not a proverb . . . But the thesis of Heracleides of Pontus (fr. 158 Wehrli = fr. 110 Schütrumpf)—that when libations were being made, the god originally pronounced the phrase three times, *"iê paian, iê paian, iê paian"*—is patently made up. As a consequence of this theory, he assigns

[287] A giant snake.

[288] Thus Crates of Mallos (fr. 23 Broggiatto); Aristarchus preferred the rough breathing.

[289] The next two columns of text in manuscript A are now either lost or so badly damaged as to be illegible. Although some of this damage had already occurred by Cobet's time, he was able to read far more than we can today, and I print the text as he transcribes it.

f μετρον καλούμενον ἀνατίθησι | τῷ θεῷ, φάσκων τοῦ
θεοῦ τοῦθ᾿ ἑκάτερον εἶναι τῶν μέτρων, ὅτι μακρῶν μὲν
τῶν πρώτων δύο συλλαβῶν λεγομένων "ἰὴ παιάν"
ἡρῷον γίνεται, βραχέως δὲ λεχθεισῶν ἰαμβεῖον· διὰ
δὲ τοῦτο δῆλον ὅτι καὶ τὸν χωλίαμβον ἀναθετέον
αὐτῷ· βραχειῶν γὰρ γινομένων εἰ δύο τὰς ἁπασῶν
τελευταίας συλλαβὰς εἰς μακρὰν ποιήσει τις, ὁ Ἱπ-
πώνακτος ἴαμβος ἔσται.

Μετὰ ταῦτ᾿ ἤδη μελλόντων καὶ ἡμῶν ἀνίστασθαι
ἐπεισῆλθον παῖδες φέροντες ὁ μέν τις θυμιατήριον, ὁ
δὲ [. . .   ]
τοῦ συμποσίου [. . .] δε
‹λιβ›α‹ν›ωτοῦ [. . .]ιμποι
[. . .   ]δὴ[. . .]
[. . .   ]ηιθυται
[. . .   ]τὰ τὸν
[. . .   ]αν. τήν
[. . .   ]ενορ...οι
[. . .   ]ὸ.. καὶ τόδε
ε[. . .]ε. τοῦ θ[υμι]ατηρίου
[. . .]και ε. τοῦ [λι]βανωτοῦ, τοῖς θεοῖς πᾶσι καὶ
πάσαις εὐξάμενος, ἐπισπείσας τοῦ οἴνου καὶ δοὺς

---

290 I.e. what we would call two spondaic feet of a dactylic hexameter (long-long long-long).   291 I.e. what we would call a
single iambic metron (short-long-short-long).

292 Clearly intended as a reference to choliambic lines, which
end short-long-long-long (rather than short-long-short-long); but
the argument is difficult to follow.

what is known as a trimeter to the god, claiming that both variations on the meter belong to him, since if the first two syllables are both pronounced long, "*iê paian*," it is a heroic metron,[290] whereas if they are pronounced short, it is iambic.[291] This makes it apparent that the choliamb should also be assigned to (Apollo); for if the initial syllables are short, but one makes the final two syllables of each metron long, it becomes the sort of iambic metron Hipponax used.[292]

After this, as we were just at the point of getting up and leaving, slaves came in, one of them carrying a censer, another[293] . . .
of the party . . .
of frankincense

and this
of the censer
. . . and . . . of the frankincense, after offering[294] a prayer to all the gods and goddesses, pouring a libation of wine,

[293] Manuscript A has again suffered damage at this point; the Epitome is of no assistance in filling in the gaps.

[294] The subject of the participles must be Larensius, and the song that follows serves *inter alia* as a final blessing for him and his counterpart in the real world, the historical Athenaeus' patron (see vol. I pp. viii–ix), whose library and personal support made production of the work that comes to an end here possible.

213

κατὰ τὸ νόμιμον ⟨τὸ⟩ ἐπιχώριον τὸ λοιπὸν τοῦ
702 ἀκράτου τῷ διδόντι ἐκπιεῖν παιδὶ ‖ τὸν εἰς τὴν Ὑγίειαν παιᾶνα ᾄσας τὸν ποιηθέντα ὑπὸ Ἀρίφρονος τοῦ
Σικυωνίου τόνδε·

Ὑγίεια, ⟨ . . . ⟩ πρεσβίστα μακάρων, μετὰ σεῦ
ναίοιμι τὸ λειπόμενον βιοτᾶς, σὺ δέ μοι
    πρόφρων ξυνείης·
εἰ γάρ τις ἢ πλούτου χάρις ἢ τεκέων
⟨ἢ⟩ τᾶς ἰσοδαίμονος ἀνθρώποις βασιληίδος
    ἀρχᾶς ἢ πόθων
οὓς κρυφίοις Ἀφροδίτας ἔρκεσιν θηρεύομεν, |
b ἢ εἴ τις ἄλλα θεόθεν ἀνθρώποισι τέρψις ἢ πόνων
ἀμπνοὰ πέφανται,
μετὰ σεῖο, μάκαιρ᾽ Ὑγίεια,
τέθαλε πάντα καὶ λάμπει Χαρίτων ὀάροις·
σέθεν δὲ χωρὶς οὔτις εὐδαίμων ⟨ . . . ⟩.

καὶ ἀσπασάμενος ἡμᾶς φιλοφρό-
[νως . . .] ἀπομάττοντας [. . .]
[. . .] οἴδασιν ο⟨ἱ πα⟩λαιοί. Σώπατρος γὰρ ὁ φλυ-
ακογράφος ἐν τῷ ἐπιγραφομένῳ δράματι Φακῆ λέγει
οὕτως·

κρεανομοῦμαι, καὶ τὸν ἐκ Τυρρηνίας
οἶνον σὺν ὀκτὼ λαμβάνειν ἐπίσταμαι.

following the local custom of giving the rest of the unmixed wine to the slave who had offered it to him to drink, and singing the following paean, composed by Ariphron of Sicyon (*PMG* 813) in honor of Hygieia ("Health"):

> Hygieia, most august of the blessed gods—may I
> dwell
> with you for the rest of my life, and may you always
> willingly remain with me!
> For if any pleasure can be got from wealth, children,
> royal power (which human beings regard as almost
> like a god), or the longings
> we pursue using Aphrodite's hidden nets,
> or if the gods have revealed any other pleasure or
> respite
> from their labors to human beings,
> all of these flourish with you,
> blessed Hygieia, and shine in the Graces'
> conversation.
> No one is happy when you are absent.

And after embracing us warm-ly[295] . . . were wiping clean . . .
. . . the ancients are familiar with. For the phlyax-author Sopater in his play entitled *Lentil-Soup* (fr. 19) puts it as follows:

> I carve my own meat, and I know how
> to consume Etruscan wine with eight guests.

[295] The subject is still Larensius, to whose consistent hospitality the quotation from Sopater (below) must be intended to apply.

c ταῦτα, φίλτατε Τιμόκρατες, κατὰ τὸν Πλάτωνα | οὐ
Σωκράτους νέου καὶ καλοῦ παίγνια, ἀλλὰ τῶν δειπνοσοφιστῶν σπουδάσματα. κατὰ γὰρ τὸν Χαλκοῦν Διο-
νύσιον·

τί κάλλιον ἀρχομένοισιν
ἢ καταπαυομένοις ἢ τὸ ποθεινότατον;

The preceding, my dearest Timocrates, were not the witty remarks of Plato's young and handsome Socrates,[296] but the earnest conversation pursued by the learned banqueters. For to quote Dionysius Chalcous (fr. 6 West²),

What is finer, as we begin
or end, than what we desire the most?

[296] Cf. *Epist. II* 314c.

INDEX OF AUTHORS, TEXTS,
AND PERSONS

This index supersedes those at the end of the first seven individual volumes of the new Loeb Athenaeus, which were prepared by different research assistants working under my supervision, and which accordingly vary somewhat in format, coverage, citation style, and the like. Almost every personal name in the index is followed by a brief identifier. Individuals of primarily historical rather than literary interest are further identified, where possible, by reference to one or more of the relevant standard prosopographies. In the case of obscure homonyms, I have generally chosen to split rather than to combine entries, although absolute consistency in this matter—as in many others—is impossible. Fragmentary authors and texts are identified by the modern editor or editors on whose numbering I have relied; for clarity's sake, I have attempted to follow the individual preferences of such editors in the use of the designations *fr.*, *F,* and the like. Occasional parentheses around numbers indicate that while the editor of the standard edition of the author or work in question regards this as a legitimate fragment or testimonium, I do not. Lowercase Roman numerals at the beginning of entries refer to page numbers in the introduction in Volume 1 (LCL 204).

Gulick included a separate index of Greek words in the final volume of his Loeb. The ongoing development of digital search tools has made a printed—and thus inevitably selective—Greek index less necessary or useful than one might have been in his day. I have accordingly chosen instead to catalog material less easily accessible via a simple TLG search or the like.

221

INDEX OF AUTHORS, TEXTS, AND PERSONS

Alcetas, *king of Macedon and notorious drinker*, 10.436e

Alcibiades, *son of Cleinias of Athens, politician and libertine (PAA 121625)*, 1.3d–e, 17e n.; 4.184d; 5.180a–b, 182a, 187c–e, 215e–16c, 219b–20a, 220c–d; 6.234e; 9.407b–c; 11.506c–d; 12.525b, 534b–5d; 13.566d–e, 574d–f; 14.643f

Alcidamas of Elis, *orator*, (Baiter–Sauppe eds.) ii.155, II: 13.592c

Alcimus of Sicily, *historian, FGrH* 560 F 1: 7.322a; F 2: 10.441a–b; F 3: 12.518b–c

Alcinous, *Homeric king of Phaeacia*, 1.9b, 13e; 5.182a, 192c; 7.284d; 12.512c, 513e

Alciphron of Maeander, *geographer*, 1.31d

Alcippe, *slave-woman of Homeric Helen*, 5.191a

Alcisthenes of Sybaris, *hedonist*, 12.541a–d

Alcius, *Epicurean philosopher*, 12.547a

Alcmaeon, *son of Amphiaraus, one of Epigoni*, 6.222d, 223c, 232e

Alcmaeonis, (Bernabé ed.) fr. 2, p. 33: 11.460b

Alcman of Sparta, *lyric poet*, 14.638e; 15.678c–d
  PMG 17: 10.416c, 19: 3.110f–11a; 20: 10.416d; 26.4: 9.374d; 39: 9.390a; 40:

9.374d; 42: 2.39a; 56: 11.498f–9a; 59(a): 13.600f; 59(b): 13.601a; 60: 15.680f–1a; 82: 9.373e; 91: 15.682a; 92: 1.31c–d; 94: 3.114f, 14.646a; 95: 4.140c; 96: 14.648b; 99: 3.81d; 100: 3.81f; 101: 14.636f; 109: 14.624b; 160: 15.678b

Alcmene, *mother of Heracles*, 11.463c, 781c, 474f, 475b–c

Alcyone, *mother of Glaucus*, 7.296b

Alcyone of Corinth, *daughter of Agemon*, 15.696f

Alcyoneus, *son of Demo and Demetrius Poliorcetes*, 13.578a

Alexamenus of Teos, *alleged inventor of dialogue genre*, 11.505b–c

Alexander, *comic poet*, (Kassel–Austin eds.) fr. 3: 4.170e–f; fr. dub. 4: 11.496c

Alexander I, *son of Pyrrhus, king of Molossia* (Berve i #38), 3.73b–c

Alexander II, *king of Macedon and brother of Philip II*, 3.112f; 14.629d

Alexander II, *king of Molossia*, 6.249d, 251c

Alexander III ("the Great"), *king of Macedon*, 1.3d, 17f, 19a, c, 20a, 22d; 2.42f, 50f, 51a, 71b; 3.124c; 4.129a, 146c–d, 148e, 155c–d, 167c, 171c; 5.201d, 202a,

225

206e; 6.231b, e, 232f, 245a
n., 245f n., 246e n., 250f–
1a, 251b, 255d; 7.276f–7a;
9.393c, 398e; 10.434a–d,
434f–5a, 437a; 11.781f,
784a–b; 12.530b, 535e,
537c–40a; 13.555a, 557c,
d–e, 565a, 578a, 586d,
591d, 594d, 603a–c, 606c–
d, 607f; 15.684e

Alexander Aetolus, *elegiac poet*
(Powell ed. = Magnelli ed.)
fr. 1, p. 121 = fr. 1: 7.296d;
fr. 2, p. 122 = fr. 2: 7.283a;
fr. 5, p. 125 = fr. 5:
15.699b–c; fr. 21, p. 129 =
fr. 18: 14.620e–f; fr. dub.
22, p. 129 = fr. dub. 24:
11.496c
(Magnelli ed.) fr. 14: 10.412f

Alexander Balas, *king of Syria,*
5.211a–d

Alexander of Alexandria, *musician* (Stephanis #102),
4.183d

Alexander of Cythera, *harp-
player* (Stephanis #105),
4.183c

Alexander of Myndus, *natural-
ist,* 2.57b
(Wellmann ed.) fr. I.4: 2.65a;
fr. I.5: 2.65b; fr. I.6:
5.221b; fr. I.7: 9.387f; fr.
I.8: 9.388d; fr. I.9: 9.389c;
fr. I.10: 9.390f; fr. I.11:
9.391b; fr. I.12: 9.391c; fr.
I.14: 9.391f; fr. I.15:
9.392c; fr. I.16: 9.393a–b;
fr. I.17: 9.393d; fr. I.18:

9.394d; fr. I.20: 9.395c–e;
fr. I.21: 9.398c

Alexarchus, *brother of Cassan-
der of Macedon and
founder of Ouranopolis,*
3.98d–f

Alexias/Alexus?, *Ionicologos,* SH
41: 14.620e–f

Alexinus of Elis, *philosopher
and author of paean in
honor of Craterus, SSR* II
C F 15 (= *SH* 40):
15.696e–f; F 19: 10.418e

Alexis of Samos, *historian,
FGrH* 539 F 1: 13.572f;
F 2: 12.540d–e

Alexis of Tarentum, *rhapsode*
(Berve i #44; Stephanis
#127), 12.538e

Alexis of Thurii, *comic poet,*
2.66f; 3.123b; 6.235e;
14.663c
(Kassel–Austin eds.) test. 12:
8.344c; fr. 2.1–8: 11.502f–
3a; fr. 2.3–9: 6.230b–c; fr.
3: 8.339c; fr. 4: 15.678e; fr.
5: 11.471e; fr. 6: 3.120b; fr.
7: 6.223f; fr. 9: 10.431d–f;
fr. 15: 3.117e–18a; fr. 15.4:
3.117c; fr. 16: 6.224f–5a; fr.
17: 7.301a; fr. 18: 7.301b;
fr. 19: 14.638c; fr. 20:
13.562d–e; fr. 21: 10.431c;
fr. 22: 14.644b–c; fr. 24:
4.169d; fr. 25: 8.336e–f; fr.
27: 9.386c–d; fr. 34:
14.650c; fr. 37: 12.544e–f;
fr. 38: 7.314d; fr. 41:
13.605f–6a; fr. 43: 3.125b;

INDEX OF AUTHORS, TEXTS, AND PERSONS

Alpheidas, *king of Athens,*
3.96d

Alpheius, *ancestor of Althephius,* 1.31c

Althephius, *gave name to Althephian vine,* 1.31c

Alyattes, *king of Lydia,* 5.210b;
13.599c

Amaltheia, *goat that nursed Zeus,* 5.198a; 11.497c,
503b; 12.542a; 14.643a

Amarantus of Alexandria, *author of* On the Stage,
8.343e–f; 10.414e–f

Amasis, *king of Egypt,* 6.261c;
10.438b; 13.560d, e;
15.680b–c

INDEX OF AUTHORS, TEXTS, AND PERSONS

INDEX OF AUTHORS, TEXTS, AND PERSONS

INDEX OF AUTHORS, TEXTS, AND PERSONS

Calanus, *Indian philosopher* (Berve i #396), 10.436f–8a

Caligula, *Roman emperor,* 4.148d

Calliades, *comic poet,* 9.401a

Callias, *comic poet,* (Kassel–Austin eds.) test. *7: 7.276a, 10.453c–4a; fr. 6: 7.286a–b; fr. 6.1: 7.306a; fr. 7: 4.140e; fr. 8: 12.524f; fr. 9: 11.487a; fr. 10: 7.285e; fr. 12: 15.667d; fr. 20: 8.344e; fr. 23: 4.176f; fr. 26: 2.57a; fr. 30: 1.22c; fr. *40: 13.577c

Callias, *son of Hipponicus of Athens, wealthy patron of sophists* (PAA 554500), 1.22f; 4.169a, 184d; 5.187f, 216d, 217a, 218b, c, 220b; 11.506f; 12.536e–7c; 15.686d–e

Callias of Athens, *author of* Literal Tragedy (PAA 553640; TrGF 233), 7.276a (= Call. Com. test. *7); 10.448b, 453c–4a (= Call. Com. test. *7)

Callias of Athens, *eponymous archon for 406/5 BCE,* 5.218a

Callias of Athens, *orator* (PAA 553610), 8.342b–c

Callias of Mitylene, *grammarian,* 3.85e–f

Callias of Syracuse, *historian,* FGrH 564 F 2: 12.542a

Callicrates, *comic poet,* (Kassel–Austin eds.) fr. 1: 13.586a

Callicrates, *flatterer of Ptolemy III,* 6.251d

Callicrates of Sparta, *engraver of cups* (Poralla #406), 11.782b

Callimachus of Athens, *eponymous archon for 349/8 BCE,* 5.217b

Callimachus of Cyrene, *scholar and poet,* 2.58f; 5.213f; 6.272b; 8.331d, 336e; 9.387f; 11.478b; 15.696f

Epigram V: 7.318b–c

HE 1105–6: 15.669c–d; 1325–6: 10.436e–f

(Pfeiffer ed.) fr. 69: 15.668b–c, e; fr. 178.11–12: 10.442f; fr. 178.11–14: 11.477b–c; fr. 200a: 3.95f; fr. 227.5–7: 15.668c; fr. 248.1: 2.56c–d; fr. 378: 7.284c; fr. 384: 4.144e; fr. 394: 7.284c, 327a; fr. 406: 7.329a; fr. 414: 9.388d–e; fr. 415: 9.389b; fr. 416: 9.394d; fr. 417: 9.395f; fr. 418: 9.391c; fr. 430: 15.669d–e; fr. 434: 6.244a; fr. 435: 14.643e; fr. 436: 1.4d–e; fr. 437: 2.70b; fr. 438: 6.252c; fr. 439: 8.336d; fr. 440: 11.496e–f; fr. 465: 3.72a; fr. 476: 1.24a–b; fr. 477: 13.571a–b; fr. 478: 2.69c; fr. 494: 1.8d–e

Callimedon "the Crayfish" of Athens, *notorious wit and glutton* (PAA 558185; Stephanis #1343), 3.100c–

253

568870; O'Connor #289;
Stephanis #1400), 10.453a–b

Cephisodorus, *comic poet*,
(Kassel–Austin eds.) fr. 2:
14.629c; fr. 3: 15.689f; fr.
3.1–3: 12.553a; fr. 5:
15.667d; fr. 8: 3.119d; fr. 9:
8.345f; fr. 11: 15.701a–b; fr.
13: 11.459d

Cephisodorus, *wandering show-
man* (*PAA* 568055;
Stephanis #1395), 1.20a;
14.615e–f

Cephisodorus of Athens, *critic
of Aristotle* (*PAA* 568030),
8.354c

Cephisodorus of Athens, *eponymous archon for 366/5 or
323/2 BCE*, 4.171d

Cephisodorus of Athens, *politician and "donkey"* (*PAA*
568060), 9.407f

Cephisodorus of Athens, *student of Isocrates* (*PAA*
568030), (Radermacher
ed.) fr. 3: 2.60d; fr. 5:
3.122b

Cephisodorus of Athens or
Thebes, *historian, FGrH*
112 F 2: 12.548e–f

Cephisodotus of Athens, *citharode* (*PAA* 567705; Stephanis #1393), 4.131b

Cerberus, *guard-dog of Underworld*, 13.597c

Cercidas of Megalopolis, *poet*,
(Powell ed.) fr. dub. 10, p.
212: 4.163d–e; fr. 11, p.

212: 8.347d–e; fr. 14, p.
213: 12.554d

Cercope, *courtesan* (*PAA*
566472), 13.587e

Cercops of Miletus, *poet*,
11.503d; 13.557a–b

Cercyon, *villain killed by
Theseus*, 13.557a

Ceyx, *friend of Heracles*, 5.178b

Chabrias of Athens, *general*
(*PAA* 970820), 12.532a–b

Chaereas of Athens, *author of
treatise on agriculture*
(*PAA* 971350), 1.32b

Chaeremon, *tragic poet, TrGF*
71 T 4: 11.482b; F 1:
13.608d; F 5: 13.608e; F 6:
15.676e; F 7: 15.679f; F 8:
13.608f; F 9: 13.608d–e; F
10: 13.608e; F 11: 15.676e;
F 12: 13.608f; F 13:
13.608e; F 14: 13.608a–c;
F 15: 2.35f; F 16: 13.562e;
F 17: 2.43c

Chaerephon of Athens, *associate of Socrates* (*PAA*
976060), 5.188c, 218e, f

Chaerephon of Athens, *parasite*
(*PAA* 975770), 4.134e,
136e, 164f–5a; 6.242f–4d,
245a, f; 13.584e; 15.685e–f

Chaeron of Pallene, *philosopher, wrestler, and tyrant*
(Berve i #818; Moretti
#432), 11.509b

Chairephanes, *restrained peder-
ast*, 1.14e–f

Chairephilus of Athens, *saltfish*

Cleomenes, *rhapsode* (Stephanis #1445), 14.620c–d

Cleomenes I, *king of Sparta* (Poralla #436), 10.427b, 436e

Cleomenes II, *king of Sparta* (Bradford p. 240), 4.142b–f

Cleomenes of Methymna, *tyrant*, 10.442f–3a

Cleomenes of Naucratis, *Alexander "the Great's" chief financial officer in Egypt* (Berve i #431), 9.393c

Cleomenes of Rhegium, *erotic poet*, 13.605e; 14.638d–e *PMG* 838: 9.402a

Cleon (nicknamed "Ox"), *citharode* (Stephanis #1456), 8.349c

Cleon, *mime-actor* (Stephanis #1457), 10.452f

Cleon, *son of Pytheas, citharode* (Stephanis #1465), 1.19b

Cleon of Athens, *politician and general* (PAA 579130), 5.215d

Cleonice, *wife of Cnopus*, 6.259b

Cleonicus, *parodist* (Stephanis #1447), 15.698a

Cleonymus, *dancer and flatterer* (Stephanis #1467), 6.254d

Cleonymus of Athens, *politician and glutton* (PAA 579410), 4.131a; 10.415d

Cleonymus of Sparta, *general* (Bradford pp. 246–7), 13.605d–e

Cleopatra, *wife of Philip II* (Berve i #434), 13.557d, 560c

Cleopatra III, *queen of Egypt*, 12.550a

Cleopatra VII, *queen of Egypt*, 4.147e–8b; 6.229c–d

Cleoptolemus of Chalcis, *father-in-law of Antiochus III*, 10.439f

Cleostratus of Tenedus, *Presocratic philosopher*, (Diels–Kranz eds.) 6 A 4: 7.278b

Clotho, *one of Fates*, 14.617a

Clytemnestra, *wife of Agamemnon*, 1.14b; 13.556c, 559c

Clytus of Miletus, Peripatetic philosopher and historian, *FGrH* 490 F 1: 14.655b–e; F 2: 12.540c–d

Cnopus, *legendary founder of Erythrae*, 6.258f–9f

Cnosion, *boyfriend of Demosthenes* (PAA 580150), 13.593a

Cobius ("Goby") of Athens, *wealthy glutton* (PAA 588990), 3.134d; 6.242d; 8.339a, e

Cobius of Salamis (PAA 588995), 7.329c

Cocalus of Sicily, *daughters murdered Minos*, 1.10e

Cocytus, *Underworld river personified*, 13.597c

Codalus, *Phrygian pipe-player* (Stephanis #1523), 14.624b

Codrus, *king of Athens*, 3.111d; 8.336f

INDEX OF AUTHORS, TEXTS, AND PERSONS

267

INDEX OF AUTHORS, TEXTS, AND PERSONS

mous glutton attacked by Hipponax, 15.698c

Eurypyle, *woman intrigued by Artemon,* 12.533e

Eurypylus, *historian,* 11.508f

Eurypylus, *Homeric hero,* 2.41b

Eurypylus, *son of Eurystheus,* 4.158a

Eurystheus, *enemy of Heracles,* 4.157f–8a; 13.603d; 15.672a

Eurytion, *centaur,* 1.10e; 6.240d n.; 14.613a–b

Eurytus, *king of Oechalia,* 11.461f

Euterpe, *mother of Themistocles (PAA 445835),* 13.576d

Euthias of Athens, *orator (PAA 431560),* 13.590d

Euthycles, *comic poet,* (Kassel–Austin eds.) fr. 1: 3.124b

Euthydemus of Athens, *author of treatises on vegetables, saltfish, and shellfish (PAA 432195),* 2.58f; 3.74b, 118b; 7.307a–b, 308e, 315f, 328d; 9.369e–f; 12.516c *SH 455:* 3.116a–c, d

Euthydemus of Athens, *eponymous archon for 431/0 BCE,* 5.217a, 218b

Euthydemus of Chios and Thurii, *title-character of Platonic dialogue and sophist (PAA 432415),* 5.187d; 11.506b

Euthynus, *cook,* 9.379e

Euthynus of Athens, *saltfish-*

vendor and glutton (PAA 433922), 3.120a; 8.342e

Euxenus of Phocaea, *married daughter of King Nanos,* 13.576a–b

Euxitheus, *Pythagorean philosopher,* 4.157c

Evenor of Athens, *physician (PAA 431340),* 2.46d

Evenus of Paros, *elegiac poet,* (West[2] ed.) fr. 1: 9.367e; fr. 1.4: 10.429f

Examue, *companion of Mimnermus,* 13.598a

Fish, *personified,* 7.301d

Folly, *personified,* 2.36d

Galateia, *beloved of Cyclops,* 1.6e–7a; 13.564e

Galateia, *beloved of Philoxenus,* 13.598e

Galateia, *mistress of Dionysius I of Syracuse,* 1.6f–7a

Galen of Pergamum, *physician and deipnosophist,* x; 1.1e, 25f n., 26c; 3.115c

Galênê, *Calm personified,* 7.301d

Galene of Smyrna, *author of treatise on wreaths or flowers,* 15.679c

Ganymede, *Trojan prince,* 2.39a n.; 10.458f–9b; 13.566d, 601e–f, 602e

Gatis. *See Atargatis*

Gelon, *tyrant of Gela and Syracuse,* 6.231f; 9.401d; 12.541f–2a

Harpies, *food-snatching mon-
sters,* 10.421f–2a with n.;
13.558a

Harpocration of Mende, *author
of treatise on cake-making,*
14.648a–b, c

Health, *personified. See* Hygieia

Hebe, *Olympian deity,* 6.245e;
10.425e; 12.513d–e

Hecabe, *queen of Troy,* 1.10b–c;
2.66a–b; 13.566d

Hecamede, *slave-woman belonging to Nestor,* 1.10b n.;
11.492e

Hecataeus of Miletus, *historian,
FGrH* 1 T 15a: 2.70a;
T 15b: 9.410e; F 9: 4.148f;
F 15: 2.35a–b; F 154:
10.447c–d; F 291: 2.70a–b;
F 292a: 2.70b; F 296:
2.70b; F 322: 3.114c;
F 323a: 10.447c; F 323b:
10.418e; F 358: 9.410e

Hecate, *Underworld deity,*
3.84b n., 110c; 4.139d n.;
6.256e; 7.313b–c, 325a, b,
d; 8.358f; 14.645b; as
Triglanthinê, 7.325d

Hector, *prince of Troy,* 1.10b,
21f n.; 2.51c; 5.178c, d;
6.226f, 236c–d; 9.396f;
10.433c, 438a; 14.660d;
15.687f, 688d

Hedyle, *poetess, SH* 456:
7.297b–c

Hedylus of Samos, *epigram-
matic poet
HE* 1837–42: 11.486a–b;
1843–52: 11.497d–e; 1853–

62: 11.472f–3b; 1863–76:
8.344f–5b; 1877–86:
4.176c–d

SH 457: 7.297a

Hegemon, *possible author of
treatise on agriculture,*
2.75d

Hegemon of Thasos, *parodist
and comic poet,* 15.698c–
9a

(Kassel–Austin eds.) test. 1:
1.5a–b; test. 2: 15.699a;
test. 4: 9.406d–7c; fr. 1:
3.108c

Hegesander of Delphi, *historian,* 3.83a–b
(*FHG* iv.412–22) fr. 1:
11.507a–b; fr. 2: 4.162a–b;
fr. 3: 6.260a; fr. 4: 6.248e;
fr. 5: 7.289c; fr. 6: 6.249d–
e; fr. 7: 6.251a–b; fr. 8:
4.167d–f; fr. 9: 6.250d–e;
fr. 10: 4.132c; fr. 11:
8.350a; fr. 12: 14.620f–1b;
fr. 13: 1.19c–d; fr. 14:
8.337f; fr. 15: 8.340f; fr. 16:
8.343e; fr. 17: 8.343c–d; fr.
18: 12.544c, d; fr. 19:
8.344a; fr. 20: 10.444d–e;
fr. 21: 11.477e; fr. 22:
10.431d; fr. 23: 10.432b–d;
fr. 24: 2.44c; fr. 25:
13.572d–e; fr. 26: 13.564a;
fr. 27: 13.592b; fr. 28:
13.584e–5a; fr. 29: 3.107e;
fr. 30: 4.174a; fr. 31:
8.365d; fr. 32: 11.479d; fr.
33: 1.18a; fr. 34: 10.419d;
fr. 35: 2.62c–d; fr. 36:

287

INDEX OF AUTHORS, TEXTS, AND PERSONS

INDEX OF AUTHORS, TEXTS, AND PERSONS

INDEX OF AUTHORS, TEXTS, AND PERSONS

307

INDEX OF AUTHORS, TEXTS, AND PERSONS

INDEX OF AUTHORS, TEXTS, AND PERSONS

INDEX OF AUTHORS, TEXTS, AND PERSONS

INDEX OF AUTHORS, TEXTS, AND PERSONS

INDEX OF AUTHORS, TEXTS, AND PERSONS

INDEX OF AUTHORS, TEXTS, AND PERSONS

Phemius, *Homeric bard,* 1.14b
n., c–d; 5.189f; 14.633c

Phereboea, *wife of Theseus,*
13.557b

Pherecles, *enemy of Mimnermus,* 13.598a

Pherecrates, *comic poet,* 9.368a
(Kassel–Austin eds.) test. ii:
13.567c; fr. 1: 10.415c; fr.
2: 15.685b; fr. 1.3–4:
6.248c; *Agrioi* test. i:
5.218d; fr. 7: 4.171d; fr. 10:
6.263b; fr. 14: 7.316e–f; fr.
26: 3.119c–d; fr. 29.2:
3.90a; fr. 30: 14.648c; fr.
32: 9.385e; fr. 33: 9.396c;
fr. 37: 6.246f; fr. 38:
9.395b; *Doulodidaskalos*
test. i: 6.262b; fr. 43:
7.305f; fr. 44: 15.699f; fr.
45: 11.480b; fr. 49: 9.396c;
fr. 50: 3.96b; fr. 57: 8.365a;
fr. 61: 3.111b; fr. 62:
8.308f; fr. 70: 13.612a–b;
Corianno test. ii: 13.567c;
fr. 73: 4.159e–f; fr. 74:
14.653a; fr. 75: 11.481a–b;
fr. 75.4: 11.479b; fr. 76:
10.430e; fr. 85: 3.75b, 80a;
fr. 86: 14.646c; fr. 89:
2.55b, 9.366d; fr. 90:
15.700c; fr. 99: 14.645e; fr.
101: 11.464f, 485d; fr. 105:
15.690d; fr. 107: 3.95d; fr.
109: 6.228e; fr. 112:
10.424b; *Miners* test. iii:
15.685a; fr. 113: 6.268e–9c;
fr. 113.13–14: 3.96a; fr.

114: 15.685a–b; fr. 117:
7.287a; fr. 125: 8.335a; fr.
128: 6.229a; fr. 133: 6.228f;
fr. 134: 11.502a; fr. 135:
11.502b; fr. 137: 6.269c–e;
fr. 138: 15.684f–5a; fr. 139:
3.78d; fr. 143: 9.395b–c; fr.
148: 8.343c; fr. 149:
15.690f; fr. 152: 11.481b–d;
fr. 152.10: 11.460c; fr. 157:
9.368b; fr. 160: 9.388f; fr.
162: 8.364a–b; fr. 163:
3.122e; fr. 164: 12.535b; fr.
167: 14.644f–5a; fr. 170:
2.55b; fr. 188: 2.67c; fr.
190: 2.56f

Pherecydes of Athens, *historian, FGrH* 3 F 13a:
11.474f; F 18a: 11.470c–d;
F 153: 13.557b

Pherenicus of Heracleia, *epic
poet, SH* 672: 3.78b

Phersephonê. *See* Persephone

Phertatos, *seller of magic
charms* (*PAA* 920450),
3.123b

Phila, *courtesan associated with
Hyperides* (*PAA* 921855),
13.587f, 590d, 593f

Phila, *wife of Demetrius Poliorcetes,* 6.254a, 255c

Phila, *wife of Philip II,* 13.557c

Philadelphus of Ptolemais, *philosopher and deipnoso-
phist,* xi; 1.1d

Philaenis of Leucas, *purported
author of treatise on sex,*
5.220f; 8.335a–e; 10.457d

324

329

INDEX OF AUTHORS, TEXTS, AND PERSONS

INDEX OF AUTHORS, TEXTS, AND PERSONS

INDEX OF AUTHORS, TEXTS, AND PERSONS

INDEX OF AUTHORS, TEXTS, AND PERSONS

INDEX OF AUTHORS, TEXTS, AND PERSONS

Theopompus of Colophon, *hexameter poet*, *SH* 765:
4.183a–b

Theoris, *courtesan associated with Sophocles* (*PAA* 513670), 13.592a–b

Theoxenus of Tenedos, *beloved of Pindar*, 13.564d–e,
601d–e

Thêr, *attendant of pampered Paphian boy*, 6.257b

Theramenes of Athens, *politician* (*PAA* 513930), 5.220b

Thericles of Corinth, *potter*,
11.470f

Thersippus, *inventor of satyr-dance* (Stephanis #1196),
14.630b

Thersites, *Homeric villain*,
13.556e

Theseus, *king of Athens*, 1.10e
n.; 7.295b, 296c; 10.454b–
f; 13.557a–b, 560c–d, 601f

Thespis, *tragic poet*, *TrGF* 1 T
11: 1.22a

355

INDEX OF PLACES AND
PEOPLES

This index includes commodities, flora and fauna, dialects, measures, and the like associated with individual cities, regions, or peoples named in the text. It does not include geographical terms used primarily as identifiers for individuals. Thus, for example, Philip of Macedon is not included here under "Macedon." Nor does this index include geographical or ethnic terms that are merely part of the titles of literary works (e.g., Aristophanes' *Lemnian Women* and Crates' *Attic Dialect*).

INDEX OF PLACES AND PEOPLES

INDEX OF PLACES AND PEOPLES

INDEX OF PLACES AND PEOPLES

INDEX OF PLACES AND PEOPLES